D1078534

Social
Structure
and Law

Volume 180 Sage Library of Social Research

RECENT VOLUMES IN . . .
SAGE LIBRARY OF SOCIAL RESEARCH

⌈Social Structure and Law⌉

Theoretical and Empirical Perspectives

William M. Evan

University of Pennsylvania

Sage Library of Social Research 180

SAGE PUBLICATIONS
The International Professional Publishers
Newbury Park   London   New Delhi

For information address:

 SAGE Publications, Inc.
2111 West Hillcrest Drive
Newbury Park, California 91320

SAGE Publications Ltd.
28 Banner Street
London EC1Y 8QE
England

SAGE Publications India Pvt. Ltd.
M-32 Market
Greater Kailash I
New Delhi 110 048 India

Printed in the United States of America

Library of Congress Cataloging-in-Publication Data

Evan, William M.
  Social structure and law : theoretical and empirical perspectives /
William M. Evan.
      p. cm. — (Sage library of social research ; v. 180)
  Includes bibliographical references and indexes.
  ISBN 0-8039-2881-5. — ISBN 0-8039-2882-3 (pbk.)
  1. Sociological jurisprudence. I. Title. II. Series.
K376.E87 1990
340'.115—dc20   90-8544
                                                          CIP

FIRST PRINTING, 1990

Sage Production Editor: Astrid Virding

Contents

PART IV. Systems Theory and the Experimenting Society

Tables

Figures

To Sarah, Robert,
Raima and Craig

Preface

Sociology of law is an expanding field in the United States, Britain, and the Continent as well as Japan. New journals are being established, new professional associations are being formed and, increasingly, courses in this field are being offered in sociology departments and law schools. In addition, in the sister discipline of anthropology, there is an upsurge of interest in "legal anthropology".

And yet, notwithstanding this intellectual ferment, there is still a good deal of confusion regarding the subject and boundaries of this field. As in the case of other disciplines, the clarification of the subject matter probably will require many years of further painstaking research. If no cumulative pattern revealing the boundaries of this field is found, a deductive process of theory construction may prove necessary to cut through the welter of theoretical, philosophical and empirical studies.

In this book of theoretical and empirical essays, I seek to contribute to the process of clarification of some of the central issues of this field. Although written over the course of many years, these essays are informed by a common underlying framework: a social-structure model. This model should not be confused with various theories of structuralism that have emerged in Europe in recent years. Nor should it be confused with a functionalist approach to the sociology of law. Rather, my model attempts to develop an integrative framework for competing

11

theories. Partially suggested by Parsons's action theory, my model can be viewed as a prolegomenon to the development of a systems theory of law. Blocking the development of such a theory are a number of unsolved theoretical and methodological problems. Until such time as a full-fledged systems theory is articulated, the present model may provide some useful theoretical guidelines for ongoing research in this field.

The fifteen chapters comprising this book are divided into four parts. In Part I, I explore a number of theories of law and society, to wit, the classical theories of Marx, Durkheim, and Weber as well as several contemporary theories of Parsons, Watson, Critical Legal Studies, Luhmann, and Teubner. Following this exploration, I draw on some of these theories in the development of a social-structure model of the interaction of legal and nonlegal institutions.

In Part II, I analyze the four components of the social-structure model: values, norms, roles and organizations. Interinstitutional analysis at the societal level—by far the most daunting problem of the social-structure model—is the focus of Part III. In the chapters in this section of the book, I undertake an empirical test of hypotheses regarding the interaction of legal and nonlegal institutions in different societies. Special attention is devoted to comparing different dimensions of legal systems as they relate to differing institutional environments.

In Part IV, I have formulated a conceptual systems model of law which may eventually lend itself to computer simulation experiments and partial empirical testing. In the closing chapter of the book, I present an argument for an experimental perspective toward law.

This book was originally intended as a companion volume to a text-reader I edited entitled *The Sociology of Law: A Social-Structural Perspective* (1980). The reader of that work will profit from studying this volume of essays which sets forth a rationale for theoretical and empirical contributions to the sociology of law.

Once again I would like to record my indebtedness to a former student, Ezra G. Levin, who is now a distinguished member of the New York bar. Many years ago he ably assisted me in various research efforts in this field. I regret that circumstances did not permit us to collaborate in writing this book.

A current graduate student, Hocine Fetni, a profound legal scholar, has graciously served as a sounding board for several chapters in this book. It is indeed a pleasure to express my gratitude to him.

William M. Evan
Philadelphia, Pennsylvania

Acknowledgments

My indebtedness to social scientists and legal scholars whose work I have consulted in writing the essays in this book is acknowledged in the references in the various chapters. There are, however, a number of debts that are not explicitly recorded in the references.

My earliest source of inspiration to pursue research in the sociology of law was the jurisprudential work of Thomas A. Cowan, Professor Emeritus of Rutgers University Law School. Another important influence was the Russell Sage Foundation, which granted me a fellowship in 1958 for the purpose of developing materials for a course in the sociology of law, which I subsequently taught at Columbia University. Yet another significant influence on my work in this field was the Research Committee on the Sociology of Law of the International Sociological Association. Founded in 1962, this committee convened frequent meetings which provided me with a forum for presenting several essays that are included in this book, namely, Chapters 10, 11, 12, 13 and 14.

Finally, I am indebted to several publishers for permitting me to reprint the following essays in the present volume:

Chapter 1. One section in this chapter is reprinted from "Macrosociology, Sociology of Law and Legal Indicators," in *Società, Norme e Valori: Studi in Onore di Renato Treves*, edited by Uberto

Part I

THEORIES OF LAW AND SOCIETY

In Search of a Macro Socio-Legal Theory

Is a sociology of law possible? This question may strike the reader as indeed perplexing in light of the marked growth of the literature in this field in the past two decades. Yet, the absence of a consensually-validated definition of the subject matter and boundaries of this field remains a basic unsolved problem. This problem is compounded by the absence of a dominant paradigm undergirding this field.

Almost three decades ago, Riesman presented a pessimistic assessment of the prospects for the development of the sociology of law:

> Sociology in its present phase can grapple with a profession or occupation; and, with its anthropological and social-psychological allies, it can seek to embrace a whole culture (if not too big); it can study stratification—and the way this shows up in jury deliberations or in the social mobility of lawyers. But, so far as I can see, sociology is not now prepared to embrace the legal order within its own categories in terms sufficiently detailed and concrete to shed new illumination. There is not only a certain intellectual impenetrability about the law, reflecting and resulting from the achievements of generations of jurists; there is an even more important factual impenetrability resulting

from the sheer overwhelming and opaque bulk of data that
must be mastered to link the empirical with the interpretive
or the ideal-typical. And in the law, and even in its mani-
fold branches, there is nothing so lucid, so condensed, so
truly theoretical, as classical price theory in economics.
Law (or what Karl Llewellyn called "law-stuff") is everywhere in its impact; it is almost everywhere in such
forms as judicialization and the use of precedent; and men
trained in law (or at least graduates of law schools) can be
found in many obviously significant social roles. No "pure
theory of law" has won anything like universal assent, or
even awareness, from students of law and jurisprudence;
nor do we have an adequate theory to tell us, beyond
semantics, when we are dealing with law, when with government, when with paralegal sanctions, and so on.

Correspondingly, to infiltrate the legal order-and-disorder
with intellect and understanding remains, in the American
scene, a task scarcely begun. (Riesman, 1962:14-15)

In effect, Riesman asserts that there are two formidable barriers to the development of a sociology of law, viz., the lack of an
adequately detailed sociological theory and the want of a theory
of the legal order to cope with the "factual impenetrability resulting from the sheer overwhelming and opaque bulk of data
that must be mastered to link the empirical with the interpretive
or the ideal-typical."

Have the intervening years negated Riesman's assessment?
Nearly two decades later, Hunt expresses a similar view:

The sociology of law has, to date, failed to develop a coherent theoretical framework within which to base its research
activities. It has failed to achieve its explicit goal of overcoming the narrow and restrictive jurisprudential tradition
within which discussion and analysis of law has been confined. . . . It takes as its starting point the 'law-society' relation but the perspective has remained underdeveloped and
unelaborated with the result that work carried out under
its label has, in general, been characterized by an eclectic

empiricism; anything that relates "law" and "society" is deemed to fall within the sociology of law. (Hunt, 1978:2)

Most researchers in this field, however, would undoubtedly agree that substantial progress has been made. And yet the problems Riesman alluded to still plague this field in some respects, witness the persistence of two problems: (1) the diversity of definitions of the sociology of law and (2) the diversity of theories pertaining to the relationship between law and society.

To document the first problem, a few definitions of the sociology of law advanced in the literature in the past fifty years will be cited:

The sociology of law is a nomographic science which aims to discover "laws" of a scientific nature concerning society in its relation to law. In this somewhat ambiguous formula, the term "law" is used with two different meanings: first, in the sense of a formula describing the causal connections between phenomena, and second, in the sense of socially imposed rules acting on human behavior. (Timasheff, 1939:19)

The Sociology of Law is that part of the sociology of the human spirit which studies the full social reality of law, beginning with its tangible and externally observable expressions, in effective collective behaviours (crystallized organizations, customary practices and traditions or behavioural innovations) *and in the material basis* (the spatial structure and demographic density of jural institutions). *Sociology of law interprets these behaviours and material manifestations of law according to the internal meanings which, while inspiring and penetrating them, are at the same time in part transformed by them. It proceeds specially from jural symbolic patterns fixed in advance, such as organized law, procedures, and sanctions, to jural symbols proper, such as flexible rules and spontaneous law.* From the latter it proceeds to *jural values and ideas which they express, and finally to the collective beliefs and intuitions which aspire to these values and grasp these ideas,* and which manifest themselves in *spontaneous "normative facts", sources of the validity, that is to say, of the positivity of all law.* (Gurvitch, 1947:48)

Sociology of law is here viewed as a branch of general
sociology, just like family sociology, industrial or medical
sociology. (Aubert, 1969:10)

The Sociology of law has as its task not only to register,
formulate and verify the general interrelations existing between the law and other social factors (law could then be
regarded as an independent or dependent variable), but
also to try and build a general theory to explain social
processes in which the law is involved and in this way link
this discipline with the bulk of sociological knowledge.
(Podgórecki, 1974:33)

The purpose of the sociology of law is nothing more nor
less than the study of how actors achieve in concerted
social action those activities which pertain to law. Law in
the context of social action is the proper object of attention,
not law generically defined and identifiable independently
of routine social activity. (Grace and Wilkinson, 1978:291)

The sociology of law seeks to explain the nature of law in
terms of the empirical conditions within which legal doctrine and institutions exist in particular societies or social
conditions. As a study aimed at the explanation of social
phenomena through analysis of systematically organised
empirical data it must concern itself centrally with understanding law as it is, rather than as it might or should be.
(Cotterrell, 1984:303)

What are we to make of this bewildering array of definitions?
We may conclude that it bears out the assessments of Riesman
and Hunt. However, at least one general, if vague, theme
emerges, viz., that the field explores the relationship between
law and society. Moreover, Aubert's formulation that sociology
of law is a branch of general sociology, in effect invites us to
consider the state of sociological theory as a source of guidance
for this specialty.

From a sociology of science perspective this diversity of
views is not a serious deficiency. As in the case of other areas of
specialization in the social sciences, research continues on the

assumption that the cumulation of knowledge will eventually point the way to a clarification of the subject matter. For this progressive cumulation of knowledge to occur, however, there is a need for a theory, or theories, to give structure to empirical findings and direct future research. This brings us to the second problem: the diversity of theories of law and society.

The concepts "law" and "society" refer to macro-structural phenomena. Is there a macro-oriented theory of law and society or a macro socio-legal theory to guide this field? As an interdisciplinary endeavor, the sociology of law relies upon or is influenced by the intellectual assumptions and propositions of general sociology and legal theory. We shall now consider the relationship of this field to both parent disciplines.

RELATIONSHIP TO GENERAL SOCIOLOGY

It is no exaggeration to state that the field of sociology lacks a systematically developed and precise theory of society. Although interest in macrosociological theory building has been in evidence for the past two decades, particularly among those concerned with comparative sociology (Eisenstadt and Curelaru, 1977), no such theory has yet been developed in sufficient detail and precision to guide empirical research. This is not to deny the fact that such macrotheorists as Marx, Durkheim, Weber, and Parsons have exerted a pervasive influence on various specialties within sociology. The field of social stratification, for example, has been greatly influenced by the theories of Marx and Weber; the sociology of religion has been influenced by the work of Durkheim and Weber, among others; and organizational sociology has until recently been dominated by the work of Weber.

The enduring contributions of Marx, Durkheim, and Weber to our understanding of the relationship between law and society derive from their formulation of an overall macro perspective.

Marx

Marx conceived of law as a component of the "superstructure" of a capitalist society. As an epiphenomenon of the superstructure, it provides a rationale or ideology for preserving the
existing class relations in a capitalist economy. Concepts of
property and contract, for example, become instrumentali-
ties for maintaining and reproducing class hegemony. In other
words, legal concepts and doctrines reinforce the position of the
ruling class and at the same time become the constituents of the
"false consciousness" from which the working class suffers. Implicit in this theory of law as a weapon wielded by the state in a
capitalist society against the working class is the assumption
that if private property were abolished and a classless socialist
society were ushered in, the state would "wither away" and,
with it, law would "wither away" as well.

As usually formulated, the Marxian theory of law and society
is not verifiable by means of empirical research. It does not
follow, however, that this theory is devoid of any empirical
implications. Questions can be raised concerning class bias in
the adjudication of civil and criminal cases, in the emergence of
significant legal norms—for example, those regarding inheritance—and in the recurrent failure of agrarian reform laws.
Likewise, it is possible to investigate a proposition counter to
the Marxian thesis, viz., that the passage of laws in a capitalist
state can potentially diminish the power of the ruling class vis-
à-vis the working class. A case in point is the enactment of the
National Labor Relations Act of 1935 in the United States which
institutionalized the rights of employees to unionize and to en-
gage in collective bargaining with employers.

Research questions such as those cited above would test the
validity of some propositions derivable from the Marxian theory of law and society. They would also orient empirical research to some significant *macrosocial* problems.

Durkheim

Turning to Durkheim's contribution to this field, one of necessity reverts to his much-debated thesis in his *Division of Labor in Society* (1933) concerning the relationship between types of laws and types of solidary relationships produced by differing systems of division of labor in society; viz., in societies characterized by mechanical solidarity there is a predominance of repressive laws, whereas in societies characterized by organic solidarity there is a predominance of restitutive laws. A number of social scientists have subjected Durkheim's thesis to empirical tests and have found it wanting (Schwartz and Miller, 1964). It is a testament, however, to the intriguing character of Durkheim's thesis that it continues to evoke the interest of researchers (Baxi, 1974; Schwartz, 1974; Sheleff, 1975). A more general formulation of Durkheim's thesis would be that societies differing along various dimensions of societal development—of which the division of labor is but one—will exhibit systematic differences in their legal systems (Evan, 1968).

In the course of developing his thesis that the division of labor is the principal source of social solidarity, Durkheim formulated his seminal idea of an "index."

> But social solidarity is a completely moral phenomenon which, taken by itself, does not lend itself to exact observation nor indeed to measurement. To proceed to this classification and this comparison, we must substitute for this internal fact which escapes us an external index which symbolizes it and study the former in the light of the latter.

> This visible symbol is law. In effect, despite its immaterial character, wherever social solidarity exists, it resides not in a state of pure potentiality, but manifests its presence by sensible indices. . . . The more solidary the members of a society are, the more they sustain diverse relations, one with another, or with the group taken collectively, for, if

their meetings were rare, they would depend upon one another only at rare intervals, and then tenuously. More-over, the number of these relations is necessarily pro-portional to that of the juridical rules which determine them. . . . We can thus be certain of finding reflected in law all the essential varieties of social solidarity. (Durkheim, 1933:64-65)

From our present vantage point, now that we take for granted the use of indicators and surrogate variables in empirical re-search, Durkheim's concept of an "index" may not warrant spe-cial attention. However, Durkheim, among his various claims to fame as the "father of modern sociology," was, to my knowl-edge, the originator of the concept of an "index," viz., an indi-rect and "external" measure of a complex dimension of social structure such as social solidarity. That he developed the con-cept of an index in connection with "juridical rules" and types of laws is of particular interest to sociologists of law and legal scholars. Under the circumstances, it is indeed surprising that to date, with few exceptions (Evan, 1965, 1968, and 1980; Merry-man, Clark, and Friedman, 1979; Lidz, 1979), this facet of Durk-heim's work has been neglected. It is my judgment that the concept of a "legal index" or a "legal indicator" merits our systematic attention if we are to become more precise in our understanding of the role of law in social change. Moreover, the concept of a legal indicator can be usefully applied to some of Durkheim's work, subsequent to his *Division of Labor in Society,* that bears on law.

In his *Professional Ethics and Civic Morals* (1958), Durkheim begins by extending the thesis he formulated on "occupational groups" that appeared as a preface to the second edition of his *Division of Labor in Society.* Concerned about the dangers of "moral anarchy" in modern life, Durkheim considers new sources of social solidarity in the emergence of professional groups and "corporate bodies" intermediate between the indi-vidual and the family, on the one hand, and the state, on the other. Each professional group develops, in the course of time, its distinctive body of "professional ethics." Durkheim's hypothesis concerning the relationship between the structure of the professional group and its professional ethics is as follows:

> In general, all things being equal, the greater the strength of the group structure, the more numerous are the moral rules appropriate to it and the greater the authority they have over their members. For the more closely the group coheres, the more frequent and intimate these contacts and the more exchange there is of ideas and sentiments, the more does a public opinion spread to cover a great number of things. . . . Accordingly, it can be said that professional ethics will be the more developed, and the more advanced in their operation, the greater the stability and the better the organization of the professional groups themselves. (Durkheim, 1958:7-8)

By way of justifying the potential contribution of professional groups to overcoming "moral anarchy," Durkheim draws a parallel with medieval guilds and envisions the possibility that professional associations would eventually take "the place of the jurisdictional area as a political unit of the region" (p. 39). To implement this quasi-syndicalist vision of the future, Durkheim refers to the need for "occupational legislation" (p. 39).

The sociologist of law who reads these posthumously published lectures over seventy five years after they were delivered may wish to take liberties in reinterpreting the text. Professional occupations seek the protection of the law to control entry to their occupations, to preserve their autonomy, and to regulate the conduct of their members, thus giving rise to the proliferation of occupational licensure laws. To what extent do developed and developing countries differ in the incidence of such laws? Can the differential incidence of such laws be interpreted as an "index" or an indicator of the trend toward a professionally based society such as Durkheim envisioned?

Weber

In comparison with the work of Durkheim and Marx, Weber's contributions to the sociology of law are appreciably more diverse and complex. Embedded in an intricate mosaic of ideal types and comparative and historical data on the emergence of legal rationality in Western civilization and on the role of law in the origins of capitalism (Weber, 1950; Rheinstein, 1954; Trubek, 1972; Collins, 1980), Weber's welter of legal conceptualizations poses a difficult challenge to the empirically oriented researcher. For example, his famous typology of lawmaking and lawfinding suggests possible research leads for comparative and historical analyses. Rheinstein, who edited and translated Weber's work on the sociology of law, lucidly summarizes his typology in the following manner:

1. *irrational*, i.e., not guided by general rules
   a. *formal*: guided by means which are beyond the control of reason (ordeal, oracle, etc.)
   b. *substantive*: guided by reaction to the individual case
2. *rational*, i.e., guided by general rules
   a. *substantive*: guided by the principles of an ideological system other than that of the law itself (ethics, religion, power, politics, etc.)
   b. *formal*:
      (1) *extrinsically*, i.e., ascribing significance to external acts observable by the senses
      (2) *logically*, i.e., expressing its rules by the use of abstract concepts created by legal thought itself and conceived of as constituting a complete system. (Rheinstein, 1954:1)

Assuming that the meaning of each of these ideal type categories can be clarified and that legal indicators can be developed for each of the types, a comparative study could be undertaken to explore differences in lawmaking and in lawfinding of such major legal systems as common law, civil law, socialist law, and Moslem law. Equally challenging would be a study of long-term trends within each of these legal systems. The findings of such an inquiry would shed light on the occurrence of the evolutionary stages postulated by Weber:

> The general development of law and procedure may be viewed as passing through the following stages: first, charismatic legal revelation through "law prophets"; second, empirical creation and finding of law by legal honoratiores. . . . ; third, imposition of law by secular or theocratic powers; fourth and finally, systematic elaboration of law and professionalized administration of justice by persons who have received their legal training in a learned and formally logical manner. (Rheinstein, 1954:303)

Another significant thesis in Weber's corpus of writings on law is the innovative role he attributes to "legal honoratiores" or "legal notables" (Bendix, 1960). Is Weber's thesis more valid for civil-law systems with its heavy immersion in Roman law, than it is for common law, let alone for socialist law or Moslem law? Once again it would be necessary to develop appropriate legal indicators to measure the degree to which legal notables—lawyers, judges, and high level civil servants—introduce new rules and new interpretations of existing legal norms in the course of administering justice.

Parsons

For decades, Parsons was the leading macrosociological theorist in the United States, making singular contributions to structural-functionalism and to a general theory of action. Focusing on the action of social systems, Parsons developed a "four-function paradigm." According to Parsons, every society faces four subsystem problems: adaptation, goal attainment, integration and pattern maintenance or latency (AGIL). The societal subsystems associated with these four functional problems are, respectively, the economy, the polity, law, religion, and education.

Following Weber, Parsons treats law as a rational-legal system consisting of a set of prescriptions, proscriptions, and permissions. The legal system, especially in highly differentiated modern societies, performs the function of a "generalized mechanism of social control" (Parsons, 1962). This function is performed vis-à-vis the economy, the polity and pattern maintenance or latency. The net effect of the pervasive normative regulation is the integration of society. As Parsons puts it: "The legal system . . . broadly constitutes what is probably the single most important institutional key to understanding . . . problems of societal integration" (Parsons, 1978:52).

With his four-function paradigm, Parsons addresses the nexus between law and society with the aid of "generalized media of interchange." The economy in a developed and differentiated society uses the medium of money for transactions. Functionally analogous media of exchange operate in each of the other subsystems, to wit, power in the polity, value commitment in pattern maintenance and influence in law.

Bredemeier, following Parsons, has analyzed in very general terms, the "outputs" of the legal system to the subsystems in exchange for certain "inputs":

1. From the political system, goals and enforcement, in exchange for interpretation and legitimation.
2. From the adaptive system, knowledge and "acceptance of queries" as research directives in exchange for organization and "demand" for knowledge.
3. From the pattern-maintenance system, conflicts and esteem in exchange for resolution and "justice." (Bredemeier, 1962:89)

Turner likewise resorts to a Parsonsian intersubsystem analysis of inputs and outputs in the course of developing an evolutionary model of law (Turner, 1980). And Parsons himself has applied his paradigm in an ambitious comparative and historical study of societies, including ancient Egypt, the Mesopotamian Empire, China, India, the Islamic Empire, and the Roman Empire (Parsons, 1966).

Suggestive as Parsons's framework is for understanding interinstitutional relations, the generalized media of interchange have not, as yet, been operationalized so as to explain how the legal system interacts with other societal subsystems. Otherwise put, since Parsons has not explicated specific linkages between the legal and nonlegal subsystems, it is difficult to discern what hypotheses can be tested against any body of data. Hence, a reasonable conclusion is that Parsons's macrosociological theory, in its present form, is actually a metatheory.

In the foregoing review of some sociological theories of law and society, two common themes have been identified: (1) that each of the theorists endeavored to comprehend the macrostructural relationships between law and other institutional systems of a society, and (2) that if the hypotheses implicit in these theories are to be empirically tested, systematic attention would have to be devoted to the development of a body of legal indicators. The current generation of sociologists of law has yet to face up to the problems engendered by both of these themes.

RELATIONSHIP TO LEGAL THEORY

Is the relationship between the sociology of law and the field of legal theory any less problematic than it is with general sociology? On its face, the question should be answered in the affirmative because the sociologist of law must take some of the legal scholars' subjects as objects of inquiry. In actuality, because of the traditions of legal scholarship, legal scholars do not generally provide an analytical basis for sociological research. Legal scholarship tends to be preoccupied with legal rules, legal principles, and their application to a multitude of specific conflict situations. As a consequence, the scholarly literature—apart from being intellectually insular—is almost entirely verbal and idiographic, with virtually no interest in a *nomothetic*, let alone *quantitative*, analysis of legal phenomena. Furthermore, there is a high degree of specialization within legal scholarship such that most scholars tend to devote their entire careers to a particular body of law, be it labor law, criminal law, contract law, family law, etc., in their own country. Those scholars specializing in comparative law are inclined to study a particular specialty, for example, family law, by comparing case studies from two or more countries (Glendon, 1975). Relatively few legal scholars seek to study the legal system of an entire society, such as the work of John Hazard (1977) and Harold Berman (1963) on the Soviet legal system. And fewer still have had the temerity to undertake systematic comparisons of total legal systems or families of legal systems, as exemplified in the work of David and Brierley (1968) and Wigmore (1928); and those who do, make no effort to relate characteristics of total legal systems to the social-structural attributes of the societies in which they are embedded.

Surveying the current scene of legal theory three distinct theoretical perspectives can be discerned: the theory of legal autonomy, critical legal studies, and autopoietic law. Each of these perspectives will be briefly reviewed and appraised for their implications for a theory of law and society.

Legal Autonomy

Traditional conceptions of the legal order and "source of law" are based on two assumptions: First, the law is a "seamless web," a relatively "closed system." Whatever processes of change occur in the law are generated from within the legal system, not from without. In other words, the change processes are immanent or endogenous and are not externally induced. Second, by definition, it is assumed that the legal system is autonomous from other systems or institutions comprising a society. Therefore, it is unnecessary to inquire into how the legal system interacts with other subsystems of a society, viz., what degree of autonomy a given legal system actually has from other societal subsystems.

Perhaps the most quintessential articulation of the theory of legal autonomy in recent years can be found in the work of Watson, a renowned legal historian and comparative law scholar.

Watson has repeated his thesis of legal autonomy in a number of monographs and articles (Watson, 1974, 1978, 1981, 1983, 1985, 1987). He contends that the growth and evolution of the law is largely determined by an autonomous legal tradition which exists and operates outside the sphere of societal needs.

> To a large extent law possesses a life and vitality of its own; that is, no extremely close, natural or inevitable relationship exists between law, legal structures, institutions and rules on the one hand and the needs and desires and political economy of the ruling elite or of the members of the particular society on the other hand. If there was such a close relationship, legal rules, institutions and structures would transplant only with great difficulty, and their power of survival would be severely limited. (Watson, 1978:314-315)

> There is a lawyer's way to approach a problem. This mode of thinking inoculates them from too much concern with the demands of society. (Watson, 1985:42)

> Law . . . is above all and primarily the culture of the lawyers and especially of the law-makers, that is, of those lawyers who, whether as legislators, jurists, or judges, have control of the accepted mechanisms of legal change. Legal development is determined by their culture; and social, economic, and political factors impinge on legal development only through their consciousness. . . . Law is largely autonomous and not shaped by societal needs; though legal institutions will not exist without corresponding social institutions, law evolves from the legal tradition. (Watson, 1985:119)

Unlike the Marxist view of law, Watson argues that the law does not advance the interests of the ruling class; instead, it reflects the "culture" of the legal elite. He bolsters his provocative thesis with a study of legal borrowing, which he refers to as "legal transplants" (1974). The fact that individual statutes, legal doctrines and entire codes have been borrowed by countries differing in cultural, political, economic and other respects provides evidence in support of his thesis of legal autonomy.

The concept of "legal transplant" has a naturalistic ring to it as though it occurs independent of any human agency. In point of fact, however, elites—legal and nonlegal—often act as "culture carriers" or intermediaries between societies involved in a legal transplant. Legal scholars who are associated with political elites may be instrumental in effecting a legal transplant. Moreover, many instances of legal borrowing involve the "imposition" of a foreign body of law by a colonial power (Burman and Harrell-Bond, 1979). Hence, it is a misnomer to describe and analyze the diffusion of law as if it were devoid of human agency. If human volition is involved, it is indeed questionable whether the borrowed legal elements do not perform a societal function—at the very least on behalf of the legal elite.

Watson's repeated assertions of his thesis concerning legal autonomy have aroused criticisms from a number of scholars, some of whom have pointed to legislation as a source of legal change that obviously relates to the social structure of a society (Abel, 1982). In two detailed replies to his critics Watson proceeds to minimize the effect and durability of legislation on legal evolution (Watson, 1983, 1987). Citing numerous historical examples of legal change via borrowing, Watson seeks to bear out his contention of the relative independence of legal systems from their political, economic and social contexts. I shall consider one of his examples—Ataturk's promulgation of the Turkish Civil Code in 1926 following the Turkish Revolution.

Watson cites the fact that, with only minor alterations, Ataturk incorporated two Swiss Civil Codes in support of his thesis. However, Watson has failed to address the following social-structural factors. After the Ottoman Empire was dissolved by the Allies following World War I, Ataturk, in the interest of modernizing the state, sought to segregate church and state and establish links with the West while retaining Turkey's distinctive historical origins in Asia. With this agenda in mind, Ataturk selected Switzerland, a politically neutral power which was a thriving commercial center in Western Europe and a country with a governance system that institutionalized a separation of church and state.

In addition, it is very likely that the legal elite involved in this legal transplant decision had intellectual and social ties with their counterparts in Switzerland. Turkish jurists, for example, may have been familiar with the Swiss Civil Code by virtue of having studied in Lausanne. Moreover, the Turkish legal elite in all probability had access to the Turkish political and economic elite and thus were in a position to exert influence on the decision to borrow the Swiss Civil Code. Thus, what seems like a random act of legal borrowing may in fact have entailed a careful and deliberate decision.

In short, there is ample reason to question the validity of Watson's thesis on legal change and legal evolution. This is indeed important for the sociology of law because the corpus of Watson's work may be interpreted as undermining the rationale for developing a theory of law and society.

Critical Legal Studies

Unlike Watson's internalist focus on the legal system and its autonomous development, the Critical Legal Studies (CLS) movement appears to pursue a dual strategy: externalist as well as internalist. CLS is externalist in its critique of the social order and of the values dominating judicial decision making. It is internalist in its fundamental critique of traditional jurisprudence and legal reasoning.

The CLS movement emerged in the late 1970s in American law schools. It brought together a diverse group of scholars with a left-of-center ideology concerned about inequality and injustice in American society. Although lacking any consensus regarding societal transformation, CLS scholars sought to identify the impact of society's dominant interests on the legal process and the impact of social and political values on legal decision making.

In his introduction to a volume of essays by CLS authors, David Kairys discusses the "basic elements" of the legal theory of this movement. Three of these elements are externalist in nature:

We place fundamental importance on democracy, by which we mean popular participation in the decisions that shape our society and affect our lives. . . . Our society allows no democracy outside this "public" sphere of our lives. For example, the economic decisions that most crucially shape our society and affect our lives, on basic social issues like the use of our resources, investment, the energy problem, and the work of our people, are regarded as "private" and are not made democratically or even by the government officials elected in the public sphere. The public/private split ideologically legitimized private—mainly corporate—dominance, masks the lack of real participation or democracy . . .

We reject the common characterization of the law and the state as neutral, value-free arbiters, independent of and unaffected by social and economic relations, political forces, and cultural phenomena. Traditional jurisprudence largely ignores social and historical reality, and masks the existence of social conflict and oppression with ideological myths about objectivity and neutrality. The dominant system of values has been declared value free; it then follows that all others suffer from bias and can be thoughtlessly dismissed. . . .

The law's ultimate mechanism for control and enforcement is institutional violence, but it protects the dominant system of social and power relations against political and ideological as well as physical challenges. The law is a major vehicle for the maintenance of existing social and power relations by the consent or acquiescence of the lower and middle classes. (Kairys, 1982:3-5)

These three externalist principles of the CLS movement have a familiar ring to them, namely, they are reminiscent of criticisms leveled by Marxists and Neo-Marxists against the legal order of capitalist societies. In addition, scholars influenced by the Frankfurt School of critical theory have expressed similar criticisms. At least one scholar contends that the intellectual precursor of the CLS movement is the antipositivist philosophical orientation of the Frankfurt School, not the empiricist and pragmatic perspective of American Legal Realism (Standen, 1986:992). In their criticism of law and social institutions as involving "belief structures" and "social reifications," CLS writers seek to transform legal consciousness and thereby transform society (Gordon, 1982). The fact that CLS writers refer to themselves as comprising a "movement" is indicative of their general social and political agenda.

By far the most distinctive contribution of the CLS movement has been its elaborate internalist critique of legal reasoning and legal process. As Kairys puts it:

> We reject . . . the notion that a distinctly legal mode of reasoning or analysis characterizes the legal process or even exists. . . . There is no legal reasoning in the sense of a legal methodology or process for reaching particular, correct results. There is a distinctly legal and quite elaborate system of discourse and body of knowledge, replete with its own language and conventions of argumentation, logic, and even manners. In some ways these aspects of the law are so distinct and all-embracing as to amount to a separate culture; and for many lawyers the courthouse, the law firm, the language, the style, become a way of life. But in terms of a method or process for decision making—for determining correct rules, facts, or results—the law provides only a wide and conflicting variety of stylized rationalizations from which courts pick and choose. Social and political judgments about the substance, parties, and context of a case guide such choices, even when they are not the explicit or conscious basis of decision. (Kairys, 1982:3)

Not only do critical legal scholars reject the notion of legal reasoning, they also reject other idealized components constituting a "legal system," viz., that law is a body of doctrine, that the doctrine reflects a coherent view of relations between persons and the nature of society, and that social behavior reflects norms generated by the legal system (Trubek, 1984:577). In contrast to an ideal model of the legal order that serves to legitimate existing hierarchical relations and to make them appear natural or inevitable, CLS scholars assert four principles that they believed accurately reflect reality about the law: indeterminacy, anti-formalism, contradiction, and marginality (Beck, 1988:436). Indeterminacy means that "legal rules or arguments, though they exist, do not determine or compel any given answers to questions about social behavior" (Beck, 1988:436). The second principle, antiformalism, rejects the alleged neutrality of legal reasoning when applied to specific cases. The principle of anti-formalism also rejects the argument that legal reasoning leads to decisions independent of value preferences and political purposes. The third principle, contradiction, asserts that "legal doctrine contradicts itself because it rests upon competing views of human relations, e.g., freedom and security." The fourth principle is marginality, namely, that "law seldom plays a decisive role in influencing social behavior" (Beck, 1988: 443).

The general conclusion CLS writers draw from "unmasking" the legal system, "trashing" mainstream jurisprudence and "deconstructing" legal scholarship (Barkan, 1987) is that "law is simply politics by other means" (Kairys, 1982:17). Such a conclusion, on its face, does not hold out any promise for developing a new, let alone heuristic, approach to a theory of law and society. On the contrary, its antipositivism combined with its search for a transformative political agenda has prompted CLS writers to view with increasing skepticism the sociology of law and research into the relationship between law and society (Trubek and Esser, 1989). At the same time, CLS has inspired the formation of the Amherst Seminar on Legal Ideology and Legal Process. Since 1982 a group of social scientists has met to develop a "critical-empirical" approach to research on law and society (Trubek and Esser, 1989). Whether they will succeed in resolving the paradigmatic conflicts, and in the process create an integrated approach to law and society, remains to be seen.

Autopoietic Law

Similar in some respects to Watson's theory of legal autonomy, but fundamentally different from the theory of the CLS movement, autopoietic law claims to be a challenging new theory of law and society (Teubner, 1988a). For the past few years, several continental social theorists who are also legal scholars have enthusiastically developed and propagated the theory of autopoietic law. A complex cluster of ideas, this theory is derived from the work of two biologists, Maturana and Varela (1980) and Varela (1979).

In the course of their biological research Maturana and Varela arrived at some methodological realizations which led them to generalize about the nature of living systems. Maturana coined the term "autopoiesis" to capture this new "scientific epistemology" (Maturana and Varela, 1980:xvii): "This was a word without a history, a word that could directly mean what takes place in the dynamics of the autonomy proper to living systems." Conceptualizing living systems as machines, Maturana and Varela present the following rather complex and abstract definition:

> Autopoietic machines are homeostatic machines. Their peculiarity, however, does not lie in this but in the fundamental variable which they maintain constant. *An autopoietic machine is a machine organized (defined as a unity) as a network of processes of production (transformation and destruction) of components that produces the components which: (i) through their interactions and transformations continuously regenerate and realize the network of processes (relations) that produced them; and (ii) constitute it (the machine) as a concrete unity in the space in which they (the components) exist by specifying the topological domain of its realization as such a network.* It follows that an autopoietic machine continuously generates and specifies its own organization through its operation as a system of production of its own components, and does this in an endless turnover of components under conditions of continuous perturbations and compensation of perturbations. (Maturana and Varela, 1980:78-79)

Given this abstract formulation of autopoiesis, Maturana and Varela draw the following four conclusions:

(i) Autopoietic machines are autonomous; that is, they subordinate all changes to the maintenance of their own organization, independently of how profoundly they may otherwise be transformed in the process. Other machines, henceforth called allopoietic machines, have as the product of their functioning something different from themselves. . . .

(ii) Autopoietic machines have individuality; that is, by keeping their organization as an invariant through its continuous production they actively maintain an identity which is independent of their interactions with an observer.

(iii) Autopoietic machines are unities because, and only because, of their specific autopoietic organization: their operations specify their own boundaries in the processes of self-production. This is not the case with an allopoietic machine whose boundaries are defined by the observer, who by specifying its input and output surfaces, specifies what pertains to it in its operations.

(iv) Autopoietic machines do not have inputs or outputs. They can be perturbated by independent events and undergo internal structural changes which compensate these perturbations. If the perturbations are repeated, the machine may undergo repeated series of internal changes which may or may not be identical. (Maturana and Varela, 1980:80-81)

A less opaque definition of autopoiesis is presented by Zeleny, one of the early advocates of this new theory:

An *autopoietic system* is a distinguishable complex of component-producing processes and their resulting components, bounded as an autonomous unity within its environment, and characterized by a particular kind of relation among its components and component-producing processes: the components, through their interaction, recursively generate, maintain, and recover *the same* complex of processes which produced them. (Zeleny, 1980:4)

Clearly these definitions and conclusions are rather obscure and high-level generalizations which, from a general systems theory perspective (von Bertalanffy, 1968) are questionable. Especially suspect is the assertion that autopoietic systems do not have inputs and outputs. The authors introduce further complexity by postulating second- and third-order autopoietic systems which occur when autopoietic systems interact with one another and, in turn, generate a new autopoietic system (Maturana and Varela, 1980:107-111). Toward the end of their provocative monograph, Maturana and Varela raise the question of whether the dynamics of human societies are determined by the autopoiesis of its components. Failing to agree on the answer to this question, the authors postpone further discussion (Maturana and Varela 1980:118).

Zeleny, however, hastens to answer this question and introduces the notion of "social autopoiesis" to convey that human societies are autopoietic (Zeleny, 1980:3).

Luhmann, an outstanding German theorist and jurist, has also gravitated to the theory of autopoiesis. According to Luhmann, "social systems can be regarded as special kinds of autopoietic systems" (1988b:15). Influenced in part by Parsons and general systems theory, Luhmann applied some systems concepts in analyzing social structures (1982). In the Conclusion to the second edition of his book *A Sociological Theory of Law* (1985), Luhmann briefly refers to the new developments in general systems theory which warrant the application of autopoiesis to the legal system. Instead of maintaining the dichotomy between closed and open systems theory, articulated by von Bertalanffy, Boulding, and Rapoport (Buckley, 1968), Luhmann seeks to integrate the open and closed system perspectives. In the process he conceptualizes the legal system as self-referential, self-reproducing, "normatively closed" and "cognitively open"—a theme he has pursued in a number of essays (1985, 1986, 1988a, 1988c). In his own words:

> The autopoiesis of the legal system is normatively closed in that only the legal system can bestow legally normative

quality on its elements and thereby constitute them as elements. Normativity has no purpose beyond this. . . . Its function is continuous making possible of self, from moment to moment, from event to event, from case to case and it is designed precisely to have no end. The system therefore reproduces its elements by its elements by transferring this quality of meaning from moment to moment and thereby always providing new elements with normative validity. In this respect it is closed to the environment. This means that no legally relevant event can derive its normativity from the environment of the system. In this respect it remains dependent on the self-generating connection of legal elements and on the limits of this connection.

At the same time, and precisely in relation to this closure the legal system is a cognitively open system. In each of its elements and in their constant reproduction it is dependent on being able to determine whether certain conditions have been met or not. By programming it makes itself dependent on facts and it can also change its programs when the pressure of facts dictates this. Every operation in law, every juristic processing of information therefore uses normative and cognitive orientations simultaneously—simultaneously and necessarily linked but not having the same function. The norm quality serves the autopoiesis of the system, its self-continuation in difference [sic] to the environment. The cognitive quality serves the coordination of this process with the system's environment. (Luhmann, 1988b:20)

This formulation is, to say the least, ambiguous. Given normative closure, how does the learning of the system's environmental changes, expectations or demands get transmitted to the legal system? Further complicating the problem is Luhmann's theory of a functionally differentiated modern society in which all subsystems—including the legal system—tend to be differentiated as self-referential systems, thereby reaching high levels of autonomy (Luhmann, 1982). Although Luhmann has explicitly addressed the issue of integrating the closed and open system perspectives of general systems theory, it is by no means evident from his many publications how this is achieved.

Another prominent contributor to autopoietic law is the jurist and sociologist of law, Teubner. In numerous publications in the past few years, Teubner discusses the theory of autopoiesis, its implications for reflexive law, legal autonomy and evolutionary theory (Teubner, 1983, 1984, 1988a, 1988b). I shall single out for discussion one of Teubner's most recent essays, "Evolution of Autopoietic Law" (1988a) because it raises two general issues: The prerequisites of autopoietic closure of a legal system, and legal evolution after a legal system achieves autopoietic closure. With respect to the first issue, Teubner applies the concept of "hypercycle," which he has borrowed from others but which he does not explicitly define. By referring to another of his recent essays (Teubner, 1988b), one can discern how Teubner is using this concept. For Teubner, all self-referential systems involve, by definition, "circularity" or "recursivity" (1988b:57). Legal systems are preeminently self-referential in the course of producing legal acts or legal decisions. However, if they are to achieve autopoietic autonomy, their cyclically-constituted system components must become interlinked in a "hypercycle," "i.e., the additional cyclical linkage of cyclically constituted units" (Teubner, 1988b:55):

> Autonomization of law means the cumulation of self-referential relations in various legal dimensions. Only after the cyclical self-constitution of all components of the legal system—elements, structures, processes, boundaries, etc.—can those components be linked up in a hypercycle. It is the constitution of such a hypercycle that produces autopoietic closure. As a result, the cycle of legal communication—legal structure—legal communication is set into motion and becomes independent from the general societal cycle of communication. (Teubner, 1988a:218)

The reader of this arcane statement who is not yet a "true believer" of the theory of autopoiesis cannot help but wonder how hypercycles can be observed, let alone measured. The legal system components, as conceptualized by Teubner—"element, structure, process, identity boundary, environment, performance, function" (1988b:55)—are general terms not readily susceptible to the construction of "legal indicators." A somewhat more descriptive statement about hypercycles is as follows:

> Procedure and doctrine are hypercyclical linkages of the relationship between norm and decision, which in this way control the self-reproduction of law. It is only once self-description and self-constitution of the system components have in this way created the necessary pre-conditions for hypercyclical coupling that the actual production of legal communication from legal communications via the network of legal expectations, controlled by legal doctrine and legal procedure, can begin. (Teubner, 1988b:66)

Single feedback loops in system-theoretic models are difficult enough to operationalize and measure. Teubner's hypercyclical linkages, involving multiple feedback loops of legal system components, would pose a daunting challenge to the empirically oriented sociologist of law.

The second question Teubner addresses—legal evolution after a legal system has attained autopoietic closure—poses a similar problem. The universal evolutionary functions of variation, selection and retention manifest themselves in the form of legal mechanisms."In the legal system, normative structures take over variation, institutional structures (especially procedures) take over selection, and doctrinal structures take over retention" (Teubner, 1988a:228). Since Teubner subscribes to Luhmann's theory of a functionally differentiated social system with each subsystem undergoing autopoietic development, he confronts the problem of intersubsystem relations in regard to evolution. This leads him to introduce the intriguing concept of "co-evolution."

> The environmental reference in evolution however is produced not in the direct, causal production of legal developments, but in processes of co-evolution. The thesis is as

follows: *In co-evolutionary processes* it is not only the autopoiesis of the legal system which has a selective effect on
the development of its own structures; *the autopoiesis of
other subsystems and that of society also affects*—in any case in
a much more mediatory and indirect way—*the selection of
legal changes.* (Teubner, 1988a:235-236)

Given the postulate of "autopoietic closure," it is not clear by
what mechanisms nonlegal subsystems of a society affect the
evolution of the legal system and how they "co-evolve." Once
again, we confront the unsolved problem in the theory of autopoiesis of integrating the closed and open systems perspectives. Nevertheless, Teubner, with the help of the concept of
"co-evolution," has drawn our attention to a critical problem
even if one remains skeptical of his proposition that "the historical relationship of 'law and society' must, in my view, be
defined as a co-evolution of structurally coupled autopoietic
systems." (Teubner, 1988a:218).

At least three additional questions about autopoietic law
should be raised. Luhmann's theory of a functionally differentiated society in which all subsystems are autopoietic raises anew
Durkheim's problem of social integration. The centrifugal forces
in such a society would very likely threaten its viability. Such a
societal theory implies a highly decentralized social system with
a weak state and a passive legal system. Does Luhmann really
think any modern society approximates his model of a functionally differentiated society?

A related problem is the implicit ethnocentrism of social scientists writing against the background of highly developed
Western societies where law enjoys a substantial level of functional autonomy, which, however, is by no means equivalent to
"autopoietic closure." In developing societies, and in socialist
countries, many of which are developing societies as well, this is
hardly the case. In these types of societies, legal systems tend to
be subordinated to political, economic and/or military institutions. In other words, the legal systems are decidedly *allopoietic.*
To characterize the subsystems of such societies as *autopoietic* is
to distort social reality.

A third problem with the theory of autopoietic law is its reliance on the "positivity" of law. This fails to consider a secular legal trend of great import for the future of mankind, viz., the faltering efforts—initiated by Grotius in the seventeenth century—to develop a body of international law. By what mechanisms can autopoietic legal systems incorporate international legal norms? Because of the focus on "positivized" law untainted by political, religious and other institutional values, autopoietic legal systems would have a difficult time accommodating themselves to the growing corpus of international law.

Stimulating as is the development of the theory of legal autopoiesis, it does not, in my judgment, fulfill the requirements for a fruitful theory of law and society. Nor does it qualify as a scientific theory. Febbrajo, in his introductory essay to the 1988 *European Yearbook in the Sociology of Law*, points out that neither Luhmann nor Teubner are concerned about the empirical basis of their theories; they justify socio-legal studies "at the level of a meta-language basically independent from direct support of empirical pillars" (Febbrajo, 1988:10).

In its present formulation, autopoietic law is a provocative metatheory. If any of its adherents succeed in deriving empirical propositions from this metatheory, subject them to an empirical test and confirm them, they will be instrumental in bringing about a paradigm shift in the sociology of law.

CONCLUSION

The classical and contemporary theories of law and society, reviewed above, all fall short of providing precise and operational guidelines for uncovering the linkages over time between legal and nonlegal institutions in different societies. Thus, the search for a scientific macro socio-legal theory will continue. There are, however, grounds for a measure of optimism at present—unlike the pessimism expressed by Riesman about 30 years ago—because of the increase in theoretical and methodological sophistication, on the one hand, and the growth of a body of empirical data on the functioning of legal systems, on the other.

CHAPTER 2

A Social-Structure Model

As is evident from the previous chapter, no single macro-socio-legal theory currently enjoys consensus among sociologists of law. Nevertheless, research continues, although handicapped by the difficulty of cumulating and generalizing empirical findings. In this chapter, I outline a model which has two advantages: (1) it points in a direction for developing an empirically testable macro-socio-legal model and (2) it generates a definition of the sociology of law.

Our point of departure is a theoretical amalgam of concepts of systems theory with Parsons's four structural components of social systems: values, norms, roles, and collectivities (Parsons, 1961:41-44; Evan, 1975:387-388). This theoretical amalgam will be referred to as a "social-structure model of law."

Any subsystem or institution of a societal system, whether it be a legal system, a family system, an economic system, a religious system, etc., can be decomposed into four structural elements: values, norms, roles, and organizations. The first two elements relate to a cultural or normative level of analysis and the last two to a social-structural level of analysis. Interactions between two or more subsystems of a society are mediated by cultural as well as by social-structural elements. As Parsons has observed, law is a generalized mechanism for regulating behavior in the several subsystems of a society (Parsons, 1962:57). At the normative level of analysis, law entails a "double institutionalization" of the values and norms embedded in other sub-systems of a society (Bohannan, 1968). In performing this rein-forcement function, law develops "cultural linkages" with other subsystems, thus contributing to the degree of normative inte-gration that exists in a society. As disputes are adjudicated and new legal norms are enacted, a value from one or more of the non-legal subsystems is tapped. These values provide an im-plicit or explicit justification for legal decision making.

Parsons's constituents of social structure, viz., values, norms, roles, and organizations, are nested elements, like "Chinese boxes", with values incorporated in norms, and both of these elements compromising roles, and all three elements constitut-ing organizations. When values, norms, roles, and organizations are aggregated, we have a new formulation, different from Par-sons's AGIL paradigm, of the sociological concept of an institu-tion. An institution of a society is composed of an ensemble or a configuration of values, norms, roles, and organizations. This definition is applicable to all social institutions, whether eco-nomic, political, religious, familial, educational, scientific/tech-nological or legal. In turn, the social structure of a society is a composite of these institutions.

By arraying the seven societal institutions listed above in a square matrix, as in Table 2.1, a number of crucial questions about a society can be addressed:

1. How congruent are the values and norms of the different institu-tions of a society? (Hypothetical scale of VN 1-5: Degree of inter-institutional congruence of values and norms.)

2. Are the institutions tightly or loosely coupled or integrated via the structure of roles and organizations? (Hypothetical scale of RO 1-5: Degree of interinstitutional interactional integration.)

3. Are there one or more institutions that dominate the other institu-tions? (Hypothetical scale of D 1-5: Degree of interinstitutional dominance.)

4. How is the legal institution related to each of the other institu-tions?

5. Does the legal institution have a measure of autonomy relative to the other six institutions, in particular to the political institutions?

Table 2.1 Inter-Institutional Relations of a Society

	Economic	Political	Familial	Religious	Educational	Scientific/ Techno- logical	Legal
Economic							
Political							
Familial							
Religious							
Educational							
Scientific/ Technological							
Legal							

Inter-institutional Rating Scales for a "Delphi Survey" or for a social indicator assessment:

VN 1-5: Degree of inter-institutional congruence of values and norms

RO 1-5: Degree of inter-institutional integration of roles and organizations

D 1-5: Degree of inter-institutional dominance

Answering each of the five questions listed above for any given society is indeed difficult. Specialists on a particular society, whether Sovietologists, Sinologists or "Americanists," would obviously have expert judgments on the foregoing five questions. Hence a "delphi survey" of a group of experts on a given society could be undertaken to elicit answers to the set of five questions and to the three interinstitutional rating scales noted in questions 1-3. Alternatively, if a set of "social indicators" could be developed, some documentary data might be unearthed describing the institutional interrelationships of a particular society (Johnston and Carley, 1981).

Questions 4 and 5 are of fundamental importance to the field of the sociology of law. A preliminary answer to these questions will be set forth in a model diagramming eight types of inter-actions or linkages between legal and nonlegal institutions (see Figure 2.1).

On the left-hand side of the diagram is a set of six nonlegal institutions each of which is composed of values, norms, roles, and organizations. If the norms comprising the nonlegal institu-tions are sufficiently institutionalized, they can have a direct regulatory impact on legal personnel as well as on the citizenry (interaction #4). On the other hand, according to Bohannan (1968), if the norms of the nonlegal institutions are not suffi-ciently strong to regulate the behavior of the citizenry, a process of "double institutionalization" (interaction #1) occurs whereby the legal system converts nonlegal institutional norms into legal norms. This effect can be seen in the rise of "blue laws" in the Colonial period, which were needed to give legal reinforcement to the religious norms that held the Sabbath to be sacred (Evan, 1980:517-518, 530-532). In addition, the legal system can intro-duce a norm that is not a component of any of the nonlegal institutions. In other words, the legal system can introduce an innovative norm (interaction #2) that does not have a counter-part in any of the nonlegal institutions (Bohannan, 1968). An example of such an innovation is "no-fault" divorce (Weitzman, 1985; Jacob, 1988).

The legal system's regulatory impact (interaction #3) may succeed or fail with legal personnel and/or with the citizenry. Depending on whether legal personnel faithfully implement the law, and the citizenry faithfully comply with the law, the effect on the legal system can be reinforcing (interaction #7) or subver-sive (interaction #5), and the effect on nonlegal institutions can be stabilizing (interaction #8) or de-stabilizing (interaction #6).

In systems-theoretic terms, the values of a society may be viewed as goal parameters in comparison with which the per-formance of a legal system may be objectively assessed. The inability of a legal system to develop "feedback loops" and "closed loop systems" to monitor and assess the efficacy of its output makes the legal system vulnerable to various types of

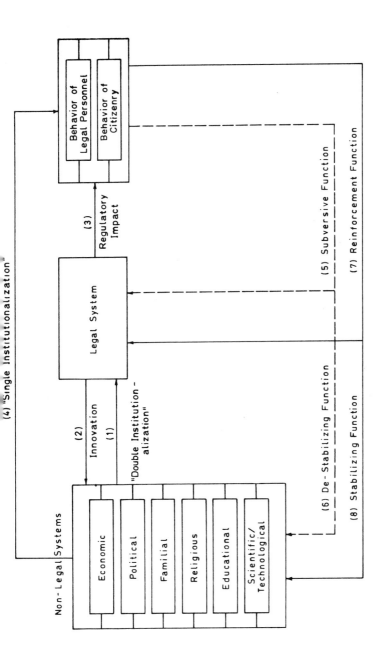

Figure 2.1 A Social-Structure Model of the Interactions of Legal and Nonlegal Institutions.

51

failures. Instead of generating "negative feedback," that is, self-corrective measures, when legal personnel or rank-and-file citizens fail to comply with the law, the system generates detrimental "positive feedback" (Laszlo, Levine, and Milsum, 1974).

What are some implications of our social-structure model? In the first place, the legal system is not viewed as only an immanently developing set of legal rules, principles or doctrines insulated from other subsystems of society, as expressed by Watson and to some extent by Luhmann and Teubner. Second, the personnel of the legal system, whether judges, lawyers, prosecutors or administrative agency officials, activate legal rules, principles or doctrines in the course of performing their roles within the legal system. Third, formally organized collectivities, be they courts, legislatures, law enforcement organizations, or administrative agencies, perform the various functions of a legal system. Fourth, in performing these functions, the formally organized collectivities comprising a legal system interact with individuals and organizations representing interests embedded in the nonlegal subsystems of society. In other words, each of the institutions or subsystems of a society—legal and nonlegal—has the same structural elements: values, norms, roles, and organizations. Interinstitutional interactions involve an effort at coupling these structural elements across institutional boundaries. A major challenge to the sociologist of law is to discover the diverse couplings or linkages—cultural and social-structural—between the legal system and the nonlegal systems in terms of the four constituent structural elements. Another challenge is to ascertain the impact of these linkages on the behavior of legal personnel and on the behavior of the citizenry, on the one hand, and to measure the impact of "double institutionalization" on societal goals, on the other.

This model will be elaborated and further analyzed in Chapter 14, where the underlying systems-theoretic framework will be explicated. In the intervening chapters the several components of this model will be discussed.

A serendipitous outcome of this model is that it suggests a definition of the sociology of law. As noted in Chapter 1, several scholars have wrestled with the problem of defining the boundaries of this field, notably, Timasheff, Cotterrell, Podgórecki, etc. My definition, which is derived from this model, is that the sociology of law deals primarily with at least eight interactions or linkages identified in Figure 2.1. Whether researchers accept this definition will be determined by its heuristic value, viz., whether it generates empirical research concerning the eight linkages.

PART II

Components of the Social-Structure Model

CHAPTER 3

Value Conflicts in the Law of Evidence

Underlying all legal norms and legal decisions, whether explicit or implicit, are values, which are conceptions of that which is desirable. These conceptions, for instance, value of property, value of individual liberty, value of privacy, value of equality, etc., are part of the cultural underpinnings of the various subsystems of a society. In other words, values are institutionally linked concepts. In each of the social institutions or subsystems of a society—be it the family, religion, the economy, the educational system, the legal system, etc.—there are dominant values guiding the respective norms, roles, and organizational components of each of these structures. Thus, for example, love and nurturance are values underlying the family; the production and distribution of wealth dominate the economy; and justice is the heart of the legal system. Each of the values may represent complex concepts of what is deemed desirable; associated with each value are diverse norms which are legal and nonlegal in nature.

In a Western democratic capitalist society, some of the primary values are free enterprise, individualism, political pluralism, civil liberties, monogamous marriage and the separation of church and state. Some of the values are embodied in the "sacred texts," as it were, of a society, such as the Magna Carta, the Declaration of Independence, and the Bill of Rights of the U.S. Constitution. Values are also reflected in the *ratio decidendi* and in *obiter dicta* of judicial decisions as well as in statutes.

Since each social institution revolves around a distinctive primary value, there is a potential for value conflicts to arise as law is called upon to resolve conflicts involving other institutions. In addition, as bodies of law evolve over time, value conflicts may arise. A case in point is the law of evidence.

The case of *Rochin v. California* (342 U.S. 165, 1951) presents us with an intriguing example of value conflicts between science and law, on the one hand, and between different legal norms comprising the law of evidence, on the other.

In *Rochin* three deputy sheriffs illegally entered Rochin's house and forced their way into his bedroom, where they found two capsules on a stand beside the bed. When the officers asked whose they were, Rochin seized the capsules and put them in his mouth. The officers then assaulted him in an effort to extract the capsules. Failing in this, they handcuffed him and took him to a hospital where, at their direction, a doctor forced an emetic solution through a tube into Rochin's stomach. This "stomach pumping" brought up the capsules, which contained morphine. The capsules were used as the chief evidence for Rochin's conviction. The decision was upheld in the appellate court but reversed by the Supreme Court of the United States on the ground that it violated the Due Process Clause of the Fourteenth Amendment.

In this case the California narcotics law, designed presumably to protect the health and morals of the public, was subordinated to the Due Process Clause, which safeguards the citizen against the abusive and arbitrary exercise of authority by the state. The conviction was reversed not because of any doubt about the validity of the evidence of violation of the narcotics law, but because of the methods by which it was obtained. Justice Felix Frankfurter, in giving the majority opinion, analogized the case to a conviction based on a coerced confession: "This course of proceeding by agents of government to obtain evidence is bound to offend even hardened sensibilities. They are methods too close to the rack and the screw to permit of constitutional differentiation." One concurring justice argued that the evidence was secured in violation of the Fifth Amendment. Another concurring justice contended that the conviction violated the Fourth Amendment, which proscribes "unreasonable search or seizure."

IN PURSUIT OF JUSTICE

In the case of *Rochin v. California,* as in all cases, the avowed objective of the court is a just decision. "Justice" is the desired end of the judicial process and one of the institutionalized means to achieve this end is the law of evidence. The concept of justice, like that of law, however, continues to be the subject of controversy in jurisprudence. Exponents of natural law conceive of justice and law as transcendental values rooted in divine will, whereas adherents of legal positivism contend that they are an expression of the will of a sovereign state.

From a sociological rather than a jurisprudential point of view, law is a body of norms with institutionalized methods of enforcement, and justice is a set of cultural values justifying these norms. Thus, justice might be called a complex of political, religious, economic, familial, and other institutionalized values—of the culture of one or more societies—which serves as the foundation of law. Or as Rene Savatier puts it, law is "the incarnation of justice and all the moral values which go with it" (Savatier, 1952:10). The courts administering justice adjudicate disputes in terms of some working conception, however accurate or inaccurate, of the values comprising justice. The empirical basis of the court's conception of the community's "sense of justice" has only recently been systematically investigated (Cohen, Robson, and Bates, 1958).

The law of evidence, from a sociological point of view, is a body of rules governing judicial investigations into questions of *fact*, designed to regularize the behavior of actors in a significant type of social situation. As one of its functions, the law of evidence purportedly assists in "the discovery of truth in trials." As an instrumental value designed to achieve the goal of justice, however, the law of evidence may come into conflict with some component values of justice. Analysis of this recurrent legal situation provides an opportunity to identify, among other things, the values, conflict of values, and hierarchy of values embodied in law and reflected in judicial decisions.

The system of rules comprising the law of evidence is a product of centuries of development toward rationalization. Legal scholars have termed this body of law a "child of the jury trial system." With the rise of the English jury system in the thirteenth century, such "irrational" methods as trial by oath, by ordeal, by battle, and by other rituals were gradually eliminated. Inquisitorial procedures by church and state were replaced by an adversarial judicial procedure. The reliance on a group of one's peers to determine the facts of a case democratized the administration of justice and provided protection against arbitrary acts by government or ecclesiastical authorities. As the law of evidence slowly evolved with common law, it underwent a process of rationalization and secularization. As Max Weber pointed out, the previous "formally irrational" trial systems, with their dependence upon magic and divine interposition, were superseded by "formally rational" procedures more in harmony with the ethos of modern science. These rational, secular, and democratic changes in the legal system—changes associated with the emergence of the liberal state—were functional requirements for the rise of capitalism (Rheinstein, 1954: xvii-lxiii, 61-64, 73, 227-228).

THE ROLE OF SCIENCE

In the modern era the value of truth is identified preeminently with the ethos of science. And in keeping with the historical trend toward rationalization in the law of evidence, the legal profession is making relatively increasing use of social science methodology in determining questions of fact. Survey data, for example, have been given judicial consideration in a number of cases, though they are still not consistently admitted as evidence. In some cases, survey data have been excluded on the ground that they violated the hearsay rule; the interviewees were not available in court for cross-examination. Content analysis has been used in several instances; and recently, psycholinguistic techniques have been employed in a criminal case to ascertain whether a confession was coerced.

Notwithstanding the long-term rationalization process in the law of evidence, a court trial has hardly been transformed into a scientific investigation. Conflicts of cultural values intrude forcibly. Whereas the search for truth in the form of verifiable and abstract knowledge is, ideally, the controlling factor in the conduct of a scientific inquiry, values other than the pursuit of truth—as illustrated in the case of *Rochin v. California*—dominate a trial.

Technical specialists do not disinterestedly investigate all available data bearing on a case and report their findings to a judge, who in turn arrives at a decision by finding the best "fit" between the data and an unambiguous law. Instead, in accordance with the adversary court system, counsel for each party presents partisanly selected data, subject to rules of admissibility of evidence, often to a jury of laymen who arrive at a verdict. A striking paradox may be briefly noted: the existing adversary court system presupposes a "perspectivistic" approach to truth, as opposed to the nonperspectivistic or objective approach which underlies the methodology of scientific inquiry as well as the inquisitorial court system current in the Middle Ages and in modern totalitarian states.

Unlike the canons of scientific inquiry, the law of evidence includes an elaborate body of rules of admissibility, some of which have the general effect of promoting the search for truth, and others of obstructing it. In the former category are rules of hearsay, best evidence rule, authentication of documents, testimonial qualifications, and impeachment of witnesses. These attempt to ensure that answers of more probative values are given to controverted questions of fact. They are also designed to exclude evidence to which lay jurors might attach too much weight.

THE CASE OF TESTIMONIAL PRIVILEGE

Testimonial privileges, on the other hand, are rules that tend to obstruct the search for truth. They include, on the one hand, privileged *acts* such as self-incrimination, and, on the other hand, *privileged communications* such as those between attorney and client, physician and patient, husband and wife, and priest and penitent.

The rationale for the testimonial privilege is phrased in terms of "social policy," viz., that values such as marital harmony and stability take precedence over the ascertainment of truth. "The basic reason the law has refused to pit wife against husband or husband against wife in a trial where life or liberty is at stake," says Justice Black, "was the belief that such a policy is necessary to foster family peace, not only for the benefit of husband, wife, and children, but for the benefit of the public as well" (*Hawkins v. U.S.*, 79 S. Ct. 136, 138, 1958.)

Similarly, it is argued that the religious values of the priest-penitent privilege and the delicacy of health considerations in the doctor-patient privilege must be protected in a court trial, even if it be at the expense of rationality in the fact-finding procedure. Thus the rules of testimonial privilege, as distinct from most rules of evidence, point to a conflict between means and ends in the law of evidence: the ascertainment of truth of litigated propositions versus the preservation of values embedded in various institutions, and also elements of the concept of justice. As a result, "truth is barred."

Testimonial privileges may be waived; they are options conceded to classes of persons to decline giving certain testimony. How often are these privileges in fact claimed? When they are claimed, how crucial does the excluded testimony *appear* to be to the structure of the evidence presented and to the judicial decision? To what extent are present rules of privileged communications held essential or desirable by the various professions and client-publics? Is the public at large in favor of an extension or a restriction of testimonial privileges pertaining to professions?

One condition necessary for the establishment of privilege is that "the *relation* must be one which in the opinion of the community ought to be sedulously fostered" (Wigmore, 1940: vol. 1, 531). With respect to the husband-wife privilege, Justice Steward in *Hawkins v. U.S.* raises a relevant empirical question: "Before assuming that a change in the present rule would work such a wholesale disruption of domestic felicity as the court's opinion implies, it would be helpful to know the experiences in those jurisdictions where the rule has been abandoned or modified."

A similar question may be asked with respect to the priest-penitent and physician-patient rules of privilege. Is the professional-client relationship at all impaired in those states which do not have these privileges? Since the confidentiality of the professional-client relationship is prescribed in the codes of ethics of all professions and is a culturally approved relationship, it is doubtful whether the relationship would be jeopardized in the absence of rules of privileged communications. In jurisdictions in which statutory provisions for these privileges or such common-law rules do not exist, are those privileges informally recognized? If they are informally recognized, is it because the courts take cognizance of the "customs" of the professions?

Apart from the explicit values which the rules of privileged communication seek to protect, it is not fortuitous that the only occupations covered are such long-established professions as law, clergy, and medicine. This may be partly a reflection of the prestige of these occupations and their organizational power to protect their vested interests. By contrast, such new professions as journalism, accounting, and social work—except in a few jurisdictions—are not covered by these privileges.

In this respect, the old profession of teaching is an anomaly. Why are teacher-student communications, particularly at the college level, not privileged? If the legal status of teaching and the new professions is explained by differential organizational power, rather than by other factors, a question arises: As these professions develop strong organizations, will they demand statutory extensions of the rules of privileged communication?

Moreover, given a general trend toward professionalization of various occupations and a further extension of occupational licensing laws, may we expect an increase in the number of occupations covered by testimonial privileges? If testimonial privileges *are* extended to an increasing number of occupations, the secular trend toward a rationalization in the law of evidence will be impeded, leading to more value conflicts between the instrumental and the terminal values of the judicial process.

If the trend toward rationalization does continue, however, testimonial privileges may be reduced or eventually eliminated. In the opinion of one legal scholar, Charles McCormick, "The manifest destiny of evidence law is a progressive lowering of the barriers to truth. . . . One may hazard a guess . . . that in a secular sense privileges are on the way out" (McCormick, 1954: 165-166). If this prediction proves accurate, value conflicts may be minimized or resolved. Two dysfunctional consequences of the testimonial privileges would also be reduced or eliminated. We would be better able to predict the results of the litigation process, which is now difficult in part because of uncertainty as to what evidence will be withheld due to testimonial privileges. The social control function of law would be strengthened in that fewer guilty persons would be able to evade punishment with the aid of the law of evidence.

However, if value conflicts are resolved in favor of more rational trial procedures, we may pay a high social cost. Some of the rules of evidence may interfere with a rational investigation of questions of fact, but they also protect the rights of the citizen against the state's monopoly of coercive power and protect values of society that presumably are widely cherished.

CONCLUSION

Thus we are faced with a dilemma. If, on the one hand, the value conflicts are resolved in favor of increasing *rational* trial procedures, some of the rights of the citizen against the state and some societal values may be threatened. On the other hand, if the value conflicts are resolved in favor of *traditional* trial procedures, to preserve some values of major institutions of our society, the rational pursuit of truth is not only obstructed but judicial predictability is lowered and social control is impaired.

Value conflicts are endemic to complex societies. The type and frequency of value conflicts will vary from one society to another. The legal system provides many problems of value conflicts, as we have seen. An analysis of rules of evidence, or even more particularly testimonial privileges pertaining to occupations, would throw light on the interrelations between selected occupations and the legal system, and it would contribute to an understanding of the rise and decline of legal norms.

CHAPTER 4

Dimensions of Legal Norms

Legal rules vary among societies, simple and complex, in many respects. Sociologists and anthropologists have sought to throw light on the diversity of legal norms and relate them to observed behavior. A number of typologies of norms have been set forth. To date, however, there is no consensus as to which typology of norms is most heuristic. In this chapter a number of dimensions of legal norms will be identified in order to develop some empirically testable propositions.

Sumner (1906) was perhaps the earliest sociologist to classify norms into folkways and mores. This distinction, however, offers little clarification of the category of norms we identify as legal norms. Legal norms, as opposed to nonlegal norms, prescribe or proscribe behavior, the violation of which is subject to sanctions by specialized personnel of a legal system. A suggestive typology of norms, developed by Morris (1956) is based on such variables as extent of knowledge, extent of acceptance, severity of sanctions provided, amount of conformity, etc.

Inasmuch as the purpose of promulgating norms is to regulate behavior, the criterion for identifying dimensions of norms is their hypothetical relationship to compliance. The focus here will be on seven dimensions of legal norms in an effort to generate propositions concerning the conditions under which members of a society comply with legal norms.

SEVEN DIMENSIONS

1. *Degree of Knowledge*

In a rational society, if one wishes to maximize compliance with law, it is necessary to allocate appropriate resources to inform people about the law, especially in light of the principle that "ignorance of the law is no defense" against conviction. In other words, in order to maximize compliance with the law, knowledge of the law should not be confined to legal personnel, viz., lawyers, judges, legislators, law enforcement professionals, administrators, etc.

Societies evidently differ substantially in the effort they expend to disseminate information about legal norms (Podgórecki et al., 1973). Totalitarian societies are relatively selective in the information they disseminate to the population, emphasizing norms that pertain to duties. On the other hand, democratic societies are less selective in their transmission of information to the population; they tend to include information about rights as well as duties. Both types of societies tend to assume that knowledge of the law is the prerogative of legal specialists and hence do not devote substantial resources to legal socialization (Tapp and Levine, 1974).

2. *Degree of Value Consensus*

There is something of a paradox with respect to the variable of value consensus as it pertains to legal norms. If there is a very high level of value consensus—approximating 100%—regarding a law, one may well wonder about the need for the law. In that case, a nonlegal norm may suffice, or as Bohannan (1968) puts it, "single institutionalization" is adequate. On the other hand, if value consensus with respect to a law is very low—approximating zero—one may wonder whether a law has any chance of being obeyed at all. Presumably, when there is a moderate level of value consensus, a legal norm is potentially useful as a means of regulating conduct (Evan, 1965b).

3. Degree of Normative Complexity

Legal norms rarely consist of brief declaratory statements such as the Decalogue. As a rule, there tend to be multiple provisions and stipulations included in each law. An example is a divorce law setting forth multiple grounds for divorce. With the emergence and diffusion of "no-fault" divorce laws in the 1970s in most of the individual states of the United States, there was a radical simplification of the law, so much so that Jacob characterizes the transformation as a "silent revolution" (Jacob, 1988). Tax law in the United States has grown more complex by several orders of magnitude since the passage of the Sixteenth Amendment to the Constitution. In 1913, when the first internal revenue code was passed by Congress, it was subdivided into 15 sections and it ran to a total of 15 pages. As amended in 1986, the code is divided into eight subtitles; in turn, each subtitle is divided into many chapters and subchapters; each subchapter is then divided into many parts and then subdivided into numerous sections. The multivolume code adds up to several thousand pages. By contrast, the Motor Vehicle Code of the Commonwealth of Pennsylvania is relatively simple: it contains approximately 500 provisions.

There are at least two constraints associated with normative complexity: cognitive and economic. It is difficult for the lay citizen and lawyer alike to digest and process information about a large number of complex laws. As legal norms become more numerous and arcane, there is an increasing willingness of the public to turn to lawyers to ascertain the law applicable to particular legal problems. In addition, as legal norms become more complex, it becomes increasingly costly to undertake broad-gauged programs of legal socialization.

4. Degree of Severity of Sanctions

It is a basic legal doctrine that a law, absent a sanction, is without force. And yet there is continuing controversy concerning the utility of a high level versus a low level of severity of sanctions for failure to comply with a law (Antunes and Hunt, 1973). A case in point is the controversy concerning the deterrent value of the death penalty. Similarly, there is a controversy concerning rape laws, with some scholars contending that the provision for severe sanctions for convicted rapists results in a tendency of juries to render acquittal decisions (Le Grand, 1973).

5. Degree of Certainty of Sanctions

Legal norms vary in the probability that violators will be apprehended, prosecuted, and punished. Given a low degree of certainty of sanctions, in part due to the lack of enforcement resources and prosecutorial discretion, potential offenders are not likely to be deterred from violating the law.

6. Degree of Enforcement Capability

Legal norms vary in the degree to which enforcement resources are allocated. For example, there is probably a higher level of enforcement capability associated with tax law as compared with narcotics law. It is also likely that societies differ substantially in their allocation of enforcement resources for different types of legal norms. Totalitarian societies expend relatively vast resources in enforcing their criminal code as compared with democratic societies.

7. Degree of Confidence in Uniformity of Enforcement of the Law

A basic assumption—widely held—about law is that justice is blind. Even without understanding fully the constitutional principle of equality before the law, citizens generally believe that laws are enforced in a uniform manner irrespective of social, economic or political position. When it becomes apparent that social class, racial, and religious factors do affect one's treatment before the law, confidence in the uniformity of enforcement is undermined and, therewith, the legitimacy of legal norms.

In selecting the foregoing seven dimensions of legal norms I am not claiming that this is an exhaustive set of dimensions. Rather, because I assume that all of these dimensions are relevant for understanding the phenomenon of compliance with the law, I have selected them for special attention. We shall now consider two types of propositions: (1) interrelations among some of these normative dimensions and (2) the relation of each of these dimensions to the variable of compliance. In each case, the *ceteris paribus* provision holds.

HYPOTHETICAL INTERRELATIONS AMONG NORMS AND COMPLIANCE

Knowledge and Value Consensus

Disseminating information about a law—along with its rationale and the rights it grants and the duties it imposes—is likely to increase the level of value consensus. However, if value consensus is defined and operationalized as "support for the law," then Sarat's study (1975) leads one to expect an inverse relationship rather than a direct relationship. Sarat's finding raises a disconcerting question about the theory of democracy, viz., the more informed citizens are about the legal system, the less likely they are to support it. Totalitarian societies evidently are convinced of the validity of this proposition, witness their tendency to avoid promulgating laws. A case in point is the recent decision of the government of the People's Republic of China, in the spirit of openness, to depart from the custom of keeping laws secret (Kristof, 1988).

Knowledge and Normative Complexity

Given the great variety of types of laws in modern societies, whether in the East or in the West, it is also not surprising that some laws are relatively simple whereas others are relatively complex. Under the circumstances, one may hypothesize that knowledge is inversely related to normative complexity: the more complex a law is, the lower the level of knowledge of the law. Because legislators are becoming increasingly aware that such a relationship exists, there has been an effort in recent years to simplify the wording of some laws.

Value Consensus and Normative Complexity

As laws become more complex and hence more "technical"— such as antitrust law, corporation law, and tax law—not only does the level of knowledge in a society decline but also the level of value consensus. Notwithstanding this hypothesized inverse relationship, normative complexity tends to make the citizenry increasingly dependent on the services of the legal profession. Those citizens who have recourse to the services of lawyers are likely to increase their value commitment to the laws in question.

Degree of Enforcement Capability and Certainty of Sanctions

As the level of enforcement capability rises, it is reasonable to assume that the degree of certainty of sanctions will also rise. Although this relationship is probably widely assumed to be true by law-enforcement personnel, many societies do not have the resources to invest in law enforcement necessary to take advantage of the hypothesized relationship. Totalitarian societies, because they are more concerned about political stability than are democratic societies, are more likely to allocate proportionally greater resources to strengthening their law-enforcement capabilities.

Value Consensus and Compliance

The Volstead Act, or the Prohibition Amendment, made many people aware—especially in the legal profession—that value consensus is directly related to compliance with a law. Many citizens and legal personnel alike were opposed to the Prohibition law, thus diminishing any chance of implementation.

Normative Complexity and Compliance

The more complex a body of law, the lower the level of compliance. This inverse relationship may arise for a number of reasons, for instance, (1) ambiguity about the meaning of a law tends to increase with complexity and (2) monitoring compliance and enforcing a multifaceted law becomes more burdensome, resulting in a lower level of compliance.

Severity of Sanctions and Compliance

A widely-held belief among most people is that the more severe the sanctions of a law, the higher the level of compliance. This view is especially common with respect to criminal law in general and the death penalty in particular. This popular judgment has been tested in a study by Antunes and Hunt (1973) of the seven crimes which comprised the FBI index. Antunes and

Hunt found that severity of sanctions accounted for a negligible amount of the variance in the crime rates.

Certainty of Sanctions and Compliance

In contrast to severity of sanctions, certainty of sanctions, or the perceived likelihood of apprehension (Zimring and Hawkins, 1971), has been found by Antunes and Hunt (1973) to be a significant deterrent to the seven crimes comprising the FBI index. In other words, Antunes and Hunt found a significant direct relationship between degree of certainty of sanctions and compliance.

Degree of Enforcement Capability and Compliance

Many a law is stillborn because of the minuscule effort expended to enforce it. This was evidently the case with respect to the Prohibition Amendment. Notwithstanding the widespread value dissensus concerning this law, it might have elicited a higher level of compliance if it had been accompanied by a higher level of enforcement capability.

TOWARD A MULTIVARIATE MODEL OF COMPLIANCE

Thus far sociologists of law have not undertaken an empirical study of the impact of several dimensions of legal norms on compliance. Although such a study is feasible, it would require launching a special data collection effort focusing on a particular field of law such as antitrust law, environmental law or laws applying to corporations. Such a study would, for example, test the effect of each of the foregoing seven dimensions of norms on compliance; it would also assess how much of the variance in compliance is accounted for by each of the seven dimensions of norms. The study by Antunes and Hunt (1973) of criminal law is an exemplary undertaking which tested several additive and multiplicative regression models.

CHAPTER 5

Role Analysis of Legal Personnel

The third component of our social-structure model of law deals with the analysis of roles of legal personnel. In complex societies, as compared to relatively simple, preliterate societies, legal systems tend to become increasingly differentiated not only with respect to the number and types of legal rules but also with respect to the number of legal roles. Whatever roles are institutionalized in a legal system, the task of the sociologist of law is to develop or apply a theory with which to analyze the behavior of legal personnel. We shall use role theory to perform this task.

ROLE THEORY

The concept of role has a long history in anthropology, sociology and psychology. In his classic formulation, Linton (1936) distinguished "role" from "status," the latter referring to a position in a social system, and the former to the behavioral aspect associated with a given position. The concepts of status and role are fundamental building blocks of social structure (Merton, 1957; Nadel, 1957). In the course of primary and secondary socialization, members of societies acquire a set of statuses and roles which link them to the various institutions of a society. "Status" refers to a normatively designated position within an institution, such as the family, education, the economy or the legal system. Associated with each status is a role which has three distinguishable elements: (1) a set of expectations or norms of conduct with implicit values, (2) a set of role orientations or attitudes of the role incumbents toward the role, and (3) observable behavior of the role incumbent.

The role expectations of legal personnel may be based on legal rules, administrative regulations, "codes of ethics," etc. Because there is often an absence of consensus on role expectations (Gross, Mason, and McEachern, 1958), role occupants exercise a measure of discretion in discharging their role obligations. The degree and type of discretion exercised by a role occupant in a legal system is partly a function of his/her role orientations or attitudes toward role expectations.

The role orientations of a lawyer, judge, prosecutor, or occupant of any other legal role are partly a function of the socialization process, which includes a formal as well as an informal phase. The formal phase may consist of a period of formal training, such as occurs in a law school; the informal phase occurs during an individual's role incumbency as he/she interacts with various "role partners" who comprise an incumbent's "role-set" (Merton, 1957:368-380). As Merton has noted, each role occupant does not necessarily interact with only one other person in a complementary role relationship—as in the case of an employer-employee relationship or a teacher-student relationship—but with a number of other role-partners who impinge on his/her particular role.

Role behavior, as distinct from role orientations and role expectations, involves overt actions—principally decision making in the case of legal roles—that may take a multitude of forms. In the case of legal roles, role behavior is not completely determined by the set of expectations or norms and the set of role orientations. At least four other factors intervene.

First are role-set relationships, which consist of a set of recurrent interactions between the role incumbent and the role partners. For example, a judge in a criminal court has ongoing relationships with fellow judges, prosecutors, defense counsel, court clerks, police officers, etc. These relationships constitute his "role-set." Second are "status-set" relationships consisting of other simultaneous statuses he or she has by virtue of relationships in various institutions such as the family, education, religion, polity, etc. The fact that members of a society, including personnel of a legal system, concurrently occupy many roles gives rise to the problem of "status-set conflicts" or, in common parlance, "conflict of interest" situations (Evan and Levin, 1966). Third are "status-sequences," viz., previous statuses and roles of an incumbent of a legal role. In the case of a judge, his prior experiences as a practicing attorney and as a partner of a prominent law firm may affect his behavior on the bench. Both status-sets and status-sequences may give rise to conflicts of interest. The fourth factor influencing role behavior is the personality of the role occupant which is a composite of unique socialization experiences around which an individual's character is formed. Collectively, these four elements, plus role expectations and role orientations, determine role behavior in general and the role behavior of legal personnel in particular.

Defining and redefining the rights and duties of individuals performing diverse roles, legal and nonlegal, in a society, is a significant, albeit taken-for-granted, function of law. Thus, the law can initiate changes in legal roles, for instance, in the length of tenure of judges, legislators and administrative agency officials.

TYPES OF LEGAL PERSONNEL

In advanced industrialized societies, one can identify a number of legal roles. First and most common is the role of the lawyer. The legal profession, especially in the United States and in a number of Western countries—in common law as well as in civil law societies—has grown substantially and has become progressively more specialized (Abel and Lewis, 1988). Codes of ethics of Western lawyers underscore their obligation to protect and promote the interests of the client, while, at the same time, in their role as "officers of the court," they have a duty to maintain the integrity of the law. Lawyers in socialist countries have no such obligations; instead, they are duty-bound to promote the interests of the party and the state.

A second common legal role is that of the judge. Recruitment to this role varies considerably. Some countries, such as Japan and the Netherlands, recruit judges by means of a specialized course of professional training, quite distinct from that of lawyers. Apart from differences in educational requirements for this role, the actual selection of candidates may be via appointment or the electoral process. In the United States, we have a combination of modes of recruitment.

A third common legal role is the legislator. Again, societies differ not only in the number of legislators they have but also in the type of political party system with which candidates seeking election are affiliated. In some countries, the legislator role is a full-time occupation, whereas in others it is not. One principal source of variation in the legislator role is whether a society has a single party system, as is true of totalitarian societies, or a multiparty system. Another source of variation is the degree of influence organized interests, other than parties, have on legislators.

A fourth legal role, as ubiquitous as lawyers, judges and legislators, is that of the police officer. Western societies differ in the ratio of police officers to the population. This ratio is very likely correlated, to some degree, with crime rates in some societies but not in others. To the extent that the primary function of police officers is law enforcement, it is reasonable to suppose that the ratio of police officers to the population is correlated with crime rates. However, if the primary function of police officers is political, in the sense of promoting the stability of the regime, no such correlation would be observed.

A fifth legal role is that of an agency administrator. In Western societies, administrators implement public policies by administering government agencies in accordance with enacted laws. In socialist societies, administrators of government agencies tend to perform their roles in compliance with policies of the party in an effort to strengthen the stability of the regime.

LEGAL PROFESSION IN THE
UNITED STATES

The first and most striking feature of the legal profession in the United States is a marked growth of the profession since World War II. In 1951 there were approximately 220,000 lawyers (Laumann and Heinz, 1977:158), whereas in 1985, according to American Bar Association estimates, there were about 655,191 lawyers.[1] In other words, the population of lawyers in the post-World War II period has virtually tripled. Comparable statistics on judges serving on both federal and state trial and appellate courts are difficult to come by. In 1970-1971 there were approximately 5,500 judges in the United States (Goldman, 1971:1); a decade later, according to the National Center for State Courts, the estimated population of judges is 28,000—more than a four-fold increase.[2] Clearly, the demand for legal and court services has greatly increased during this period. Has the volume of conflicts requiring adjudication increased disproportionately to the growth of the economy, the government and the population? Notwithstanding the substantial rate of growth of the judiciary in the past decade, it constitutes only about 4% of the legal profession. By contrast, in West Germany, for example, the judiciary accounts for about 20% of the legal profession (Rueschmeyer, 1973:34).

A second noteworthy feature of the legal profession in the United States is its internal differentiation. In the absence of longitudinal data one can only surmise that in the course of the twentieth century the process of specialization within the profession has increased. According to a recent comprehensive study of the Chicago bar, the differentiation within the profession is "systematically structured and . . . [the] structure is determined largely by the impact of client interests" (Heinz and Laumann, 1978:1141). The stratification of the bar is based on various dimensions, including field of specialization, prestige of specialties, income, organizational setting of practice, type of law school attended, etc. One-half of the lawyers in Chicago work in fields categorized as the "corporate client sector" (e.g., antitrust, business real estate, business tax, securities, patents, public utilities, etc.); the other half work in fields designated as the "personal/small business client sector" (e.g., general litigation, personal real estate, personal tax, probate, divorce, personal injury, etc.) (Laumann and Heinz, 1977:224-229).

The prestige or deference accorded different specialties varies greatly. At the top of the prestige order, "big business" specialties predominate, viz., securities, tax, antitrust (defendants), patents, antitrust (plaintiffs), banking and public utilities. At the bottom of the prestige ranking are specialties that provide services to individuals, such as general family practice, divorce, personal injury, consumer and criminal law. Correlated with the prestige ordering of specialties are such variables as whether practitioners attended an "elite" law school or a "local" law school, percentage of blue collar clients, percentage of law practice income derived from major corporations, percentage of lawyers practicing in large firms, percentage of solo practitioners, etc.

The above findings by Laumann and Heinz are consistent with those of other researchers who have studied the metropolitan American bar (Smigel, 1969; Carlin, 1962, 1966). Rueschmeyer summarized one aspect of these studies as follows:

> The top of the stratification system in the metropolitan American bar is held by the partners of large law firms, while the bottom, which is very large, is occupied by the majority of individual practitioners and small-firm lawyers. By and large, these two groups work and live in different worlds in virtually every respect. (Rueschmeyer, 1973:49)

The stratification profile of the legal profession that has emerged from research in the past two decades dovetails with the observations of a historian who traced the development of the profession:

The emergence and proliferation of corporation law firms at the turn of the century provided those lawyers who possessed appropriate social, religious, and ethnic credentials with an opportunity to secure personal power and to shape the future of their profession.

In the years before World War I the structural transformation of the legal profession neared completion. White Anglo-Saxon corporation lawyers were concentrated at the professional apex, and new-immigrant metropolitan solo practitioners were restricted to the professional base. Ethical norms were promulgated; whether enforced or not they distributed status and morality according to social origin and type of professional practice. (Auerbach, 1976:21, 62)

Comparable stratification studies of the judiciary in the United States have yet to be undertaken. It is very likely, however, that the stratification of the bench corresponds closely to the hierarchical structure of authority of the court system. At the state trial court level are judges who usually attain their office through victory in a partisan election. Their social background as well as their legal experience and expertise are of a relatively modest nature. At the state appellate court level judges are sometimes appointed by governors but more often elected in partisan as well as in nonpartisan elections (Goldman, 1971). In either case, their professional caliber as well as the social class level are likely to be higher than those of judges at the trial court level. It is also very likely that a substantial proportion of federal district court judges is somewhat superior in professional knowledge to state appellate judges. At the federal appellate court level the professional caliber is apt to be appreciably higher than that at the district court level and, in some instances, comparable in quality with the select few justices appointed to the Supreme Court.

A third feature of the legal profession is the relatively low level of mobility between the top and bottom strata (Rueschmeyer, 1973:51). Although entry into the profession by disadvantaged minorities and women entails a significant measure of upward mobility, the barriers to reaching the top stratum are formidable. "In New York, less than 2% of those who did not start out in large firms ended up working there. Downward mobility is more frequent" (Rueschmeyer, 1973:51). Horizontal mobility, involving a temporary leave of absence for a tour of duty in a government position, is available to the legal elite. Some members of prestigious corporate law firms are offered positions in the executive branch of the federal government, are appointed by a governor to the bench, or are offered an opportunity to run for elective office at the local, state or federal level.

LINKAGES BETWEEN LEGAL AND NONLEGAL ELITES

Given the social stratification of the bar and the bench in the United States (and presumably in many other countries as well), what linkages, if any, are there between the legal elite and the elites of other social institutions? A plausible hypothesis is that elite lawyers have "cosmopolitan role sets"—that is, relationships with geographically dispersed and high social status "role partners" who have a commitment to the ideal norms of the profession—whereas nonelite lawyers would have "local role sets." Inasmuch as corporate lawyers comprise most of the elite of the legal profession, they have, by definition, recurrent interrelationships with corporate clients, many of whom are members of the corporate elite. In the course of providing professional services to corporate clients in such areas as antitrust, securities or corporate taxes, corporate lawyers have occasion to interact with federal regulatory officials, some of whom are members of the government elite.

Mills, who advanced the thesis that there is a national "power elite" consisting of the top leaders in the three dominant institutions of the United States—the military, the corporation and the federal government—paid particular attention to the role of the lawyer (Mills, 1956). First, a not insignificant proportion of corporate executives are recruited from the legal profession. Second, and more generally, the corporation is in constant need of legal advice:

> Today, the success of the corporation depends to a considerable extent upon minimizing its tax burden, maximizing its speculative projects through mergers, controlling government regulatory bodies, [and] influencing state and national legislatures. Accordingly, the lawyer is becoming a pivotal figure in the giant corporation. (Mills, 1956:131)

Mills also looked upon the corporate lawyer as an indispensable member of the "inner core of the power elite" (Mills, 1956: 289) who helps integrate the elites from the military, the corporation, and the government.

> The corporation lawyer and the investment banker perform the functions of the "go-betweens" effectively and powerfully. By the nature of their work, they transcend the narrower milieu of any one industry and accordingly are in a position to speak and act for the corporate world or at least sizable sectors of it. The corporation lawyer is a key link between the economic and military and political areas. (Mills, 1956:289)

Domhoff, who continued Mills's efforts to document the existence of a "power elite," also affirms the prominent role of the corporate lawyer: "We conclude that the large businesses and law firms which dominate the American economy are the keystone of the power elite" (Domhoff, 1967:61).

ASCERTAINING THE ROLE ORIENTATIONS
OF LEGAL PERSONNEL

One way of arriving at a profile of the role structure of a legal system is to inquire, by means of a sample survey, into the role orientations of legal personnel. The purpose of such an inquiry is to ascertain whether the personnel of a legal system have an institutionalized and professional role orientation or whether

Table 5.1 Comparison of Role Orientations of
Legal Personnel

Lawyers	Judges	Legislators	Police Officers	Agency Administrators
1. Officers of the Court	Law Interpreter	Delegate	Scrupulous Enforcement	Public Interest Fiduciary
2. Client-Orientation	Law Maker	Trustee	Even-Handed Discretion	Bureaucratic Self-Preservation
3. Self-Orientation	Pragmatist	Politics	Discriminatory Discretion	Special Interest Commitment
4. Corrupt Orientation	Corrupt Orientation	Corrupt Orientation	Corrupt Orientation	Corrupt Orientation

NOTE: Orientations 1 and 2 are almost equally institutionalized; orientation 3 is looked upon with some suspicion—it is a quasi-deviant orientation; orientation 4 is clearly deviant.

they have a deviant or corrupt role orientation. Since no such systematic comparative empirical research has been undertaken, I shall outline such a study by hypothetically comparing the five legal roles discussed above. Table 5.1 summarizes four different role orientations of lawyers, judges, legislators, police officers and government agency administrators. The first and second rows in the table set forth relatively institutionalized and professionalized role orientations. In the third row, a moderate amount of deviant behavior is represented, whereas in the last row a full-fledged corrupt role orientation is identified, namely, the exploitation of the legal role for personal gain in violation of the norms underlying the legal role.

A high frequency of deviant and corrupt role orientations among the role incumbents of a legal system is indicative of the failure of legal socialization. Such a situation has profound consequences for the legitimacy of the legal system. If legal personnel fail to perform their roles as fiduciaries, they also fail as role models for the citizenry. In that event, we can expect a low level of perceived legitimacy of the legal system and a low level of compliance with the law on the part of the citizenry as a whole. We can also expect that the legal system is fundamentally flawed and that the law may be in the process of being superseded by the exercise of political power.

Comparative research on the role orientations of legal personnel of societies differing in significant structural characteristics would very likely reveal basic differences in the functioning of their legal systems.

NOTES

1. Personal communication, October, 1989.
2. Personal communication, May 1982.

CHAPTER 6

Administrative Law and Organization Theory

Even in the legal systems of nonliterate societies it is possible to discern some organizational elements, for instance, a council of elders performing a judicial function. Organizational analysis, the fourth component of our social-structure model of law, involves an analysis of values, norms, and roles as they affect the functioning of organizations within a legal system. In analyzing a court, a legislature, an administrative agency or some other organizational component of a legal system, it is important to attend to that system's structural design, that is, its internal organizational relationships (Pugh et al., 1968; Blau and Schoenherr, 1971) as well as external organizational relationships (Evan, 1976).

More than two decades ago, a debate on behavioral science and administrative law between the political scientist Grundstein and the eminent authority on administrative law Kenneth Culp Davis was aired in the pages of the *Journal of Legal Education* (Grundstein, 1964; Davis, 1964). Grundstein argued that administrative law had, in effect, reached a dead end in its development and was on the verge of being transformed with the help of behavioral science theories and methodologies and, in particular, through systems analysis and simulation. Davis countered by pointing out that traditional administrative law was an evolving discipline; that although some contributions in behavioral science were impressive, others were vacuous; and that if "behaviorally-oriented research" produces anything of value, "it will be readily and easily absorbed into administrative law research" (Davis, 1964:151). As a disinterested observer from another discipline, I must confess that I found Davis's arguments more persuasive.

My purpose in this chapter, however, is not to resume this debate but rather to examine (1) some trends in American administrative law, (2) some trends in organization theory, (3) an organization-set model of the administrative process, and (4) several potentially fruitful research strategies. Although the focus will be almost exclusively on American administrative law, the analysis will have implications for comparative research on legal systems (Merryman, 1974). An underlying assumption of this chapter is that the sociology of law can perform the midwife role in the birth of a new style of research linking administrative law with organization theory.

THE EXPANDING ROLE OF
GOVERNMENT ADMINISTRATION

Before considering some trends in American administrative law, several brief observations are in order concerning the expanding role of government administration. As Galanter puts it, "throughout the world, there has been a proliferation of governmental responsibility and a growth of new areas of law" (Galanter, 1966).

Weber's theory of bureaucracy is concerned with characterizing organizations in terms of his ideal type of bureaucracy and with the rise of bureaucracy as an indispensable element in the development of modern Western societies. In the intervening decades since Weber's work appeared, it has become apparent that his analysis may be as relevant for centrally planned economies as for market economies and for societies in the process of development as well as for those that are highly developed. In their effort to achieve modernization, developing countries are all too often severely hampered because of their failure to design an effective system of government bureaucracy as an integral component of their legal system. In his analysis of 11 features of a modern legal system, Galanter might explicitly have included the development of a rational-legal system of government administration.

Davis has captured the pervasiveness of government administration, in the United States, with the following observation:

> The ordinary person probably regards the judicial process as somewhat remote from his own problems; a large portion of all people go through life without ever being a party to a lawsuit. But the administrative process affects nearly everyone in many ways nearly every day. The pervasiveness of the effects of the administrative process on the average person can quickly be appreciated by running over a few samples of what the administrative process protects against: air and water pollution; excessive prices of electricity, gas, telephone, and other utility services, unreasonableness in rates, schedules, and services of airlines, railroads, street cars, and buses; disregard for the public interest in radio and television and chaotic conditions for broadcasting; unwholesome meat and poultry; adulteration in food; fraud or inadequate disclosure in sale of securities; physically unsafe locomotives, ships, airplanes, bridges, elevators; unfair labor practices by either employers or unions; false advertising and other unfair or deceptive practices; inadequate safety appliances. (Davis, 1972)

In terms of the sheer number of administrative agencies at the federal level, in 1949 the Code of Federal Regulation listed 155 agencies; in 1973 the number had virtually doubled—even if allowances are made for multiple listings (Davis, 1958; Office of the Federal Register, 1972). At the state and local levels there are undoubtedly many thousands of administrative agencies, and their growth for this period has in all likelihood been similar. Small wonder then that the case load of the federal agencies far outstrips that of the federal courts. For example, in 1963, according to Davis:

The number of civil cases filed in all federal district courts was 63,630 and the number of civil trials was 7,095. In the agencies the number of cases filed is in the millions, but stripping down to the small portion of the cases involving "an oral hearing with a verbatim transcript" and "the determination of private rights, privileges, or obligations," and excluding determinations solely on written applications or on oral presentations in the nature of conference or interview, the number is 81,469 cases disposed of. (Davis, 1971)

Admittedly the 11:1 ratio of administrative to judicial cases is crude. However, even if further refinements are made—as Davis suggests—to make the statistics more nearly comparable, the ratio would still be heavily weighted in the direction of administrative adjudication. This comparison suggests that it might be instructive to develop a cross-national time series for a sample of nation-states, both developed and developing, to test the hypothesis that as the level of economic development increases, the ratio of administrative cases to judicial cases increases. Associated with this hypothesized relationship are such features of modern legal systems as increasing technical complexity and increasing requirements for professional personnel, both of which may be more true of administrative agencies than of courts (Galanter, 1966:155-156).

SOME TRENDS IN
AMERICAN ADMINISTRATIVE LAW

In his 1970 supplement to his treatise on American administrative law, Davis reaffirms his original definition of administrative law, that it is "the law concerning the powers and procedures of administrative agencies, including especially the law governing judicial review of administrative action" (Davis, 1971). However, he acknowledges that a more comprehensive view of the subject is now required; instead of focusing exclusively on regulatory agencies, particularly those that are independent agencies, it is equally necessary to attend to agencies in the executive branch and, more generally, to *all* administrative agencies, whether federal, state or local.

This major extension in the scope of this field requires a classification of agencies by type of function other than that of regulation. For example, is it sufficient to classify agencies according to whether their primary purpose is to regulate an industry (e.g., the Interstate Commerce Commission), provide benefits (e.g., the Social Security Administration), render a service (e.g., the U.S. Postal Service), give grants (e.g., the National Science Foundation), or award government contracts (e.g., an office of procurement of the Department of Defense)? Schwartz and Wade, in their comparative analysis of administrative law in Britain and the United States, distinguish between regulatory and benefactory agencies. Britain's agencies are largely of the latter type since their method of economic regulation entails nationalizing industry or establishing special public corporations (Schwartz and Wade, 1972).

In the course of defining administrative law, Davis also indicates what it is not, to wit:

> Apart from judicial review, the manner in which public officers handle business unrelated to adjudication or rule making is not a part of administrative law; this means that much of what political scientists call "public administration" is excluded. Administrative law is also confined to arrangements involving rights of private parties; it does not extend to internal problems affecting only the agencies and their officers and staffs. (Davis, 1971:3-4)

These exclusions, as we shall see, unnecessarily constrict the purview of scholars in administrative law.

Another distinctive feature of Davis's 1970 supplement to his treatise is his delineation of four stages of development of the discipline. The first stage dealt with the constitutional bases of the administrative process; hence the concern with the doctrine of delegation of power from the legislature to the administrative agency and with the separation of powers, in view of the fact that agencies were accorded legislative, judicial, and executive functions. The second stage focused on problems of judicial review, which gave rise to many doctrines pertaining to the reviewability of administrative actions and to the scope of review. The third stage, which characterizes the present state of the field, is concerned with procedures in rule making and adjudication as reflected in the passage in 1946 of the Administrative Procedure Act. During the current stage a plethora of procedural doctrines has been the center of attention, for example, institutional decisions, subdelegation of powers within the agency, separation of functions within the agency, due process requirements, sovereign immunity, and tort liability of public officials. It is the intensive preoccupation with such diverse procedural doctrines that has prompted some political scientists, for example Grundstein, to complain that "procedure has been an obsessive concern of American administrative law and research has been subordinated to this concern with procedure" (Grundstein, 1964:122).

The fourth stage, to which Davis wishes to direct the field, would be concerned with an understanding of discretionary justice (Davis, 1969). He admits that his treatise, which is concerned with formal procedure and judicial review, deals with only 10% to 20% of the administrative process.

> Yet *the strongest need and the greatest promise for improving the quality of justice to individual parties in the entire legal and governmental system are in the areas where decisions necessarily depend more upon discretion than upon rules and principles and where formal hearings and judicial review are mostly irrelevant.* The reason the literature of administrative law, as well as that of jurisprudence and of public administration, has almost completely neglected the vital 80% or 90% is that the subject is so exceedingly elusive. (Davis, 1971)

How the transition to the new stage will be made—by means of conventional methods of legal research and legal doctrines or with the help of new methods and theories borrowed from other disciplines—Davis does not say. Judging from his ongoing comparative study of discretionary justice in five countries, Davis is evidently willing to depart from conventional modes of legal research (private communication, 1973).

A quite different perspective on trends in American administrative law is reflected in the work of Schwartz and his British collaborator, Wade. Schwartz notes that:

> Administrative Law until now has been concerned almost entirely with property rights and the extent to and the manner in which they might be regulated by governmental power. The Administrative Law of the future must direct itself to the rights of the person, seeking to ensure a place for the individual vis-à-vis the state in the type of society toward which we are evolving (Kass, 1966:77).

Schwartz's formulation is related to the worldwide interest in the Scandinavian ombudsman concept as an institutional device to protect citizens against administrative injustice (Davis, 1961; Gellhorn, 1965, 1968; Rowat, 1968; Peel, 1968; Evan, 1973).

Wade's transatlantic perspective on changes in administrative law is also noteworthy:

> To an English lawyer it is interesting to see how in a few years the emphasis in American administrative law has shifted. Formerly it seemed to be preoccupied, at the federal level at least, with tempering the control of the big regulatory agencies over powerful businesses such as power companies, airlines, broadcasting networks and stockbrokers. The agencies in time became the allies of businesses and there resulted what was called "a welfare state for the wealthy." Today the preoccupation is with social and communal welfare, most of all for the poor. The courts are prodding the administrators into adopting fair rules and fair procedures for enforcing them. The doctrines worked out for the welfare of the wealthy are reaching down the scale into regions where, apparently, arbitrary power used to reign. (Schwartz and Wade, 1972:313)

Yet another trend in American administrative law is the increasing concern with assessing the performance of administrative agencies, particularly of regulatory bodies. This problem has evoked the interest not only of legal scholars but also of economists, various government commissions and consultants, and consumer advocates.

Economists have conducted an extensive amount of research on the economic effects of regulation and have generally concluded that it either has no impact or that it produces no net benefit relative to costs. Thus, for example, Stigler and Friedland, in their study of electrical utilities found no significant effects either with respect to rates or to rates of return on investment; MacAvoy has observed no net benefits from the regulation of public utilities; and Joskow, in his study of the property insurance industry, also emerged with the negative finding as to the impact of regulation, so much so that he encourages states to eliminate formal rate regulation (Stigler and Friedland, 1962; MacAvoy, 1970; Joskow, 1973).

Among the two relatively recent appraisals of regulatory commissions in an effort to "reorganize" and "reform" them so that they will more faithfully fulfill their legislative mandate, those by Landis and the Ash council are especially noteworthy. Deploring the delay in disposition of administrative cases, time-consuming procedures, and the failure to delegate routine problems, Landis made a variety of recommendations principally aimed at augmenting control by the executive branch over the independent agencies (Landis, 1960). A decade later, the Ash council again recommended greater presidential rather than congressional control over the agencies, and, in addition, proposed merging transportation agencies (the ICC, the CAB, and the FAA) and subdividing the FTC into two agencies, one dealing with antitrust activity and one with consumer protection (President's Advisory Council on Executive Organization, 1971).

Consumer advocates, notably Ralph Nader and his associates, have exposed the failure of various regulatory agencies to promote the "public interest." They have documented in some detail that some of these agencies, such as the ICC and the FDA, have been "captured" by the regulated industries (Fellmeth, 1970; Turner, 1970).

To be sure, administrative law scholars have themselves critically evaluated some of the agencies. In his statistical study of antitrust enforcement of the Department of Justice, Posner charges the department with making little effort to identify monopolistic markets, with not seeing to it that its decrees are complied with, and with not keeping any useful statistics on its own activities (Posner, 1970:419). He concludes his indictment with the telling assertion that it is "inappropriately run as a law firm, where the workload is determined by the wishes of the clients (in this case most unhappy competitors, aggrieved purchasers, and disgruntled employees), and where the social product of the legal services undertaken is not measured" (Posner, 1970:419).

Jaffe, a distinguished authority on administrative law, criticizes the "broad delegation model" of administrative agencies, that is, that they operate more effectively when the legislative mandate is vague rather than well defined. In the course of advancing his conception that "the political process . . . provides the milieu and defines the operation of each agency," Jaffe formulates several potentially testable propositions that would gladden the heart of any social scientist reading his article:

> Where the ends and means of an agency's role are highly defined, elaborately rationalized—as is the case with tax or social security—the effects of the political process on the agency are marginal though rationalization could never go so far as totally to exclude political choice. . . . Such agencies are to be judged in terms of their fair, uniform, and zealous application of well-articulated law; the very precision of the law may help to reduce pressures from the regulated. . . .

> Where in form or in substance the legislative design is incomplete, uncertain, or inchoate, a political process will take place in and around the agency, with the likely out-

come a function of the usual variables which determine the product of lawmaking institutions. . . .

An agency faced with an uncertain congressional mandate may do no more than it believes Congress expects it to do, which may, in fact, be nothing. (Jaffe, 1973:1188-1190)

Another recurrent problem in assessing the performance of administrative agencies is the nature of the relationship between the regulatory agency and the client organizations it is charged with regulating. Schwartz and Wade have formulated an intriguing "life cycle" hypothesis concerning this relationship that, as in the case of Jaffe's formulation, is empirically testable:

The influence of regulated upon regulators tends to increase progressively as the regulatory commissions go through what has been seen to be their typical "life cycle." The federal commissions have all gone through periods of youth, maturity, and old age, with their development dominated by what has been termed the progressive law of ossification. It is only during its youthful phase that the commission is vigorous in fighting for the public interest. As time goes on, it loses its early enthusiasm, and administrative aggressiveness is increasingly replaced by apathy. During the phase of maturity, the regulated direct their energies toward taking over the regulators and the commission tends more and more to equate the "public interest" with the interests of the regulated groups. This tendency is carried further in the commission's old age, when it has more or less come to terms with those whom it is ostensibly regulating. Over the years there develops a relationship which can be described only as regulatory symbiosis: regulators and regulated have learned to live with each other and have, in fact, grown intimately dependent on each other. (Schwartz and Wade, 1972:32-33)

Two other developments in American administrative law are noteworthy. In 1964 a new federal administrative agency—the Administrative Conference of the United States—was established for the purpose of studying administrative agencies and for collecting and disseminating information about them (Davis, 1971). This agency subsequently adopted many recommendations, including one pertaining to the "compilation of statistics on administrative proceedings by federal departments and agencies" (Davis, 1971:1). To implement this decision, the Administrative Conference has recently developed a "caseload accounting system for administrative agency proceedings" which would make it possible to compare various agencies on this dimension of performance (Halloran, 1974). In a recent report in which this system is presented, the author compares the average number of cases disposed of per year by hearing examiners—now upgraded and designated "administrative law judges"—in 16 federal agencies, with the average number of cases terminated per year by judges of the U.S. District Courts. According to this study, the performance of federal judges is significantly higher than that of administrative law judges (Halloran, 1974:8).

Finally, the Board of Governors of the American Bar Association, following the recommendation of its Section of Administrative Law, has created a Center for Administrative Justice. The goals of the Center include: "the provision of a central source of information and research materials pertaining to administrative law at all levels of government . . . and [the] conducting of basic research both on its own and on behalf of governmental agencies or private organizations" (Davis, 1973). If these goals are fulfilled in an imaginative manner, we would have another source of data on the functioning of administrative agencies.

From the perspective of the sociologist of law and the organization theorist, the foregoing discussion of trends in American administrative law suggests an increasing sensitivity to problems of administrative law in action. It also suggests that the perennial problems of administrative agencies are unlikely to be solved within the framework of the dominant paradigm in American administrative law. This much is clear from the ongoing work of such administrative law scholars as Davis, Posner, Freedman, and others (Posner, 1972; Freedman, 1972). Do the recent trends, however, make this field more receptive to the contributions of organization theory?

SOME TRENDS IN ORGANIZATION THEORY

Compared with administrative law, the field of organization theory appears to be highly abstract, diffuse, and even chaotic. In spite of its name, there is no *one* commanding theory but a variety of theories differing in scope—some quite narrow, some middle range, and some grand in design. It is an interdisciplinary field on which diverse social sciences, management sciences, and even engineering have converged because of the challenging problems of better understanding and designing complex organizations. It has its roots in the work of the classical school, including Taylor and Fayol in scientific management, and Gulick, Urwick, and others in public administration (March and Simon, 1958). Weber, whose theory of bureaucracy has had a pervasive impact on the course of research in this area, has a close kinship with the classical school in his emphasis on the structure of organizations. In fact, in the empirical work of sociologists in the past two decades, we encounter the first significant trend in the field, namely, the concern with delineating organizational structure. Instead of using Weber's ideal type of bureaucracy, various dimensions have been conceptualized pertaining to his rational-legal, monocratic system of authority. As a result, such organizational variables as the following have been operationalized: centralization of decision making, administrative intensity (which includes the classical notion of "span of control" and various ratios of managerial to nonmanagerial personnel), the degree of formalization (i.e., the emphasis on written rules governing the conduct of bureaucratic personnel), and the degree of professionalization of personnel because of the bureaucracy's reliance on expertise.

In the work of Blau and his students, the concern with structural variables is clearly in evidence (Blau, 1973; Heydebrand, 1973; Meyer, 1972; Blau and Schoenherr, 1971). They have established interrelationships among such variables as organizational size, professionalization of personnel, functional and departmental specialization, and administrative intensity. For example, they have found that, as organizational size increases, so does functional and departmental specialization.

The Aston group, that is, Pugh and his colleagues, has similarly focused on structural variables in their study of a sample of organizations in Britain (Pugh et al., 1968, 1969; Hickson et al., 1969). They have investigated the interrelationships among such variables as functional specialization, formalization, administrative intensity, and centralization of decision making. In short, a dominant trend has emerged involving a *quantitative-structural* analysis of organizations.

In the course of pursuing this style of research, it has become evident that it is important to test hypotheses interrelating structural variables in organizations differing in function, hence the new *comparative* trend in organization theory. Another facet of this trend is the realization of the need for testing whether the structural relationships observed by Blau, Pugh, and their respective colleagues hold in other countries as well (McMillan, 1973; Hickson et al., 1974; Evan, 1975).

In his recent compilation of 30 comparative studies, all involving a quantitative-structural mode of analysis, Heydebrand included only two conducted in government organizations, one dealing with state public personnel agencies of civil service commissions and the other with finance departments of state and local governments as well as with public personnel agencies (Heydebrand, 1973). By comparison, 11 of the studies pertained to professional and service organizations such as hospitals and colleges, and 8 dealt with business organizations. Clearly, sociologists have paid scant attention to the study of administrative agencies, a notable exception being Blau's study of a federal enforcement agency and a state employment agency (Blau, 1955). The pioneering work of Selznick on the TVA, using the case method to analyze dynamic processes, has not been followed up until the recent work of his student, Nonet, on California's Industrial Accident Commission (Selznick, 1949). In his historical analysis of this agency, Nonet discerns a process of "legalization," that is, the "growth of the relevance of law in practical problem-solving, as well as to the elaboration of legal rules and doctrines that occurs in this process" (Nonet, 1969:2). This study is perhaps the clearest recent example in the literature of an effort to integrate concepts from organization theory and the sociology of law, on the one hand, with some concepts from administrative law, on the other.

A third trend in organizational research, in part an outgrowth of the quantitative-structural trend, is a concern with *longitudinal analysis* (Holdaway and Blowers, 1971; Hage, 1974; Kimberly, 1974). Instead of studying relations among structural variables cross-sectionally, it is becoming increasingly clear that a longitudinal mode of analysis is essential. If there is a positive relation between centralization and formalization, does this persist over time or does it change, and if so, in which direction? Only a longitudinally designed study can throw light on such a question.

A fourth trend in organization theory is the increasing attention to *interorganizational relations,* especially since the principal focus of the quantitative-structural research discussed above has been on *intraorganizational relations.* In the work of Litwak, Downs, Evan, and others, we observe this recent emphasis in the field (Litwak, 1970; Downs, 1967; Evan, 1966, 1972, 1976).

In his perceptive study of decision making of government bureaus, Downs starts with the supposition that "every organization's social functions strongly influence its internal structure and behavior, and vice versa. This premise may seem rather obvious, but some organization theorists have in effect contradicted it by focusing their analyses almost exclusively on what happens within an organization" (Downs, 1967:2). One of the important concepts and variables to emerge from the literature on interorganizational relations is organizational autonomy as it is related to the environmental forces impinging on a given organization.

It is the interorganizational trend in this field *in conjunction with* the quantitative-structural, comparative, and longitudinal trends that can open the way for a new line of research on administrative agencies of potential value to both administrative law and organization theory.

AN ORGANIZATION-SET MODEL OF
THE ADMINISTRATIVE PROCESS

In our brief discussion of recent trends in administrative law and organization theory, various concepts have been alluded to. It may now be instructive to juxtapose a "baker's dozen" concepts in each field, as I have done in Table 6.1. In only 5 of the 13 —those that are asterisked—is there any conceptual correspondence. Thus, for example, institutional decisions presuppose a high degree of centralization in decision making, whereas subdelegation of power entails decentralization of decision making. Similarly, rule making is close to the concept of formalization; the concern with the separation of functions—legislative, adjudicative, and executive—involves a process of departmental specialization; administrative discretion reflects in part a pattern of informal organization, namely, one that is not officially prescribed or sanctioned and entails a process of innovation.

To go beyond the mere drawing of interdisciplinary conceptual parallels requires a model in terms of which some of these concepts can be used, thus building a bridge between the two disciplines (Evan, 1962d; Evan and Schwartz, 1964). A first approximation will be attempted here.

The organization-set model that I have formulated elsewhere has two underlying assumptions. First, organizations, in general, and administrative agencies, in particular, are systems of interrelated elements interacting with other systems in their environment; hence an application of a systems perspective is required. This assumption is similar to Downs's premise and to Jaffe's view that "each agency functions in a political milieu" (Jaffe, 1973:1189). A second assumption is that an organization's performance, however it may be conceptualized and measured, is a function of (1) its goals, (2) its internal organizational structure, (3) the role orientation of its members, and (4) its mode of interaction with its environing organizations.

The point of departure of this model is a consideration of several concepts in role theory developed by Merton and by Gross, Mason, and McEachern (Merton, 1957; Gross, Mason, and McEachern, 1958). Instead of selecting a status as the unit of

Table 6.1 Selected Concepts in American Administrative Law and
Organization Theory

American Administration Law	Organization Theory
1. Delegation of powers	1. Organizational size
2. Separation of powers	2. Organizational age
3. Judicial review	3. Complexity of task structure
4. Substantial-evidence rule	4. Technological complexity
5. Primary jurisdiction	5. Organizational effectiveness
6. Sovereign immunity	6. Organizational autonomy
7. Officer tort liability	7. Functional specialization
8. Administrative due process	8. Administrative intensity (bureaucratization)
*9. Institutional decisions	*9. Centralization of decision making
*10. Sub-delegation of power	*10. Decentralization of decision making
*11. Rule making	*11. Formalization
*12. Separation of functions	*12. Departmental specialization
*13. Administrative discretion	*13. Informal organization and innovation

*These items are examples of a degree of interdisciplinary conceptual parallelism.

analysis and charting the complex of role relationships in which the status occupant is involved, as Merton does in his analysis of role-sets, I take as the unit of analysis an organization or a class of organizations and trace its interactions with various organizations in its environment, that is, with elements of its "organization-set." Following Gross, Mason, and McEachern's use of the term "focal position" in their analysis of roles, I have referred to the organization or class of organizations that is the point of reference as the "focal organization" (Gross, Mason, and McEachern, 1958:50-56; Evan, 1966:178). As in the case of role-set analysis, the focal organization interacts with a complement of organizations in its environment, that is, its organization-set. A systems analysis perspective, however, suggests that the organization-set be partitioned into an "input organization-set" and an "output organization-set." By an input organization-set, as the term suggests, is meant a complement of

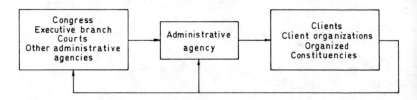

Figure 6.1 An Organization-Set Analysis of an Administrative Agency

organizations that provides various types of resources to the focal organization. Similarly, by an output organization-set is meant all organizations that are the recipients of the goods and/or services, including organizational decisions, generated by the focal organization. Furthermore, a systems analysis requires that we trace feedback effects from the output organization-set to the focal organization and thence to the input organization-set, or directly from the output to the input organization-set. These feedback effects can, of course, be positive or negative, as well as anticipated or unanticipated.

The four components of the model—focal organization, input organization-set, output organization-set, and feedback effects—may be jointly conceived as comprising an interorganizational system.

For purposes of illustration, if we take as a focal organization an administrative agency such as the FCC (see Figure 6.1), the input organization-set includes: the Congress through its enabling act, the Appropriations Committee, and so on; the Executive Branch, including the president who appoints the chairman and commissioners, and the various executive departments; the courts whose past decisions become guides and constraints on the agency's future actions; and other administrative agencies that may either support, help, or compete with the FCC for scarce resources. The degree to which the FCC is effective in managing the input organization-set, which is very likely plagued with conflict and uncertainty, affects its internal structure and in turn its capacity to perform its regulatory functions.

The output-set consists of many thousands of radio and television stations whose licenses and programming are regulated by the FCC's decisions, various trade associations, and a bar association of attorneys in the communications industry.

The success with which the FCC manages its multifaceted relations with the members of its output organization-set in turn has feedback effects on the FCC as well as on the input organization-set, which again triggers the cycle of interorganizational systemic relations (Sutherland, 1949).

Managing the boundary relations of the FCC with its input organization-set and its output organization-set are its various boundary personnel, principally attorneys who conduct investigations, administrative law judges, and liaison officers with Congress and the Executive Branch. At least two role attributes, expertise and loyalty, determine the behavior of the boundary personnel and cumulatively affect the performance of the FCC. If the boundary personnel are not high-caliber professionals, they will fail to apply the relevant agency rules or legal principles to the problems and facts at hand; and if the norms governing their conduct—their normative reference group—are derived from the regulated industry, rather than from the agency, they will again fail to perform their function with fidelity to the FCC's mandate. Greatly aggravating the dilemmas of the boundary personnel, as Jaffe points out, is the broad delegation of powers in terms of the concept of public interest (Jaffe, 1973).

In short, with the help of the organization-set model supplemented with relevant structural variables, it would be possible to study a sample of administrative agencies differing on such dimensions as type of delegation of power (broad versus narrow), life-cycle position, volume of rule making, scope of jurisdiction (federal, state, or local agency), and so on. Such an inquiry would be able to test propositions of interest to both administrative lawyers and organization theorists. One hypothesis, for example, is as follows:

Administrative agencies with a low degree of organizational autonomy will—all other things being equal—have:

1. a high degree of centralization of decision making;
2. a high degree of formalization;
3. a high probability of rendering decisions in favor of organizations that can exercise substantial power over the agency;
4. a low proportion of professionals with a high commitment to the legislative mandate; and
5. a low level of performance, for example, as measured by the case load of its personnel.

To further clarify how the organization-set model would be applied in an empirical study of administrative agencies, 25 variables, illustrating the four components of the model, are enumerated in Table 6.2. Variables 1 to 6, which are indicators of the input organization-set, include a composite measure of organizational autonomy (Variable 6), namely, of the administrative agency. Variables 7 to 17, which are indicators of the structure of the focal organization, resemble those Blau, Pugh, and their respective colleagues have employed in their studies. The four output organization-set variables (22 to 25) include a composite measure of the degree of regulatory resistance to the focal organization (Blau and Schoenherr, 1971:27-29; Heydebrand, 1973:7-11; Pugh et al., 1968). Finally, the four output variables (18 to 21), which include a composite measure of organizational effectiveness of the agency, would provide a basis for ascertaining negative and positive feedback effects of the interorganizational system.

It should be evident that the list of 25 variables is only a first approximation—particularly those purporting to measure agency effectiveness—to the kind of effort that would be required in any empirical application of the model. With the aid of a carefully selected and operationalized inventory of organization-set variables, it would be possible to test two general hypotheses of interest to administrative lawyers as well as to organization theorists, to wit:

1. The structure of an administrative agency (Variables 7 to 17) is a function of the input organization-set variables (1 to 6) and of the output organization-set variables (22 to 25).

Table 6.2 Some Illustrative Organization-Set Variables for Studying Administrative Agencies

---

Input Organization-Set Variables

1. Type of legislative mandate (broad vs. narrow)

2. Size of input organization-set (i.e., number of organizations)

3. Degree of homogeneity of input organization-set

4. Network configuration of input organization-set (e.g., presence of coalition formation against the focal organization)

5. Degree of adequacy of input resources

6. A composite measure of the degree of organizational autonomy (based on Variables 1 to 5)

Focal Organization Variables

7. Organizational size

8. Organizational age

9. Complexity of task structure

10. Technological complexity

11. a. Functional specialization

    b. Degree of boundary role specialization

12. Degree of professionalization of personnel

13. Type of normative reference group orientation of boundary personnel (i.e., focal organization vs. external organization)

14. Centralization of decision making

15. Formalization

16. Departmental specialization

17. Administrative intensity

Output Variables

18. Cost per administrative action

19. Number of administrative actions per professional employer

20. Percentage of administrative actions reviewed by courts per year

21. A composite measure of the degree of organizational effectiveness of the focal organization (based on Variables 18 to 20)

Output Organization-Set Variables

22. Size of output organization-set

23. Degree of homogeneity of output organization-set

24. Network configuration of output organization-set (e.g., presence of coalition formation against the focal organization)

25. A composite measure of the degree of conflict of the output organization-set with the focal organization (i.e., degree of resistance to regulation—based on Variables 22 to 24)

---

2. The effectiveness of an administrative agency is a function of its organizational structure (Variables 7 to 17), its input organization-set (Variables 1 to 6), and its output organization-set (Variables 22 to 25) (Evan, 1976c:15-28).

RESEARCH STRATEGIES

To test any facet of the foregoing model would obviously require the most efficient methods available. At least four social science methodologies are clearly relevant. The first is the application of the sample survey method such as Blau and his colleagues as well as the Aston group use in conducting quantitative-structural research. This would involve drawing a sample of administrative agencies, mapping the nature of their interactions with their organizational environment, and measuring the effects of their internal structure and the role orientations of its boundary personnel on its legislative, adjudicative, and executive functions.

A second research strategy is that of the case method as exemplified by the outstanding studies of Selznick and Nonet (Selznick, 1949; Nonet, 1969). Rather than trying to establish quantitative relationships among variables, the focus is on discovering dynamic processes with the help of a given model. Thus, Selznick's use of "cooptation" to throw light on the environmental constraints on the TVA and Nonet's concept of "legalization" illustrate the potential benefits from this mode of research.

A third and least exploited research strategy in this context is that of experimental methodology. Organizational experiments pertaining to intraorganizational and interorganizational phenomena can be conducted with the aid of laboratory as well as field studies (Evan, 1971). Thibaut, Walker, and Lind, in the course of testing the relative merits of the adversary versus the inquisitorial mode of adjudication, have made a case for the use of laboratory experimentation to simulate decision making in courts as well as in administrative agencies:

The laboratory method seems best adapted to studies of institutional modes of conflict resolution since these modes embody standardized rules and procedures that can be experimentally replicated in simplified form. In our society the courts and administrative agencies are of course the principal institutional devices for resolution of social disputes. Thus, the obvious application of the suggested laboratory method entails the simulation of a court or administrative process and the introduction of planned variations of substantive or procedural rules in a way that permits exact measurement of the effects attributable to the variations (Thibaut, Walker, and Lind, 1972:387)

As for field experiments, Schwartz, Campbell, and Zeisel have advocated the desirability of conducting such research (Schwartz, 1961; Campbell, 1970; Zeisel, 1973). It does not require a fertile imagination, particularly on the part of some economists who have argued in favor of deregulation of selected industries, either to perform a "quasi-field experiment," such as Campbell has urged, or, more ambitiously, to seek to persuade relevant administrative agencies to modify in a controlled manner their internal structures or policies—to the extent, of course, that this would not violate the law.

Almost as neglected as experimental methodology in the study of legal phenomena is the use of computer simulation, a technique that is slowly attracting the attention of legal scholars (Sigler, 1968; Merrill and Schrage, 1969; Drobak, 1972). Instead of conducting field experiments—that entail substantial costs and difficulties—to test alternative policies of court administration, law enforcement, administrative adjudication, and the like, it is possible to represent real and hypothetical states of various dimensions of legal systems by means of computer simulation. Although organizational research has thus far made only modest use of simulation models, several studies suggest potentially fruitful applications of this methodology to problems of administrative agencies (Bonini, 1963; Cohen and Cyert, 1965; Rowe, 1968:173-175). In fact, the organization-set model outlined above, and the 25 illustrative variables operationalizing the model (see Table 6.2) provide the wherewithal for testing an array of functional relationships in a sequence of computer simulation runs.

Although I would obviously not rule out the relevance of conventional legal research, it would be important to select with care a sample of administrative decisions involving *formal adjudication* as well as a sample of decisions involving *informal proceedings*, which, of course, is Davis' principal argument for research on discretionary justice.

CONCLUSION

The burden of this discussion is that the sociology of law can be instrumental in forging a link between administrative law, on the one hand, and organization theory, on the other. If a research partnership were developed between these two disciplines, administrative lawyers would learn how the organizational environments of administrative agencies interact with the internal organizational structures to affect the agencies' legislative, judicial, and executive functions. Organization theorists, on the other hand, in coming to grips with the complex environmental processes impinging on administrative agencies, would significantly advance their knowledge of interorganizational relations and, in addition, contribute to the integration of organization theory and macrosociological theory, inasmuch as the functioning of any administrative agency invariably entails a complex of legal, political, and economic interactions.

In sum, if the argument advanced in this chapter were taken seriously by researchers in both disciplines, organization theory would make significant strides, particularly in modeling and explaining interorganizational phenomena; and administrative law would probably evolve more rapidly into Davis's fourth stage of discretionary justice, which in turn might usher in a fifth stage of "administrative law in action," informed by concepts, propositions, and models derived from organization theory (Davis, 1971).

CHAPTER 7

Organizations and the Limits of Effective Legal Action

The concept of law as an instrument of social engineering is hardly a new idea. First popularized by Roscoe Pound (1923) more than 60 years ago, it is a notion widely held by legal officials and citizens alike. The credo is that for any problem that arises in a society there must be a solution; and the law is the principal source of remedy. Although this boundless faith in the efficacy of law is probably more widespread in the United States than in some European countries, it is very likely also common in virtually all nation-states, capitalist as well as socialist. Ironically, Pound (1917), the father of the idea of the use of law as social engineering, also identified what he calls the "limits of effective legal action." Among these limits, Pound, however, does not mention the power of organizations to neutralize and act as a countervailing force to the power of the law.

Organizations, as aggregations of substantial reservoirs of resources and hence of power, have the capacity to affect the decisions and behavior of others. This is true of organizations *within* and *without* the legal system. In the American legal system, the powers of administrative agencies, for example, are spelled out in enabling legislation. Whatever discretionary power such agencies may exercise, they cannot, as a rule, exceed the powers enumerated in the statutes under which they operate. When and if they exceed such powers they are subject to controls in the form of judicial review by federal courts and of legislative amendments by Congress. Although, in principle, courts are more powerful in the sanctions they can invoke than administrative agencies, they frequently limit their discretionary powers to conform to standards of fairness or justice commonly held by fellow judges.

In contrast to administrative agencies and courts, organizations outside the legal system, depending on the magnitude of their resources, seek to exert their influence over the interpretation and implementation of a law. In the process of exerting such influence, organizations external to the legal system can in effect succeed in varying degree in limiting the efficacy of a law.

AN AMERICAN CASE

The Conflict Between the Amalgamated Clothing and
Textile Workers Union and J. P. Stevens and Co.

To explore the relationships between organizations and the law outlined above, I shall consider the history of the conflict between the Amalgamated Clothing and Textile Workers Union (ACTWU) and J. P. Stevens and Co. (JPS). In recent labor law history in the United States this conflict stands out as the most protracted and the most rancorous (Gamson, 1966). It highlights the power of organizations within and without the legal system to limit a law's effectiveness.

Since the early 1960s, the ACTWU, in its effort to unionize workers in the South—where some textile companies relocated their mills to escape the costs of unionization—has encountered sustained and vigorous resistance from the second-largest textile manufacturer in the country, JPS. To counter and undermine the union's organizing campaign, JPS's basic strategy has been to discharge employees sympathetic to the union. The company's strategy is in clear violation of the National Labor Relations Act (NLRA),which states that "It shall be an unfair labor practice for an employer to interfere with, restrain, or coerce employees in the exercise of their rights guaranteed" under this Act. One such right is the right to join or form a union. Between 1963 and 1977, JPS has engaged in actions which have led to more than 1200 violations of the law. During this period the National Labor Relations Board (NLRB) has initiated approximately 130 cases against JPS. In each of the cases the NLRB has found JPS guilty of violating the rights of workers to organize a union. When JPS appealed the decisions of the NLRB in federal appellate courts, these courts have in general upheld the findings of the NLRB that JPS has "flagrantly" violated the labor laws. Specifically, the company has been found guilty of threatening plant closings, coercive interrogation of workers, denying overtime to union supporters, discriminatorily altering working conditions, electronic spying on union organizers, downgrading union members' jobs, dismissing employees who testified before the NLRB, etc.

After many years of campaigning to organize employees of JPS, ACTWU in 1974 won a representational election in a plant in Roanoke Rapids, North Carolina. Thereafter negotiations for a contract began between officials of the union and the company. These negotiations continued for about six months at which point the union officials concluded that their counterparts in the company were not "bargaining in good faith." The union submitted a complaint to the NLRB averring unfair labor practices against JPS. This charge was eventually upheld by the NLRB, viz., that JPS was bargaining in bad faith. To enforce its order to JPS to bargain in good faith, the NLRB initiated a lawsuit in a federal appellate court against JPS. The court upheld the NLRB's order and, in turn, ordered JPS to bargain in good faith. Thus far, however, no collective bargaining contract has been signed in Roanoke Rapids, North Carolina. This court order, like others, has not been obeyed by the company and has, to date, led to three contempt citations by the courts (Bartosic and Lanoff, 1972). In the last of these three contempt citations, in 1978, the federal court threatened to invoke penalties of fines and jail sentences against JPS executives.

In short, ACTWU has won innumerable administrative and judicial battles against JPS only to discover that they had won a hollow victory. As one ACTWU attorney summed up the state of the dispute with JPS from 1963 to the present: "You win, you win, you win, but you never really win."

An Assessment of the Efficacy of the Law and the Resources of the Organizational Actors

Why the "hollow victory" on the part of ACTWU, the party to the dispute, which the NLRB as well as the federal appellate courts have acknowledged has been deprived of its rights under the National Labor Relations Act? To answer this question we shall assess the relative resources of the several organizational actors in this dispute.

The National Labor Relations Board. The NLRA does not empower the NLRB to enforce its own orders. This administrative agency, like all others, must have recourse to the federal courts to enforce its orders. Second, the sanctions or remedies available to the NLRB, according to NLRA, are very limited: it can issue a "cease and desist order" in the event, for example, of an unfair labor practice; in the case of an unfair employee discharge, the employer may be ordered to reinstate the employee with "back-pay" so as "to make things whole," that is, to restore the status quo ante. The NLRB does not have the authority under the act, for example, to impose punitive penalties for unfair labor practices in the form of double or triple damages. Nor has Congress been willing to revise the act to grant the NLRB more effective sanctions when confronted with "flagrant" violations of the law.

The courts. The federal appellate courts, to which the board turns to enforce its orders, also contribute to the hollow victory of the union. Although the courts have almost always upheld the decisions of NLRB against JPS, their qualifications and their demurrers have had the effect of encouraging JPS to continue its litigational strategy against the unions. Nor do the courts accompany their decisions with sanctions that have any teeth in them. Instead, the sanctions to which the courts have thus far resorted are of a symbolic character exclusively. Even in the case of the three contempt of court decisions against JPS for disobeying court orders, the courts stopped short of imposing fines and/or jail sentences on the company executives. The reluctance of courts to penalize corporations for disobeying its orders, in turn, has to do with a disinclination to punish executives— members of a social class similar to that of judges themselves— and more generally to the dilemmas that arise in handling corporate violations of the law. Since a corporation is, by definition, an impersonal entity lacking "a soul so it cannot be damned," yet enjoying the privileges of "corporate personality" and "limited liability," the courts tend to refuse to punish individual executives for illegal actions committed by them on behalf of the corporation. In this respect, the legal doctrines associated with the corporation function as impediments to the efficacious enforcement of the law.

J. P. Stevens. How shall we assess the relative resources and the respective strategies of the two principal organizational actors in this dispute, viz., JPS and ACTWU? Clearly, JPS, a huge corporation, has far more resources and "staying power" than ACTWU. Apart from its house counsel in its legal department, it can afford to hire several large law firms employing hundreds of lawyers to devote their talents to contesting all complaints and lawsuits initiated by ACTWU and the NLRB. Thus, its litigation strategy—without regard to costs of lawyers' fees—can prolong the dispute and ensure hollow victories for ACTWU for many years to come, as they, in effect, have done since 1963. JPS claims that ACTWU has unfairly singled it out as a "target" for unionization, claiming, in effect, that by resisting the union demands for collective bargaining, it is promoting competition in the textile industry and protecting the interests of consumers as well as the company (Guzzardi, 1978).

ACTWU. The union, for its part, has chosen JPS, rightly or wrongly, as the firm in the industry which offers the highest probability of achieving the union's goal of unionization, which would then more easily diffuse to the rest of the industry. Apart from its field staff of union organizers and business representatives, ACTWU has a legal staff of about a dozen lawyers at its headquarters who handle all legal problems of the union, not only those involving the dispute with JPS. Hence, its litigation resources are much smaller than those of its adversary. Its strategy to unionize firms in the South and the sun-belt was in part arrived at because of the migration of textile plants from the North to the South.

After more than 15 years of scoring "hollow victories" against JPS, ACTWU is evidently modifying its strategy against JPS. First, it has concluded from its dispute with JPS that its antagonist is not acting alone to protect its economic interests vis-à-vis the union. Instead, ACTWU has inferred from JPS's conduct that it is engaged in collusive activity with other textile manufacturers as well as with other corporations to ward off the common enemy, viz., the union. Hence, the coalition of industry forces, spearheaded by JPS, according to ACTWU, constitutes a violation of antitrust law. Thus, the union's revised litigation strategy includes an antitrust suit brought in 1977, in addition to pressing its charges of illegal antiunion conduct on the part of JPS. A second strategy that appears to be emerging from ACTWU is to supplement its litigations with a legislative lobbying strategy to reform the National Labor Relations Act. This strategy is much more difficult to implement; it presupposes a capacity of the union to build a coalition of organizations to lobby effectively for labor law reform. Such coalitional activity, of necessity, engenders counter-coalitional behavior on the part of pro-corporate forces (Evan, 1976a). Judging from the failure of Congress to pass a recent bill aimed at reforming NLRA to strengthen the hands of the unions, JPS and other companies are, thus far, more successful in countering this union strategy.

A third strategy of ACTWU in its battle against JPS may be characterized as political and interorganizational in nature. In 1978, ACTWU brought pressure on some large banks in which it had its deposits, for example, Hanover Trust Co., to persuade its board of director members, who are officials of JPS, not to run for re-election. By thus eliminating JPS officials from the boards of directors of major banks, ACTWU sought to "isolate JPS from the financial community."

A fourth strategy of ACTWU against JPS is also political in nature and is closely linked to the third strategy. Since 1976, ACTWU has launched a boycott campaign to persuade retailers not to purchase such JPS products as sheets, towels, pillowcases, and carpets. Thus far, with the help of church organizations, college student organizations, and other unions, ACTWU has succeeded in persuading the managers of 2,000 retail establishments to boycott JPS products. The union acknowledges that its boycott has limited economic impact because of two compelling facts: JPS is a multinational corporation with many subsidiaries abroad that are beyond the reach of the current boycott campaign; in addition, at least two thirds of the company's products are sold directly to manufacturers who either use them to manufacture their own products, such as seat covers for automobiles, or else market JPS products under their own brand names, for instance, Sears or J. C. Penney. Hence, the potential benefit of the boycott campaign to ACTWU may be more symbolic than economic.

In short, will the four-pronged strategy of ACTWU succeed in converting its hollow victories into a genuine victory?[1]

A BRITISH CASE

Is the conflict described between JPS and ACTWU unique? If, in fact, it is unique, it would not be useful as a source of data for generalizing about industrial relations or about the sociology of law. The difficulties of generalizing from such phenomena were recently noted by a student of industrial relations:

Consider, for example, the fate of the British 1971 Industrial Relations Act and its consequences for British industrial relations. A system of legal regulation of industrial relations which works successfully in one country, may be a failure in another which has a quite different background. Indeed, very few theoretical propositions in industrial relations are universal truths capable of general application without regard to the context in which they operate. This is not to say that we must not strive for "general" theories with universal applicability; it is rather to argue that greater attention should be paid to stating the limitations of theory relating to contextual factors. (Singh, 1979)

I shall cite one case from Britain—the Grunwick dispute concerning union recognition, which has become a *cause célèbre* (James and Simpson, 1978; Dickens, 1978).

Unlike the United States, where the National Labor Relations Act has institutionalized union recognition since 1935, the first such statutory provision in Britain was contained in the Industrial Relations Act of 1971 (Hart, 1978). When this law was repealed by the Labor government in 1974, statutory recognition was included in section 2 of the Employment Protection Act of 1975. In accordance with this law, an administrative agency, the Advisory, Conciliation and Arbitration Service (A.C.A.S.), has the duty to inquire into an application for union recognition and to make a recommendation followed by an effort to conciliate the dispute. With these differences in mind, we now consider a recent dramatic union recognition conflict in Great Britain.

The dispute at Grunwick Processing Laboratories Limited, a mail-order photographic processing and printing company employing about 500 employees, the majority of whom are women, began in August 1976 with the dismissal of one employee and the walkout of several other employees. The dispute quickly escalated when 50 additional employees joined the walkout; within a few days, the number of employees on strike increased to 137. The striking workers then sought the help of the Association of Professional, Executive, Clerical, and Computer Staff (APEX), a "white-collar" union which was "known in the labor movement for its right wing views and . . . a supporter of moderate policies" (Scarman, 1977:5). Shortly after joining the dispute, APEX made a formal request to the company for union recognition. Grunwick not only rejected the union's request for recognition but also dismissed all the striking employees. APEX responded by submitting an application for union recognition to A.C.A.S. in October 1976, in accordance with section 2 of the Employment Protection Act of 1975.

After conducting an inquiry, A.C.A.S. recommended union recognition. The company challenged the decision in the courts, losing at the trial court level but winning in the appellate courts. Grunwick was determined to do battle with APEX and A.C.A.S. by resisting unionization which, combined with the prolonging of the strike for many months, prompted the union to resort to a program of "industrial action." Among the actions undertaken were mass picketing, which resulted in some violence, and an arrangement with the Union of Post Office Workers whereby they agreed to "black the mail" (i.e., to refuse to handle the mail) of Grunwick. These actions gave rise to a variety of legal proceedings such as prosecutions of picketers, proceedings arising out of the "blacking of mail," action by the Post Office to forestall its threatened resumption, and a Court of Inquiry under the Industrial Courts of 1919 (James and Simpson, 1978; Scarman, 1977). The final legal defeat sustained by APEX occurred when A.C.A.S. appealed the decision of the appellate court to the House of Lords, which eventually declared this agency's recommendation for union recognition null and void.

In both the United States and British cases, national regulatory agencies (NLRB as well as A.C.A.S.) had virtually no sanctions at their disposal when confronted with a reluctant employer who was strongly opposed to union recognition. In this respect, the sanctions provided by the Employment Protection Act of 1975 are no different from those in the Industrial Relations Act of 1971 (James, 1977:39). Both laws are grounded on a principle of voluntarism supported by advice, conciliation, and arbitration. Neither law takes account of the judicial approach to union recognition which was recently summarized as follows:

There is a unifying theme underlying the judgments in the appellate courts. This is an approach which seeks to minimize the impact on individual interests of statutory provisions which are intended to further workers' collective interests. This judicial attitude has a long history in cases concerning provisions which provide protection against common law restraints. Its emergence in a case concerning provisions which establish positive collective rights will not therefore surprise anyone familiar with the history of legal intervention in British industrial relations. This history has also shown the limits of the efficacy of amending legislation in the face of such judicial views. (James and Simpson, 1978:577)

Interestingly enough, the reluctance of American appellate courts to impose civil or criminal sanctions against employers guilty of violating the National Labor Relations Act bears a similarity to the orientation of British appellate courts in cases involving union recognition.

CONCLUSION

The protracted conflicts between JPS and ACTWU and between Grunwick and APEX sketched above pose a challenge to sociology of law, organization theory and policy analysis. Are there any general propositions that can be derived from these disputes that would be applicable to broader classes of problems such as the formation, interpretation, and administration of laws? Under what conditions is a law effective in regulating the conduct of organizations, especially organizations that are not components of the legal system?

Several propositions suggest themselves from the foregoing analysis:

1. Interactions between organizations, whether *within* or *without* the legal system, influence the enactment, interpretation, and administration of a law. Thus, during the Depression, conflict between labor and management in the United States reached a level of intensity which prompted Congress to defuse it by passing the National Labor Relations Act in 1935. After World War II, when labor had virtually achieved a high degree of countervailing power vis-à-vis management and had assumed a militant stance, Congress saw fit to revise the NLRA so as to abridge the power granted to labor.

2. A law, in its very formulation, as well as in its implementation, can inadvertently limit its own efficacy. The National Labor Relations Act failed to specify significant sanctions in the event of violation of the act. Nor has the administrative agency, the NLRB, created by the act, exercised any discretionary rule making to increase the probability that labor and management would comply with the law.

3. The organizational design of an administrative agency can have the unanticipated effect of limiting its efficacy. The internal structure of the NLRB, differentiating the staff into prosecutorial and adjudicatory functions, probably leads to intraorganizational conflict which may result in a tendency to moderate its mode of administration of the law.

4. Interorganizational dependency can unanticipatedly limit the effectiveness of a law. The fact that the NLRB's decisions are dependent on federal appellate courts for enforcement of the board's orders and are also potentially subject to judicial review may induce the agency to adopt a moderate strategy in administering the law.

5. If there is an imbalance in resources between organizational adversaries that are subject to legal regulation, and if legal agencies, whether Congress, administrative agencies, or the federal courts fail to provide sanctions and remedies that compensate for the asymmetry in organizational resources, these factors inadvertently limit the efficacy of the law in question. In other words, to the extent that a law fails to equalize the power of organizational contestants (Nader and Serber, 1976), the actual interpretation and administration of a law is influenced by the asymmetry of organizational power.

6. If the power imbalance of organizational contestants directly or indirectly influences the interpretation and administration of a law, then it further tends to impair the efficacy of the law.

7. As the efficacy of a law diminishes, there is a tendency for the weaker organizational adversary to seek recourse to *political* rather than *legal* remedies.

In sum, organizational factors, within and without a legal system, affect the efficacy of a law. To the extent that the efficacy of a law is impaired and the legitimacy of a law wanes, a disadvantaged party loses confidence in the fairness of the legal process and resorts to political action, namely, the use or threatened use of power, coercion and violence. Thus, the enactment of laws and their implementation have fateful consequences for social order (Evan, 1980).

NOTE

1. In 1980, J. P. Stevens & Company ended the 17-year struggle to prevent unionization of its workers by signing a contract with the Amalgamated Clothing and Textile Workers Union.

Part III

INTERINSTITUTIONAL AND COMPARATIVE ANALYSIS

CHAPTER 8

Public and Private Legal Systems

Interinstitutional analysis is, by definition, more complex than intrainstitutional analysis, which focuses on the values, norms, roles and organizations comprising an institution or a subsystem of a society. From the vantage point of interinstitutional analysis, a legal system is, at any point in time, a function of its interactions with the particular configuration of nonlegal institutions in a given society. Since the configuration of institutions in a society changes over time and differs from one type of society to another, we would expect to observe corresponding differences in legal systems. Hence, there is a need for a comparative as well as an historical perspective in the study of legal systems.

In this chapter I shall consider some implications of a conception of law and legal systems that is not exclusively identified with the state (Ehrlich, 1936; Weber, 1954). By examining the organizational components of legal and nonlegal institutions, some significant hypotheses are generated for research in the sociology of law.

A TYPOLOGY OF LEGAL SYSTEMS

For present purposes, we shall classify legal systems along two dimensions. Implicit in our discussion is a distinction between legal systems on the basis of jurisdiction, namely, whether they are public or private. A public legal system has its locus in the formal structures of the state such as the judiciary, the legislature, the executive, and the administrative agency; its jurisdiction extends to all inhabitants of the territory of a society. A private legal system, on the other hand, has its locus in a formal organization relatively independent of the state; its jurisdiction officially extends only to the organization's members.

The second basis of classification involves a vague, multidimensional but important distinction between democratic and undemocratic types of legal systems. A democratic legal system includes at least three attributes: (a) the separation of powers, (b) "procedural due process of law," and (c) the consent of the governed. The first two attributes have the function of delimiting the authority exercised over the members or the "laity" of the social system. Through the separation of powers, the three normative functions are so distributed as to prevent a concentration of authority in one and the same status.

Procedural due process of law, as distinct from substantive due process, relates to a complex of norms protecting the rights of parties in the prosecution and adjudication of a dispute (Forkosch, 1958: 176-195; Hale, 1952: 228-239). Incorporated in the Bill of Rights in 1791, the Due Process Clause protects the citizen against the exercise of arbitrary power by the federal government. These rights were extended after the Civil War, via the Fourteenth Amendment, to citizens vis-à-vis their state governments. Parties to a dispute are assured a "fair" and "impartial" trial through such guarantees as the right to notice of hearing, the right to confront witnesses and to cross-examine them, and the right to introduce evidence on one's behalf (Forkosch, 1958: 212). The significance of this constitutional doctrine for democracy has recently been underscored by a legal scholar who states that "due process may almost be said to be a sufficient cause for our democracy" (Forkosch, 1958:173). Justice Frankfurter has expressed a similar view in asserting that due process is one of the "indispensable conditions for the maintenance and progress of a free society" (Forkosch, 1958:189, n. 43).

Consent of the governed, the third attribute of a democratic legal system, not only affords the laity a veto power through the electoral process but also implies the right to dissent. Institutionalization of dissent protects the minority among the laity as well as among the officials performing specialized normative functions (Lipset, Trow, and Coleman, 1956).

A democratic legal system as defined here—one characterized by the separation of powers, procedural due process, and consent of the governed—maximizes the probability that the institutionalized rights, immunities, and privileges of all members of a social system are protected. On the other hand, an undemocratic legal system, or one lacking these three properties, provides for none of the safeguards against unlimited and arbitrary authority. The occupant of one and the same status in a social system may perform legislative, executive, and judicial functions; there is no institutionalized procedure for impartially adjudicating disputes; and the occupants of statuses that do not have specialized legal functions, the laity, have little or no formal veto power over the officials performing executive, legislative, and judicial functions. Weber's monocratic type of bureaucratic organization is obviously closer to the undemocratic than to the democratic type of legal system (Weber, 1947).

These two dimensions for classifying legal systems yield four ideal types: (1) public democratic, (2) public undemocratic, (3) private democratic, and (4) private undemocratic. Examples of public legal systems that are formally democratic are the municipal, state, and federal courts, legislatures, and executive branches of government in the United States and other countries with polylithic states. By contrast, the public legal systems of societies with monolithic states are formally undemocratic. Private legal systems that are formally democratic are exemplified by such organizations as trade unions, professional associations, and trade associations. With respect to its employees, the industrial or business organization is an example of a private undemocratic legal system.

This typology of legal systems suggests several general classes of problems for the sociology of law. First, what are some

significant structural and functional similarities and dissimilar-
ities among legal systems, public and private? Second, what are
the interrelationships between public and private legal systems?
Third, what are the interrelationships between public legal systems? Fourth, what are the interrelationships between private
legal systems? Fifth, under what conditions do legal systems,
whether public or private, undergo transformation from an undemocratic into a democratic type, and vice versa? Sixth, under
what conditions do legal systems, democratic or undemocratic,
undergo transformation from a public to a private type and vice
versa? Although the typology may point to other problems,
those enumerated have the merit of dealing with basic problems
of normative and structural change about which we have relatively little systematic knowledge.

HEURISTIC VALUE OF THE TYPOLOGY

We shall briefly consider four classes of problems suggested
by our typology which readily lend themselves to the identification of problems of sociological significance. This discussion is
intended merely to illustrate the kinds of problems that a developing sociology of law might embrace.

Comparative Study of Legal Systems

Comparative studies have been made by legal scholars of
public legal systems, either of total systems (judicial, legislative,
and executive components) or of subsystems. Thus, for example, Wigmore examines a great variety of public legal systems;
Orfield compares the public legal systems of Scandinavian
countries; and Hoebel compares the public legal systems of several preliterate societies (Wigmore, 1928; Orfield, 1953; Hoebel,
1954). An illustration of a comparative study of a subsystem of public legal systems is McRuer's work on judicial process (McRuer, 1957). Since these studies tend to be descriptive

in nature, they provide data only for comparative sociological analysis.

Characteristically, Weber developed a classification of analytical categories for his comparative and historical analysis of different public legal systems (Weber, 1954). His fourfold classification—concerned with law making and law finding, two of the three normative processes—is based on the interrelationship between two dimensions: formal-substantive and rational-irrational (Weber, 1954:xlvii-lxii). We may infer from Weber's analysis that democratic legal systems may have the attributes of either a formally rational or a substantively rational system, though perhaps not of a formally irrational or a substantively irrational type.

The three attributes of a democratic legal system discussed above—separation of powers, procedural due process of law, and consent of the governed—provide the bases for a comparative study of public and private legal systems. In the case of public legal systems we may examine the structural differences and similarities between the democratic and the undemocratic. For example, do democratic legal systems have a higher rate of turnover in key specialized statuses? Is this true of legislative and executive statuses but not of judicial statuses, which may require greater stability of tenure to guarantee the incumbents the necessary autonomy in their role performance? Correlatively, is the status sequence (Merton, 1957) of occupants of specialized statuses in democratic legal systems characterized by a higher rate of transition to nonlegal or lay statuses than is the case in undemocratic legal systems?

Other differences between these two types of legal systems may be observed in the structure of the legal profession, the judiciary, and the civil service. A legal profession that does not enjoy a high degree of autonomy vis-à-vis the state cannot effectively train recruits to uphold the normative system in a disinterested manner. Similarly, if the court system is organized on the principle of a chain of command, the lower courts are not likely to venture independent interpretations of law for fear that they may be overruled by the higher courts. This hierarchical mode of organization facilitates extralegal control of the judiciary. If the civil service is not sufficiently professionalized, and hence does not administer the law efficiently and in accordance with universalistic standards, it, too, is susceptible to extralegal control. Are such propositions true?

Related questions may be raised about private legal systems. The high degree of variation among formal organizations of a private character points to a general problem: in what types of private organizations do we find an approximation to a democratic legal system, and in what types an approximation to an undemocratic legal system?

A distinction between administrative organizations and voluntary associations, as advanced by Moore (Moore, 1957; Evan, 1957) provides a fruitful preliminary approach to this problem. In administrative or work organizations, in which membership is a direct source of livelihood, the legal system tends to be undemocratic. Authority with respect to normative processes is not limited by any of the three attributes of a democratic legal system. Ruml, for example, in analyzing the structure of corporate management, observes that "the Someone who represents the Company [to potential stockholders] gets his authority from a superior source in the Company's management, a source which combines *legislative, administrative, and judicial powers*" (Ruml, 1950). In voluntary associations, on the other hand, in which membership is generally based on shared norms and values, a democratic legal system tends to predominate. To take but one subclass of voluntary associations, occupational associations are likely to be closer approximations to the democratic type of legal system than are industrial organizations.

A more refined typology of formal organizations than the distinction between administrative organizations and voluntary associations is obviously necessary. A comparison between an industrial organization and a university, both of which are administrative organizations, would show marked differences in their legal systems, with the former resembling an undemocratic legal system and the latter a democratic legal system. This contrast is due to differences in organizational goals—the production of goods versus the creation and dissemination of knowledge—and to a corollary difference in occupational structure. A university generally has a higher proportion of professional personnel than an industrial organization; this is conducive to the growth of an "occupational community" (Lipset, Trow, and Coleman, 1956) with norms and a social structure consistent with that of a democratic legal system.

Voluntary associations, as in the case of administrative organizations, also differ greatly. Thus a comparison of a professional association with a trade union would probably yield evidence that the former more closely approximates a democratic legal system than the latter, if only because the norms of a professional occupation engender the development of a more cohesive and self-governing occupational community.

A comparative approach to private legal systems might fruitfully inquire into the extent of members' knowledge of norms, the extent of their acceptance of the norms, and the extent of nonconformity. How different are private legal systems in their profiles on these three variables? With respect to knowledge of norms, it may be hypothesized that the laity of an undemocratic legal system is likely to be more informed about the duties pertaining to its status and less informed about its rights, privileges, and immunities, whereas in a democratic legal system no such difference obtains, or the reverse may be true. It may also be hypothesized that in a democratic legal system a higher proportion of the laity approves of and conforms to the norms.

Such comparative inquiry would probably show that the number of persons who perform the functions of legislators, executives, judges, and lawyers in private legal systems is larger than we generally assume; it would probably identify a larger number of litigants, a higher incidence of litigation, and many more sanctions being invoked than we tend to associate with the organs of public legal systems.

Interrelationships Between Public and Private Legal Systems

The relationship between public and private legal systems has usually been conceived of, and examined in terms of, the role of pressure groups in the legislative process, or in terms of the government's regulation of private organizations, especially business organizations. It also has long been observed that public legal systems confer upon private legal systems rights, duties, privileges, and immunities through the process of granting a charter of incorporation, license, permit, franchise, and so on (Berle, 1958). Several modes of interrelationship, however, have been neglected.

First is the increasing tendency for the norms of private legal systems to be judicially recognized. For example, in medical malpractice suits the code of ethics of the American Medical Association is likely to be invoked; in a suit involving the internal relations of a trade union, the union's constitutional provisions are accorded legal status by the court; or in a suit by a student against a college or university, the institution's disciplinary rules are judicially recognized. Such judicial recognition, particularly under a system of common law, results in precedents, that is, in the growth of new legal norms guiding judicial decisionmaking. The adoption, as it were, of the norms of private legal systems by public legal systems is functionally equivalent to the conferral of rights on private legal systems.

A second interrelationship is the diffusion of norms in letter or spirit from private to public legal systems. Although such diffusion is probably less common than judicial recognition of the norms of private legal systems, this is an important source of growth of the norms of public legal systems. An example of such diffusion is the incorporation of the "law merchant" into common law and statutory law (Jaffee, 1937). Diffusion of norms should be distinguished from the process associated with the concept of pressure groups. Whereas the concept of pressure groups connotes an "enactive" and intended process of change, diffusion connotes a "crescive" and unintended process. The tempo of effect of pressure groups on public legal systems may be gradual or rapid. The suffragette movement is an example of a pressure group whose effect was gradual as compared with the "right-to-work law" pressure groups whose effect, at least in eighteen states, was relatively rapid. By contrast, the diffusion of the "law merchant" to the public legal system was a very gradual and unintended process. Another distinction is that pressure groups are associated primarily with one or two structural components of public legal systems, namely, legislatures and administrative agencies, whereas the diffusion mechanism applies to all structural components of public and private legal systems.

A third form of interrelationship between public and private legal systems involves the flow of personnel between the two legal systems. Public legal systems, of necessity, recruit officials of private legal systems who have the required expertise to administer laws transferred from or modeled after those of private legal systems, as in the case of professionals serving on occupational licensing boards, or business executives serving in such administrative agencies as the Securities and Exchange Commission, Federal Trade Commission, or Interstate Commerce Commission (Jaffee, 1937:231; Hamilton, 1957).

Private legal systems in turn seek to recruit professionals with experience in public legal systems, possibly because of their knowledge of "secrets of the office." Thus, for example, corporations and trade unions may wish to recruit officials of the National Labor Relations Board in the hope that it will help them in their relationships with the agency. Such transfers of personnel may lead to a transfer of norms between public and private legal systems. In other words, the status sequence of officials of public and private legal systems probably serves as a mechanism for the transmission of norms from one type of system to another.

A fourth interrelationship between public and private legal systems is the emergence of administrative agencies in response to the emergence of private legal systems. In the United States, where this development occurred later than in some European countries, there has been a steadily increasing multiplication of administrative agencies or independent regulatory agencies since the establishment of the Interstate Commerce Commission in 1887. Regulation by administrative agencies entails a conferral of both rights and duties on private legal systems.

Private legal systems are obviously not all of equal importance as sources of new legal norms and organs in public legal
systems. Those which are rooted in certain institutional spheres
have greater effect on public legal systems than others with
different institutional bases. For example, the legal systems of
trade associations, professional associations, and trade unions,
because of their links with economic institutions, presumably
have more effect on public legal systems than the legal systems
of, say, educational, familial, or recreational organizations.

The converse of this mode of interrelationship, namely, the
impact of the public legal systems on private legal systems, is
well known. However, two interrelationships are noteworthy.
First is the diffusion of "procedural due process of law" from
public to private legal systems. This process is more readily
observable in trade unions than in corporations—for example,
in the growth of internal and external appellate review procedures in trade unions such as the Upholsterers International
Union and United Automobile Workers (United Automobile
Workers, 1957). Berle, however, claims that:

> There is being generated a quiet translation of constitu-
> tional law from the field of political to the field of economic
> rights. . . . The emerging principle appears to be that the
> corporation, itself a creation of the state, is as subject to
> constitutional limitations which limit action as is the state
> itself. (Berle, 1952:942-943; 1954:77ff.)

If in fact this process of institutionalization is under way, we may
expect that public legal systems will eventually impose a duty
on corporations to conform to procedural due process of law in
their internal relations.

The second interrelationship, even less obvious, is the emergence of private legal systems as unanticipated consequences of
decisions by public legal systems (Evan and Schwartz, 1964).
Two contrasting examples of this process will suffice: the rise of
the League of Women Voters following the passage of the Nineteenth Amendment, with its functional consequences for the
public legal system; and the formation of the White Citizens'

Councils, following the desegregation decision of the United States Supreme Court, with their dysfunctional consequences for the public legal system.

Interrelationships Among Private Legal Systems

The proliferation of private organizations, and hence private legal systems, particularly in the United States (Boulding, 1953), has resulted in an increase in the frequency and types of inter-organizational relations. Of the various types of interrelations two will be mentioned because of their effect on public legal systems. One interrelation entails a marked inequality of power in the relationships between two or more private legal systems; the other, an approximation to a balance of power. In the former type of relationship, the weaker party may choose one of several alternatives: submit to the domination of the superordinate power; seek alliances—as in the case of international relations—to effect a shift in the balance of power; or have recourse to a unit of a public legal system to redress wrongs of the more powerful private legal systems or to augment its relative power. The latter course of action is illustrated by the National Automobile Dealers Association's efforts, through the courts and legislatures, to curb the power of the three large automobile manufacturers to dictate the terms of contracts and to cancel contracts (Palamountain, 1955). In other words, inequality in power relationships among private legal systems is a major source of pressure on public legal systems to introduce normative and organizational changes.

Where there is an approximation to a balance of power between two or more private legal systems, that is, where organizational relationships are of a coordinate rather than a superordinate-subordinate character, one possible consequence of the relationship is the growth of a degree of consensus regarding goals that eventuates in a merger or a federation. In the absence of a high degree of consensus regarding goals, an approximation to a balance of power may lead to the growth of a partial legal system for the purpose of resolving intersystem conflicts. Private tribunals for labor and commercial arbitration are notable examples of this process. The more the parties approach an equality of legal and power status, the more effective these tribunals are as conflict-resolving mechanisms. It may be hypothesized that if the formal legal equality of the parties in these tribunals is not accompanied by equality in economic and political power, the effectiveness of the arbitral process is diminished (Evan, 1959).

Such mechanisms develop among private legal systems because of the incompetence of units of public legal systems to cope with the technical problems of private legal systems, the cost and delay of litigation, the lack of legislation or precedents applicable to the novel problems confronting private legal systems, or because of the importance of maintaining flexible relationships, which action by components of public legal systems would make difficult (Shulman, 1955; Shister, 1956). Bypassing the courts, private arbitration tribunals handle 70%—according to one estimate—of all civil litigation in the United States (Mentschikoff, 1952:698). And in the case of labor arbitration, the grievance machinery is administered by a large number of management and union personnel, for example, approximately half a million shop stewards perform the function of "counsel" for aggrieved workers (Chamberlain, 1958:609). It is small wonder that this private judiciary with its evolving body of private law is recognized by public legal systems. For instance, the New York Civil Practice Act takes cognizance of private arbitration tribunals, specifies procedures, and makes their awards enforceable by the courts.

Transformation of Legal Systems

Reconceptualizing law and legal phenomena in these general normative and social-structural terms generates the insight that the frontier of growth of the law in a modern industrial society such as the United States is in private as well as in public legal systems. In addition, it suggests several general hypotheses regarding the transformation of legal systems.

First, as private legal systems extend their sphere of jurisdiction beyond their institutional base, the potential for competition and conflict with other private legal systems in the affected institutional sphere increases. Thus, for example, as corporations, trade unions, and churches increase their political activities, their relations with one another and with political parties may become marred with conflict. And conflict, in turn, may continue unresolved; it may elicit efforts at cooptation of the leadership of the threatening organization; or it may call forth the mediating action of other private legal systems or of public legal systems. In the event the public legal system intervenes, new norms arise, whether through legislative enactment, judicial decision, or executive or administrative action. We may also hypothesize that the more each private legal system seeks to extend its sphere of jurisdiction, the more safeguards are thereby erected against the monopolization of power by public legal systems. However, a democratic public legal system can, among other things, protect the rights of the laity of private legal systems against the exercise of arbitrary and autocratic authority.

Second, the progressive differentiation of specialized statuses, with respect to the normative processes, results in an acceleration of the rate of growth of norms in public and private legal systems. However, the multiplication of rules and officials that we associate with the trend toward bureaucratization do not necessarily endanger the rights of the laity if limitations on authority are preserved through the three democratic mechanisms—separation of powers, consent of the governed, and procedural due process.

Third, private legal systems of a democratic type are transformed into undemocratic types under such *exogenous* conditions as the following: (a) if there is a monopolization of power in a given institutional or subinstitutional sphere; or if there is an oligopolization of power in the absence of countervailing private legal systems; (b) if relationships with other private legal systems are principally with those of an undemocratic type of superior economic or political power. Conversely, private legal systems of an undemocratic type are transformed into democratic types under such *exogenous* conditions as the following: (a) if countervailing power in the form of a private legal system develops within a given institutional or subinstitutional sphere to counteract monopolization or oligopolization of power among private legal systems; (b) if relationships with other private legal systems are primarily with those of a democratic type or with those of an undemocratic type of equal or inferior economic or political power.

Fourth, public legal systems of a democratic type are transformed into undemocratic types under such *exogenous* conditions as the following: (a) if the autonomy of private legal systems declines to the point where they cannot challenge the authority of the public legal systems; (b) if there is a monopolization of power among private legal systems in the various institutional or subinstitutional spheres, or if there is an oligopolization of power without the development of countervailing private legal systems; and (c) if most private legal systems are transformed from democratic into undemocratic types.

In the last two hypotheses, with their implicit *ceteris paribus*, we have drastically limited the exogenous conditions of a legal system to relationships with other legal systems in the environment and to the structure of these systems. Obviously other exogenous as well as endogenous factors are operative in the transformation of a legal system from a democratic to an undemocratic type and vice versa (Lipset, 1959).

CONCLUSION

The traditional view of law as an integral part of the state has tended to obscure the fact that law exists in nonstate contexts as well. Adopting the legal perspective of Ehrlich and Weber, we have presented a sociological conception and typology of legal systems that bridges the developing field of the sociology of law with that of formal organization. To illustrate the research potentialities of this approach, we have examined four problem areas suggested by our typology: comparative study of legal systems, interrelationships between public and private legal systems, interrelationships among private legal systems, and the transformation of legal systems.

Inquiry into the processes whereby public and private legal systems are transformed will throw light on the general sociological problem of the conditions under which new norms and organizational structures arise and old norms and organizational structures decline. Of particular significance and promise is a comparative study of the structure and functioning of private legal systems and their interrelationships with private and public legal systems. Although these problem areas in the sociology of law may appear new, Ehrlich, one of the earliest students in this field, indirectly suggested them early in this century when he asserted that "the center of gravity of legal development . . . from time immemorial has not lain in the activity of the state but in society itself, and must be sought there at the present time" (Ehrlich, 1936:390). In a sense, Ehrlich's perspective, combined with the approach outlined in this chapter, suggests the need for research on the conditions under which political pluralism—as a type of social system, not as a political philosophy—survives or perishes.

CHAPTER 9

An Analysis of Labor Arbitration Decisions

One of the major social trends in the United States in the past fifty years is the growth of the institution of collective bargaining. The violence and turbulence of the conflicts between "labor and capital" of the Haymarket days, of the steel strike after World War I, and of the "little steel" strike of 1937 have been gradually superseded by collective bargaining agreements between "labor and management." These agreements set forth a variety of substantive and procedural rights and duties of both parties. Thus, *power* relations, though not entirely displaced, have been supplemented with *bargaining* relations.

With the replacement of the entrepreneur by the corporate manager, the ideological principle of "open shop" slowly gave way to a reluctant acceptance of some form of union security which offered greater assurance of harmonious industrial relations (Bendix, 1956:267-274). Contributing to this ideological shift was the National Labor Relations Act of 1935, which guaranteed workers the right to collective bargaining. This law produced the *intended* effect of markedly accelerating the growth of trade unionism.

A key element of the institution of collective bargaining, which according to some students is of singular although unheralded significance for the development of industrial relations, is the grievance procedure (Chamberlain, 1955:609-610). This provides for the right of both parties to institute complaints or grievances alleging actions in violation of the collective bargaining agreement. For workers, in particular, the right to redress wrongs via the grievance machinery has meant the establishment of "civil rights" in industry. These rights afford workers protection against the exercise of arbitrary authority on the part of management. This has been likened to the application of the constitutional principle of due process (Lazar, 1953:1). The grievance machinery constitutes a multi-step procedure for resolving conflicts, with the final step being arbitration. The decision of the arbitrator, a third party, whether an individual or a board selected by both parties, is binding.

Although voluntary labor arbitration in the United States dates back to the 1860s, it was not until the 1930s that it became a prominent social mechanism for resolving industrial disputes (Witte, 1952:1-16, 43). In 1944, 73% of all labor-management agreements contained an arbitration clause in contrast to 83% in 1949, and about 90% in 1957 (Moore, 1953:262; Whitney, 1957). The recent growth of grievance arbitration may be interpreted as evidence of labor union's approximation to management in power and bargaining strength. In fact, it may be hypothesized that a necessary condition for the emergence of *effective* labor arbitration—and this may well be true of international arbitration as well—is an approximation to equality in the relative power and bargaining strength of the parties. It is the effect of the relative bargaining strength of the parties on labor arbitration awards which will be preliminarily and illustratively explored here.

Arbitration: A Private Tribunal

The grievance procedure and specifically the arbitration of grievances comprise an autonomous system of adjudication (Shulman, 1955:1007). Instead of resorting to courts to redress wrongs, labor and management have established a private tribunal presided over by a "judge" called an arbitrator whose decisions are enforceable in a court of law. The arbitrator is officially charged with the responsibility for settling disputes in accordance with the "private law"[1] developed by the parties. This body of private law is contained in the collective bargaining agreement, which, as in the case of any law, requires interpretation. In addition to the provisions in the collective bargaining agreement, arbitrators may take into account decisions of similar cases involving the same or different sets of labor-management parties. Thus, there is a tendency toward the growth of precedent, though not nearly to the same extent as in common-law courts.

This private tribunal has several distinctive features which are noteworthy. Unlike litigation in court, the parties to arbitration must continue to "live with one another" during and after the dispute. In a typical lawsuit, each litigant is concerned with a past transaction. Each desires to win the suit regardless of the basis on which the decision is made. But an arbitration award that merely designates one side as the winner and does not achieve the solution which both parties, particularly the loser, find acceptable has not settled the issue. Arbitration is a process by which the parties seek a settlement to a labor dispute which will make it possible for them to continue their necessarily sustained relations with a reasonable degree of harmony.

Another notable feature of arbitration is that both parties choose the judge in a deliberate and self-conscious manner such as does not occur in a "public tribunal." This means that the arbitrator must command the respect and trust of both parties. He must not only be fair-minded but also knowledgeable of the parties' problems and industry. As a consequence, the permanent arbitrator, umpire, or impartial chairman, as distinct from the temporary arbitrator, has become increasingly common.

Since an arbitrator is selected by the parties, and the parties have to maintain an enduring relationship, it is reasonable to expect that the arbitrator would take into account extra-arbitral considerations—just as a judge on occasion takes account of extrajudicial factors—in the process of finding the facts in a controversy and in interpreting the relevant contract provisions. At least one student of labor arbitration has mentioned in passing the possibility that arbitrators consider the bargaining strength of the parties in the process of reaching a decision:

> The degree and direction of pliability of a contract, when its application is arbitrated, may have their roots in a recognized bargaining balance. . . . All that is suggested is that the liberality or narrowness with which a contract is interpreted, even in the face of equivalent language, and the diversity in scope accorded to the arbitration authority are frequently explicable in terms of the collective bargaining balance. (Gollub, 1948:vi)

And an industrial sociologist has asserted that "arbitrators frequently seek to settle disputes on a basis of a balance of power between management and labor. Some arbitrators conceive of their function as just determining what the balance of power is and then getting management and labor to recognize and act on it" (Schneider, 1957:329).

These assertions may be viewed, until confirmed by research findings, as in the nature of an hypothesis. If we compare three logically possible sets of parties with respect to bargaining strength, this hypothesis leads us to expect that: (a) when the parties are equal in bargaining strength, arbitration awards tend to be equally divided between the parties; (b) when management is superior in bargaining strength, more arbitration awards are made in favor of management than of labor; and (c) when the union is superior in bargaining strength, more arbitration awards are made in favor of the union than of management. In short, this hypothesis asserts that the arbitral process departs from the judicial model of decisionmaking on the basis of the merits of the case, emphasizing instead the relative bargaining strength of the parties as a determinant of the decision process.

A Provisional Test of the Hypothesis

The clarity and simplicity of the hypothesis belie the difficulties encountered in testing it. These consist in obtaining a reliable body of data on arbitration awards and in selecting labor-management parties of equal and unequal bargaining strength. This chapter will therefore present of necessity only some preliminary and incomplete findings bearing on the hypothesis.

Data on Arbitration Awards. The arbitration award, the dependent variable in the hypothesis, poses no conceptual problems. The award is for one or the other of the two parties, a form of compromise, or a refusal to make an award because the arbitrator wishes to defer the decision or does not think the grievance falls within his jurisdiction. The problem that arbitration awards raise is largely an operational one: How to obtain a reliable sample or a population of awards for sociological analysis? Several collections of awards have been published since 1946.[2] These are highly selective containing only those cases assumed to be of general interest to the field and which both parties have agreed to release for publication. The selective bias in these collections of cases virtually destroys their value for research purposes.[3]

A second source of arbitration awards is the archive of the American Arbitration Association. Since its founding in 1926, the American Arbitration Association has been conducting labor as well as other types of arbitration. However, only recently has an effort been made to process its arbitration records for research purposes. This processing is still in progress and the data have not yet been released to scholars. A third source is the Bureau of Labor Statistics which, on occasion, reports an analysis of arbitration awards.[4]

In view of these obstacles, it was necessary, for the purpose of this pilot study, to select several sets of labor-management parties which either granted access to their files or provided the necessary data. The selection of the sets of labor-management parties, however, in turn entailed a decision regarding the measurement of relative bargaining strength.

Selection of parties. The independent variable in our hypothesis, the relative bargaining strength of the parties, poses conceptual as well as operational problems. What criterion or criteria shall we use for distinguishing between the bargaining strength of an employer and a trade union? Our tentative answer was in terms of a group property which Merton calls "completeness" (Merton, 1957:314-315). This property "refers to the ratio of actual members of a group or organization to its potential members, i.e., to those who satisfy the operative criteria for membership" (Merton, 1957:314). This group dimension is clearly applicable to trade unions: what is the degree of unionization in a plant, a firm, or an industry? However, it is not at all apparent how this group property applies to an industrial organization. We have taken the liberty of interpreting this dimension as relating to an industrial organization's "share of the market" (Chamberlain, 1955:233-236).

The operational problem of finding examples of the three possible sets of parties was solved, after consultation with labor arbitrators, by selecting the Ford Motor Company and the United Automobile Workers of America (UAW), on the one hand, and the Affiliated Dress Manufacturers and the International Ladies' Garment Workers' Union (ILGWU), on the other. The former set of parties, it was presumed, represents an approximation to equality in bargaining relations, and the latter an inequality in bargaining relations, with the union being superior. A suitable example of the third logical type, one in which management is superior, was not found because of the dearth of arbitration cases. The arbitration records of General Electric and various electrical unions (IBEW, IUE, and UE) and those of Dan River Mills and Textile Workers Union of America proved unusable because of the small number of arbitration cases. A possible inference from the fact that we did not succeed in locating an example of a relationship in which management is superior in bargaining strength, and one which involves a sufficient number of arbitration cases for statistical analysis, is that under this condition arbitration is very poorly developed. Often the collective agreement in such cases imposes restrictions on the use of the arbitration machinery, such as by confining it to workers who have been employed for at least one year.

With respect to the bargaining position of the first of the two sets of parties selected, the Ford Motor Company—one of the "big three" automobile manufacturers—controls 28.7% of the market for cars and trucks in the United States (Moody's Industrial, 1957:2883). For an oligopolistic industry, this is indeed a high degree of "completeness" and represents a high degree of bargaining strength. Adding materially to the bargaining strength of Ford Motor Company is the virtual alliance of the "big three" manufacturers as regards collective bargaining negotiations. On the other hand, the UAW, a union with approximately a million members, and with union-shop agreements, includes in its membership—according to one source—97% to 99% of all hourly workers employed at the Ford Motor Company. Thus its degree of "completeness" is likewise very high. It may be argued that this hardly entitles us to *equate* the parties in bargaining strength; perhaps all we can say is that there is an *approximation* to equality in the bargaining strength of the parties.

The first contract between the Ford Motor Company and the UAW was signed in 1941 after several years of a violent power struggle. In 1943, the Office of the Umpire was established, the first umpire appointed being the late dean of Yale Law School, Harry Shulman, who served until 1955.

In our second set of parties, the women's garment industry presents an entirely different labor-management situation from that of the automobile industry. Instead of an oligopoly, this industry is highly competitive. In fact, the discontinuance rate is said to be 20% per year (Raskin, 1959). The share of the market of any one of the 5,006 dress manufacturers (U.S. Bureau of the Census, 1954:23C-3)—and we limit ourselves to this branch of the industry—in the country is so small and precarious, and their position vis-à-vis the ILGWU with 450,000 members is so weak, that they have organized themselves into employer associations. Of the five associations which comprise the New York City "dress market," one, the Affiliated Dress Manufacturers, has a membership of 240 employers. In the absence of any statistics on this association's share of the market, we may estimate on the basis of its proportion of the total number of dress manufacturers in the industry, that it is roughly 5%. On the other hand, the ILGWU, which has union-shop agreements, includes in its membership about 90% of the potential employees. Even if we consider that this manufacturers' association derives latent bargaining strength from the other four associations, which jointly control approximately 68% of the dress market in the country, we may, nevertheless, conclude that the ILGWU has a higher measure of "completeness" and hence a stronger bargaining position than the Affiliated Dress Manufacturers.

The first contract between the Affiliated Dress Manufacturers and the ILGWU was signed in 1929, five years after the Office of the Impartial Chairman for the New York City dress industry was established. Since 1936 the incumbent of the office of the umpire has been Harry Uviller.[5]

Selection of discharge cases. Grievances referred to arbitration include problems involving job classification, assignment of work, suspension, promotion, transfer, merit increase, payment for vacations, sick leave, insubordination, etc. Some of these problems may be viewed as trivial or critical by one or the other of the parties. While it is possible that our hypothesis may apply to some classes of grievances and not to others, it seemed that discharge cases, because they are the most serious of grievances, at least from the employees' point of view, were the best cases on which to test this hypothesis. We would expect that the factor of relative bargaining strength would least affect a grievance where a person's job is at stake, for discharge is the most severe sanction that management can invoke in disciplining its employees. In fact, a student of arbitration refers to it as the functional equivalent in industry of "capital punishment" (Skilton, 1952; Gollub, 1948:15). Rather than sustain discharges, arbitrators, even when they find the employee guilty of the alleged misconduct, tend to reduce the penalty to suspension or loss of pay. Consequently, they have been criticized by management for substituting their own judgment for that of management and for exceeding their authority (Gray, 1948:209-213).

The limitations on management rights to discharge range from none at all—which is, of course, the rule in the absence of a bargaining relation—through the requirement for "proper" or "just" cause for discharge to a statement of specific conditions under which management has the right to discharge. The Ford-UAW agreement contains the customary "just" cause provision: "The company retains the sole right to discipline and discharge employees for cause, provided that in the exercise of this right it will not act wrongfully or unjustly or in violation of the terms of this agreement" (*Collective Bargaining Agreement, UAW-Ford Motor Co.*, 1955). In the agreement between the Affiliated Dress Manufacturers-ILGWU, the discharge clause reads: "The employer may discharge its workers for the following causes: incompetency, misconduct, insubordination in the performance of his work, breach of reasonable rules to be jointly established, soldiering on the job" (*Collective Agreement, Affiliated Dress Manufacturers-ILGWU*, 1958-1961). Ordinarily, it may be assumed that limiting discharge by stating explicitly the causes is a greater restriction on management prerogatives than simply requiring "cause" or "just cause" for discharge. However, the rules and procedures in a particular industry governing the interpretation of "just cause" may in fact limit management's scope of action just as much—if not more so—than a written set of requirements for discharge.

The findings. The data on discharge cases for the two sets of parties were obtained, respectively, from the Office of the Impartial Chairman of the Dress Makers' Joint Council-ILGWU and the Office of the Umpire of the Ford Motor Company-UAW. The data comprise a population rather than a sample of discharge cases. The time period covered in these cases differs for the two sets of parties. For the Affiliated Dress Manufacturers-ILGWU the time period extends from 1936 to 1957; for Ford-UAW it runs from 1946 to 1958. This difference in the years covered, however, does not affect the findings, for the results are the same when the ten-year period from 1936-1945 is eliminated in the case of the Affiliated Dress Manufacturers-ILGWU.

As shown in Table 9.1, 76% of the awards were made in favor of the union in the Affiliated Dress Manufacturers-ILGWU cases

Table 9.1 Arbitration Awards in Discharge Cases in Two Sets of
Labor-Management Relations

	Percent of Awards in Favor of:			
	Union	Manage-ment	Neither	Total Cases
Affiliated Dress Manufacturers-ILGWU (1936–57)	76	22	2	92
Ford Motor Co.-UAW (1946-58)	38	62	–	1,026

as compared with 38% in favor of the union in the Ford-UAW
cases. Thus, the results are only partially consistent with the
hypothesis. The ILGWU, which was characterized as having a
higher degree of bargaining strength, does have a much higher
proportion of arbitration awards in its favor. But, in the case of
Ford-UAW, we find a 62-38 distribution in favor of management
instead of a closer approximation to the expected 50-50 distribution. Does it follow from these findings that part of the hypothesis is untrue?

A preliminary analysis. Obviously, if we are to avoid converting our hypothesis into a tautology, we cannot draw any in-
ferences from the distribution of arbitration awards about the
relative bargaining strength of the parties. The departure from
an equal distribution in the Ford-UAW cases suggests that factors other than relative bargaining strength may be operative.
Additional support for this conclusion is provided by a study of
arbitration cases conducted by the Bureau of Labor Statistics
involving a set of parties, which, in terms of our measure of
"completeness," we may rate as roughly equal in bargaining
strength, viz., Bethlehem Steel Company and United Steelworkers' Union. For the 10-year period of 1942-1952, 89 discipline
cases are reported (U.S. Department of Labor, Bureau of Labor
Statistics, 1942-1952). Of these cases, a special tabulation by the
Bureau of Labor Statistics shows that only 17 involved the discharge penalty; of these cases, in turn, 76% were decided in
favor of management, 18% in favor of labor, and 6% for neither
party.[6] This pattern of awards, involving an admittedly small

number of cases, shows an even more marked departure from the expected 50-50 split, and, as in the Ford-UAW situation, also points to the operation of factors other than relative bargaining strength.

Among these factors, three will be mentioned which may account for the slightly deviant distribution of the Ford-UAW cases. The first factor is the possible differential in expertise of the representatives of the parties participating in arbitration proceedings. Particularly in oligopolistic industries, such as automobiles, management may in some instances employ superior staff specialists, if only because they can afford to pay better salaries than the unions in such industries.[7] Management representatives may, therefore, prove more effective in marshaling the necessary evidence in arbitration proceedings. On the other hand, in competitive industries, such as the women's garment industry, the union may be in a position to employ more competent staff specialists. It is, of course, only a conjecture that this factor applies to the Ford-UAW relationship and that it has affected the pattern of distribution of arbitration awards.

A second factor, which may be more important than the first, is that a union which is especially responsive to its membership, such as the UAW, may press a grievance to arbitration not because it is convinced of the merits of the case but as a means of assuaging the injured feelings of the worker. Hence, it is possible that many of the UAW discharge cases were so weak that the chances of an award in favor of the union were consequently reduced.

A third factor is that the arbitrator's role and role performance may differ in respect to the degree to which they are guided by a "legalistic" approach. In general, a permanent arbitrator, whose title is an "umpire," has more restricted powers than an arbitrator known as an "impartial chairman."

> The titles are associated with quite different concepts of arbitration. Umpireships tend to be narrower in outlook than impartial chairmanships. That is, the latter more frequently permit a wider scope of authority for the arbitrator, a lesser emphasis on the language of the contract, and

more frequent resort to mediated settlements. (Bernstein, 1954:304)

That the role of the umpire in the Ford-UAW relationship is clearly circumscribed is evident from the provisions in the collective bargaining agreement (*Collective Bargaining Agreement, UAW-Ford Motor Co.*, 1955:44-45). This presumably constrains the umpire to resort to a narrow construction of the contract.

Related to the third factor is the occupational background of the arbitrators in our two sets of labor-management relations. Although both Harry Shulman of the Ford-UAW and Harry Uviller of the Dress Manufacturers-ILGWU are lawyers by training, the fact that the former was the dean of Yale Law School and the latter a one-time executive of a trade association, might have made a "legalistic" approach to arbitration more congenial to the former than to the latter. An illustration of the possible difference in their approach is the manner in which they respectively handled a discharge case involving an alleged theft. Uviller of Dress Manufacturers-ILGWU reinstated the worker on the grounds that, in his judgment, the facts did not prove that the worker intended to misappropriate the employer's property (*Joint Board of Dress and Waistmakers' Union of Greater New York v. Aywon Dress Co., Inc.-Affiliated Dress Manufacturers*, 1939). Thus the decision was based on an appraisal of the facts of the case and did not involve an explicit interpretation of any clause in the collective agreement. On the other hand, Shulman of Ford-UAW, after a discussion of the criminal-law distinction between petty and grand larceny, admits that the penalty of discharge appears to be too severe in the five cases in question, but then claims that under the terms of the contract he is powerless to modify the penalty. He, therefore, sustains the discharge in three of the cases, apparently mediates one of the cases, and reinstates one of the aggrieved on the ground that he is not guilty of the alleged wrongdoing (Umpire, Ford Motor Co., and UAW-CIO, 1948). If, as is generally true of labor arbitration (Whitney, 1957: 109), the UAW initiates more grievances than does the Ford Motor Company, Shulman's tendency toward a "legalistic" approach may redound to the advantage of management and thereby contribute to the slight deviation from a 50-50 distribution in the arbitration awards. The Ford-UAW relationship seems to be more akin to a "legalistic" rather than to a "bargaining" relationship, whereas the reverse is true for the Affiliated Dress Manufacturers-ILGWU.

An arbitrator's "legalistic" approach may, in turn, reflect a "legalistic" relation between labor and management which may develop out of a bargaining relation between two parties capable of wielding considerable economic and political power, as is true in heavy industry such as automobiles. "Legalism" betokens a commitment by the parties to both institutional norms and institutional means. Under conditions which remain to be specified, a "legalistic" relation between labor and management may be conducive to the growth of a "legal" relation, which we shall interpret to mean a high degree of consensus between the parties on goals, norms, and means.[8]

The analytic distinctions between "legalistic" and "legal" relations, on the one hand, and "power" and "bargaining" relations, on the other, bear further consideration in relation to the arbitration process. As was indicated above, when a power relationship obtains between a union and a company—or, for that matter, between any two organizations—there is a low degree of consensus with regard to goals, norms, and means. In such a situation, it is not uncommon for the parties to use illegitimate authority, such as force or fraud, to protect or promote their *interests.*

As a bargaining relation develops, consensus on goals remains low; similarly, consensus on norms may be fairly low, which is why the grievance machinery is often overburdened. On the other hand, consensus on means may be fairly high; for instance, work stoppages are curtailed and grievances are processed. In the course of bargaining about the terms of employment, each party agrees to sacrifice a favored object or course of action.

A variant of a bargaining relation and possibly a sequel to a mature bargaining relation is what we called a "legalistic" relation. This interorganizational state is characterized by a high degree of consensus on both norms and means. In fact, "legalism" involves a heightened awareness of existing *rights* of the parties as embodied in the growing corpus of norms comprising the collective bargaining agreement. Increased sensitivity to the provisions of the contract in turn may inhibit actions in violation of the "private law." Sabotage and slowdowns become as difficult for workers to undertake in concert and with the consent of the union as lockouts are for management. As the degree of consensus on goals between labor and management increases, a "legalistic" relation is transformed into what we have termed a "legal" relation, that is, one in which both parties share, in considerable measure, a commitment to common goals, norms, and means. The relationship between each of the four modes of labor-management relations to the pattern of arbitration awards and to the incidence of arbitrated grievances is presented in Table 9.2.

In the transformation of a labor-management relationship from one in which "bargaining" or "legalism" predominates to one in which "law" predominates, a permanent arbitrator may play a significant role. If the arbitrator maintains and articulates his or her commitment to a set of potentially common goals, norms, and means, she or he may help socialize the parties into these principles of actions.[9] If she or he should succeed in this effort, the pattern of arbitration awards, as is hypothesized in Table 9.2, would decreasingly bear any relationship to the relative bargaining strength of the parties. Moreover, and virtually by definition, the higher the degree of consensus between the parties on goals, norms, and means, the lower the incidence of grievances of various kinds, including grievances referred to arbitration. Thus, in a labor-management relationship which is predominantly "legal" in character, it is hypothesized that there would be a lower incidence of arbitrated grievances than in a "legalistic" or a bargaining relation (see Table 9.2).[9]

A case in point is the development of a "legal" relationship between Hickey-Freeman Company and Amalgamated Clothing Workers of America (Strauss, 1949), a set of parties which in regards to relative bargaining strength is not unlike Affiliated

Table 9.2 Type of Labor-Management Relations* by Patterns of Arbitration Awards and Incidence of Arbitrated Grievances

Type of Labor Management Relations	Consensus**			Patterns of Arbitration Awards	Incidence of Arbitrated Grievances
	Goals	Norms	Means		
Power	−	−	−	No arbitration process	Zero
Bargaining	−	−	+	Dependent on relative bargaining strength	High
Legalistic	−	−	+	Slightly dependent on relative bargaining strength	High
Legal	+	+	+	Independent of relative bargaining strength	Low

*Only four logically possible types of labor-management relations are discussed in this chapter. It is not thereby implied that the remaining four logical types are all null classes; in fact, types (−+−) and (++−) may be empirically significant and related to the four types analyzed.

**High degree of consensus is designated by (+) and low degree by (−).

Dress Manufacturers-ILGWU. With the signing of the first contract in 1919, an arbitration system was established providing for an office of an impartial chairman to which an economist, William Leiserson, was appointed. Leiserson not only made arbitration awards which were deemed "fair and equitable" but also took pains to explain his decisions, "thereby creating a code of industrial ethics which could give guidance to both union and management representatives" (Strauss, 1949:12). After writing an opinion on an arbitration case, Leiserson would offer to appear at management conferences and union meetings in order "to hammer out, on the anvil of free discussion, general acceptance of the principles which he helped to form" (Strauss, 1949: 16). In 1922, Leiserson's decisions were distilled into a series of rules on major labor-management problems. As these norms became generally known and accepted, the number of grievances referred to arbitration began to diminish. From 1930 to 1948, when the report on this labor-management relationship was written, not a single grievance was referred to arbitration (Strauss, 1949:17). By socializing the parties into the goals, norms, and means implicit or explicit in his arbitration opinions, Leiserson helped them to develop a "legal" relation and hence a capacity to resolve their conflicts without the intervention of a third party. And in performing his role as an arbitrator with expertise, Leiserson thereby worked himself out of a job, which is allegedly "the goal of all competent and successful arbitrators" (Copeloff, 1948; Bernstein, 1954:312).

SUMMARY AND CONCLUSION

A preliminary and illustrative analysis of labor arbitration cases involving the discharge penalty was conducted for two sets of parties. The hypothesis that relative bargaining strength is a determinant of the arbitral decision process was clearly confirmed for the Affiliated Dress Manufacturers-ILGWU, but only partially confirmed in the case of Ford-UAW. In an effort to account for the slight deviation from the expected distribution of arbitration awards, a distinction was drawn between "legalistic" and "legal" types of labor-management relations; these types were compared with "power" and "bargaining" relations. The differences among these types of relations are manifested in their profiles on three dimensions: goals, norms and means.

The utility of these concepts for an analysis of labor arbitration—and possibly other interorganizational phenomena as well—awaits further research. Additional sociological inquiry into the problem explored in this chapter would have to overcome the data deficiencies encountered in this study. In particular, a large sample is necessary—instead of the N of 2—of labor-management parties equal and unequal in relative bargaining strength, controlled for such variables as type of arbitration clause, type of discharge clause, type of arbitrator (permanent versus ad hoc; umpire versus impartial chairman), and so on. Furthermore, a multi-dimensional measure of bargaining strength, more refined than our single dimension of "completeness," may prove more discriminating. For example, an index based on the three group properties of completeness, size, and stability of membership may turn out to have more predictive power than our unidimensional index.

The analytic distinctions among the four types of labor-management relations point to problems of a broader scope than those which evoked them. For example, are the sequences of types of labor-management relations patterned? Is there a secular trend toward the transformation of labor-management relations from those in which power predominates to those in which "law" predominates? Or is there a cyclical process at work, possibly related, for example, to business cycles, or changes in internal organizational structure? Since conflicts over some values—for instance, allocation of profits to wages, dividends, investment, etc.—are probably endemic in labor-management relations, these may erupt and generate a movement from "legal" relations to "legalistic," bargaining, or even to "power" relations. What types of changes in labor-management relations in fact occur over time and what the conditions for changes of different types are, constitute significant theoretical as well as practical problems in interorganizational relations.

ADDENDUM

In the intervening years since this paper was published, labor arbitration has become progressively more institutionalized in the American industrial relations system. As of the present, more than 95% of all collective bargaining contracts include a provision for the arbitration of disputes (Goldberg, 1989:9). The issue addressed in this chapter, namely, the impact of relative bargaining power of the parties on the arbitration decision process, is still relevant, especially in view of the secular decline of union memberships (Kochan, 1987).

Another noteworthy trend is the emergence of nonarbitral conflict-resolution mechanisms to avoid the adversarial and win-lose underpinnings of the arbitration process. Experiments with "alternative dispute resolution" techniques are becoming increasingly common. These include "expedited arbitration," mediation, "med-arb," conciliation and conference procedures

(Goldberg, 1989; Schlossberg, 1988:22; Ury, Brett, and Goldberg, 1988).

NOTES

1. For an analysis of the internal law of private organizations and its relation to the law of the state, see Evan, 1962b:165-184, or Chapter 8 in this book.

2. See, for example, *American Labor Arbitration Awards*, 1946.

3. For example, Shulman (n.d.) presents 221 opinions referring to 383 out of a total of 2,340 cases for the period 1943-1946.

4. See, for example, U.S. Department of Labor, 1942-1952; Moore and Nix, 1953.

5. The data on ILGWU were obtained from an official of this union.

6. Personal communication from the Bureau of Labor Statistics, April 20, 1959.

7. For an analysis of the role of the staff specialist in industrial organizations and in unions, see Moore (1951:304-305, 310-311, 333-335).

8. For an analysis of deviant behavior in which the concepts "goals," "norms" and "means" are used in much the same manner as in this section, see Dubin, 1959:148-149. See also some related observations, bearing on the "movement from power to justice," in Selznick, 1959:122-123.

9. See Schulman, 1956:251, for a discussion of the "educational functions" of the permanent arbitrator

CHAPTER 10

Legal Indicators and Comparative Law

In Chapter 1, I alluded to the importance of developing appropriate legal indicators to test propositions derivable from classical theories of law and society and from current work in macro-socio-legal theory. Omitted from these allusions is the acknowledgment of the need to inquire into the relationships between legal indicators and nonlegal indicators. This question first occurred to me in 1964, when I wrote a paper titled "Toward a Sociological Almanac of Legal Systems" for a meeting of the Research Committee on the Sociology of Law of the International Sociological Association (Evan, 1965a). At the subsequent meeting of this committee in 1966, on the occasion of the Sixth World Congress of Sociology, I presented a follow-up paper in which I reported the preliminary results of a statistical analysis interrelating nine indicators of legal systems and ten indicators of nonlegal subsystems of society (Evan, 1968).

These papers appeared shortly after the emergence of the field of "social indicator" research. Since the early 1960s, there has been a rapidly growing interest in social indicators (Bauer, 1966; Sheldon and Moore, 1968). The impetus for what has become known as the "social indicator movement" in the United States and elsewhere is the growing demand for information to monitor social changes and to evaluate public policies and programs (Sheldon and Land, 1972; Johnston and Carley, 1981). Along with the policy-oriented work on social indicators is an interest on the part of some social scientists to construct analytic indicators for the purpose of modeling social systems (Land and Spilerman, 1975).

This movement has spawned a number of invaluable compendia of social indicators, such as those of Banks and Textor (1963), Russett et al. (1964), Taylor and Hudson (1972), and a publication by the U.S. Department of Commerce (1980). The bulk of the indicators contained in these compendia are objective measures of social systems pertaining to demographic, economic, educational, political, and communication variables. Only in the past few years have subjective indicators been added on the "quality of life," such as aspirations, fear of crime, and concerns about environmental problems.

MEASURES OF ATTRIBUTES OF LEGAL SYSTEMS

Conspicuously lacking in these handbooks, however, are measures of attributes of legal systems—with the exception of some criminal statistics. How might one explain this lacuna?

First, law is primarily a qualitative discipline preoccupied with the interpretation and evaluation of rules and doctrines.[1] "The general unconcern about quantitative legal information among lawyers both explains and perpetuates the relative unavailability of legal measurements" (Merryman, Clark, and Friedman, 1979:14). Transforming the masses of qualitative data lawyers deal with—for instance, statutes, judicial decisions, and administrative actions—requires special social science research methods with which legal scholars are unfamiliar.

Second, all social indicators, including legal indicators, are not value-neutral; the very process of measuring—even objectively—a significant dimension of society can have implications for public policy and the potential for becoming "political" (Henriot, 1972; Carley, 1981). For example, the Equal Employment Opportunity Commission in the United States is charged with the responsibility of implementing Title VII of the Civil

Rights Acts of 1964, which prohibits employment discrimination on the basis of race, religion, ethnicity, or sex. This agency, to my knowledge, does not publish any data on the number of sex discrimination complaints and suits per year that are filed against employers by women nor the percentage of such actions decided in favor of the plaintiffs. Such a legal indicator, if it were publicized, might have the effect of increasing the rate of complaints submitted and suits filed, which, in turn, might arouse the enmity of employers, who, in turn, might lobby Congress to abridge the budget, if not the mandate, of this agency. It might also have the undesirable consequence—from the vantage point of some government administrators—of heightening the awareness, on the part of the public, of the gap between legal prescription and legal reality, thus potentially impairing the level of legitimacy of the legal system. In other words, "any objective system of social indicators may damage or threaten established policies or favored positions by producing unwelcome evidence of deteriorating conditions, unmet needs, inefficient or ineffective programs, glaring inequities, and the like" (Johnston and Carley, 1981:551).

Not infrequently, social scientists are refused access to quantitative data because the data are deemed "too sensitive." Thus, in their comparative study of law and social change in six countries, Merryman and his colleagues were compelled to abandon efforts to obtain quantitative data on police and internal security systems. "Most governments will not allow access to such information, particularly not to a foreign research project" (Merryman, Clark, and Friedman, 1979:24).[2]

RESEARCH OPPORTUNITIES IN COMPARATIVE LAW

Clearly, the underlying rationale for developing legal indicators is to enable the sociologist of law to test hypotheses about the relationships between law and society within a *comparative* framework. For example, is Weber's theory about the predominance of formal rationality in civil-law as compared with common-law countries valid? *In principle*, this theory could be tested by means of quantitative data, though the methodological difficulties would be enormous. However, because comparative law has traditionally been qualitative and descriptive in its intellectual style, we would not expect scholars in this field to undertake comparative quantitative analyses of the substantive content of rules of law in different countries or in different legal family systems (Merryman, Clark, and Friedman, 1979:25; Glendon, Gordon, and Osakwe, 1982). A noteworthy development in comparative law, though entirely in the qualitative tradition, promises to generate a rich source of data of potential value to the quantitatively oriented sociologist of law. In the early 1960s, the ambitious seventeen-volume "International Encyclopedia of Comparative Law" was conceived (Drobnig, 1972; Sprudzs, 1980).[3] The global scope of this compendium, covering an array of substantive and procedural categories of law, prepared by hundreds of scholars drawn from the major families of legal systems, may stimulate new research in comparative law and may help to create "a generally accepted supranational legal terminology" (Drobnig, 1972:118).

Notwithstanding the qualitative and descriptive tradition in comparative law, comparativists do occasionally formulate analytical propositions that can only be tested with the aid of quantitative data. Take, for example, the eminent comparative law scholar Max Rheinstein. In the following statement, Rheinstein advances a proposition that is almost Weberian in its prolixity and grandeur:

> To the student of comparative law it is an impressive experience to realize how little the private law systems of the world differ from one another. Wide divergencies exist in public law, between democratic and authoritarian countries, between private enterprise countries and socialist countries. In the latter, the field of private law is narrower than in the former, but insofar as private law exists, it is of striking similarity, irrespective of whether the country is one of free enterprise or of socialist planning, whether it is democratic or authoritarian. (Rheinstein, 1972:6)

What is one to make of an hypothesis such as this, even if one were to set aside the inherent ambiguities involved in distinguishing between public and private law across national and legal systems? To illustrate the potential for a possibly fruitful intersection of interests between comparative law and the sociology of law, I have selected, for consideration, seven substantive fields of law—property, corporation, labor, inheritance, tax, family, and criminal law. At least four of these fields (property, family, inheritance, and labor) may be classified as private law in some societies. In Table 10.1, I have formulated a number of *illustrative* legal indicators that could be constructed by means of a content analysis (Berelson, 1954; Holsti, 1969) of the relevant statutes of a sample of countries. Admittedly, any serious effort to develop quantitative comparative legal indicators would run the risk of ethnocentric biases (Glendon, Gordon, and Osakwe, 1982:10), because of ignorance and/or unarticulated value premises. The scores derived from such an analysis could then be correlated with two types of quantitative measures: (1) social indicators pertaining to economic, demographic, political, educational, and communication variables; and (2) other legal indicators, such as the ratio of lawyers to population, ratio of courts to population, and the volume of societal conflicts as measured by the number of cases (per population) pertaining to the seven substantive fields that are adjudicated in a given time period.[4]

This hypothetical inquiry would, no doubt, require the resources of a team of comparative legal scholars and sociologists of law. If it were ever undertaken, it would have the salutary effect of linking up comparative law with macro-socio-legal theory, on the one hand, and with social indicator research, on the other (Evan, 1968:125).

There are at least two promising theoretical developments in macrosociology which may facilitate this type of research. Gouldner's penetrating analysis of the concept of functional autonomy in social systems, viz., that "there are *varying degrees* of interdependence which may be postulated to exist among the parts of a system," is pregnant with implications for the sociology of law (Gouldner, 1959:254-263). Another strand of macro-sociological theory of potential significance for this

Table 10.1 Illustrative Legal Indicators Applied to Seven Substantive Fields of Law

Field of Law	Hypothetical Indicators to Be Derived from a Content Analysis of Statutory Provisions
Property Law	Degree to which propertied classes are favored over propertyless classes (e.g., in landlord-tenant or land-owner-peasant relationships); degree of protection of private ownership of property vs. public ownership of property.
Corporation Law	Degree to which the charter of incorporation enables corporations to govern themselves with a minimum of intervention from the state, shareholders, customers, or employees.
Labor Law	Degree to which workers' rights are institutionalized to unionize, to bargain collectively, to protect themselves against arbitrary and capricious treatment by management, and to strike; degree to which unions are made responsible to their members; degree of protection against management's control over corporate decisions.
Inheritance Law	Degree to which the state facilitates or inhibits intergenerational transmission of wealth; degree to which testator's wishes are to be followed.
Tax Law	Degree of progressivity of tax rates, viz., placing a higher burden on wealthy individuals and enterprises.
Family Law	Degree to which divorce is restrictive; degree of protection against child abuse and wife abuse; degree to which spouses within marriage are accorded equal property rights and the legal power to enter into contracts.
Criminal Law	Degree to which defendants are accorded due process protections in the criminal law process.

subdiscipline is Blau's work on social structure (Blau, 1977a: 26-54; 1977b), inspired by Simmel's concept of "quantitative sociology."

CONCLUSION

In this chapter, my principal objective was to exploit developments in comparative law and the field of social indicators research for the purpose of furthering the growth of knowledge in the sociology of law. Also, a case was made for applying macro-socio-legal theory to seven substantive fields of law in the context of an inquiry in quantitative comparative law. The conjunction of these specialties, viz., macro-socio-legal theory, comparative law, and social indicators research, I believe, would provide an especially heuristic point of departure for research in the sociology of law.

ADDENDUM

Among the collections of indicator data regularly published, there is a marked dearth of comparative social and legal indicators. For example, the last volume of social indicators for the United States, published by the U.S. Bureau of the Census, was for 1980 and has since been discontinued. By contrast, there is a vast amount of economic indicator data annually published by the International Monetary Fund (IMF), the World Bank and the United Nations (IMF, 1989; World Bank, 1989; United Nations, 1988). And in recent years a substantial body of science and technology indicator data has appeared (Organisation for Economic Co-operation and Development, 1988; National Science Board, 1987). How does one explain the absence of any regularly published series on legal indicators? Does the answer lie in a supply-demand relationship, or is it much more complicated than that?

NOTES

1. For a contrasting conception of law, see Black, 1976.

2. In my preliminary comparative study to test the feasibility of interrelating legal and social indicators for a large number of countries, I included a *qualitative* legal indicator on the role of the police in legal systems (Evan, 1968:16). This indicator was derived from a compendium by Banks and Textor, 1963, who, with the aid of the judgments of a group of experts, constructed a dichotomous indictor as to whether the police in a given society performed a predominantly political or law-enforcement function.

3. I am very grateful to Professor Mary Ann Glendon for calling my attention to this invaluable data source for the sociology of law.

4. For an example of a quantitative comparative study of human rights, see Strouse and Claude (1976).

CHAPTER 11

Analyzing Indicators of Legal Systems

Comparative research on legal systems has, for many years, been virtually the exclusive domain of comparative legal scholars. The range of scholarship of comparativists is indeed wide. At one extreme, some comparativists concentrate on specific problems in a limited number of legal systems, such as the dismissal of civil servants in the United States, Britain and France (Joelson, 1963). At the opposite extreme, some scholars undertake encyclopedic analyses of legal systems, as represented in the work of Wigmore (1928) and David (1964). One of the virtues of comparative law, as Kahn-Freund observed in his inaugural address at Oxford, is that "it allows a scholar to place himself outside the labyrinth of minutiae in which legal thinking so easily loses its way and to see the great contours of the law and its dominant characteristic" (Kahn-Freund, 1966).

SOCIOLOGY AND COMPARATIVE LAW

From a sociological perspective, much of the research in comparative law is concerned exclusively with legal doctrine, is descriptive in nature, or is insufficiently oriented to the interplay of legal institutions with other institutions in society. Thus far, however, few sociologists or other social scientists have ventured into the field of comparative law. Some notable exceptions are Hoebel's comparison of the legal systems of five preliterate societies (Hoebel, 1954), Rose's study of the impact of law on voluntary associations in the United States, France and Italy (Rose, 1961), and Rabinowitz's implicit comparative analysis of the legal profession in Japan and in Western countries (Rabinowitz, 1956).

All comparative lawyers, except for those with a sociological orientation (Hall, 1963), would probably dismiss any social science study that purports to supplement the extant approaches in their field. It is, therefore, incumbent upon the sociological trespasser to indicate what he expects to contribute to cross-national research on law.

The sociologist attracted to this type of comparative research can bring to bear some of his distinctive theoretical and methodological biases. Theoretically, the sociologist might wish to investigate, for example, the differing role of law in social change as a function of the degree of bureaucratization, the degree of rigidity of the social stratification system, and the degree of social system integration. Because law pervades all the other institutional subsystems of society, a macro-sociological approach which takes into account the aggregate characteristics (Lazarsfeld and Menzel, 1961; Retzlaff, 1965) of a legal system would illuminate the relationships law has with other subsystems of society.

Methodologically, the sociologist would be interested in systematically collecting data on a sufficiently large number of societies to test propositions of theoretical and/or practical interest. He might even wish to test some propositions formulated by comparative lawyers. For example, Kahn-Freund recently advanced the tantalizing, if somewhat ambiguous, proposition that "under similar social, economic, cultural pressures in similar societies the law is apt to change by means of sometimes radically different technique" (Kahn-Freund, 1966:45). Assuming this proposition were operationalized, the sociologist would put it to a systematic and quantitative test rather than resort to the case method often employed by legal scholars.

A DATA ARCHIVE OF LEGAL SYSTEMS

With presuppositions such as these in mind, in 1964 at a meeting of the Research Committee on the Sociology of Law of the International Sociological Association I proposed that a data archive of legal systems be developed (Evan, 1965a).

To be sure, the bookkeeping systems of nation-states, the United Nations, and various international organizations yield vast quantities of statistics. For example, the United Nations publishes data on mortality, fertility, manufacturing, newspaper circulation, etc.; the International Labor Organization publishes statistics on unemployment, number of man-hours lost from strikes, etc. However, the bulk of available data provides surprisingly little grist for the mill of the sociologist interested in cross-national research on legal systems. This is true even if one construes the concept of a legal system in very broad terms, as I have done, namely, as "a set of institutions comprising norms, roles, and patterns of behavior pertaining to judicial, legislative, executive, and administrative processes of a society" (Evan, 1965:336).

Translating this broad conception of a legal system into a set of quantitative indicators to permit cross-national comparisons is in itself a complex undertaking (Bauer, 1966). There is a strong temptation to focus only on those attributes of legal systems that readily lend themselves to quantification, such as the number of lawyers and judges, and ignore qualitative phenomena that require quantification and may even be more important, such as the degree to which norms of procedural due process are institutionalized (Evan, 1962c) and govern judicial decision making.

An even more serious obstacle to developing a set of indicators is the diversity of meaning and behavior associated with seemingly unequivocal terms such as lawyer, policeman, and homicide. Lawyers differ substantially in professional training and function, with some countries making a distinction between a barrister and a solicitor while others do not. A police officer may be a local, regional, or national official; he or she may be known or unknown to the public; and he or she may perform a predominantly law-enforcement function or a political function (Banks and Textor, 1963). As for the meaning of homicide, the United Nations has for some years wrestled with problems of defining major criminal offenses in order to make possible the collection, analysis and presentation of international criminal statistics (Ancel, 1952; U.N. Economic and Social Council, 1959).

The problems of developing cross-national definitions of terms and comparable quantitative indicators pose a formidable intellectual challenge. This is evident when one examines the provisional list of 36 quantitative indicators included in the proposal that gave rise to the present study (Evan, 1965a). This list of items may give the impression of an aimless endeavor. However, though a data archive must have some theoretical underpinnings, it must also lend itself to the multiple purposes of various potential users if it is to be a useful archive.

EXPLORATORY ANALYSIS OF ILLUSTRATIVE DATA

By way of illustrating, rather than demonstrating, the feasibility and utility of such a data archive, a small body of data has been compiled from United Nations sources, a document by the World Peace Through Law Center (1965) and several other sources. The legal indicators are quantitative as well as qualitative in nature. Among the quantitative indicators are law schools per 1,000 population, law professors per 1,000 population, lawyers per 1,000 population, legislators per 1,000 population, divorce rate, suicide rate, and illegitimacy ratio. Among the qualitative indicators are role of police—whether a predominantly political or law-enforcement function—and a classification of legal systems often used by comparativists, namely, civil law, common law, socialist law, and Moslem law (David, 1964).

In order to explore the interrelationships of legal institutions and other institutions or social processes, some data on as many nations as possible were collected, principally from United Nations sources and from the handbook of the Yale Political Data

Program (Russett et al., 1964; Deutsch et al., 1966). Ten quantitative indicators of nonlegal institutions were selected:

1. level of industrialization, which consists of an average rank on three highly intercorrelated variables, namely, GNP per capita, energy consumption per capita, and percentage of labor force engaged in agriculture;

2. degree of urbanization, as measured by the percentage of population living in cities of over 20,000;

3. level of education, which consists of an average rank on three highly intercorrelated variables, namely, students enrolled in higher education per 100,000 population, primary and secondary school pupils as a percentage of the population aged 5-19, and percentage literate of population over 15 years of age;

4. date of political independence;

5. age of marriage as measured by the median age of grooms;

6. percentage of Christians in the population;

7. percentage of Moslems in the population;

8. degree of professionalization of the labor force, as measured by the percentage of professionals and technical personnel in the labor force;

9. degree of bureaucratization of the labor force, as measured by the percentage of administrative, executive, and managerial personnel in the labor force; and,

10. the size of the military establishment as a percentage of the population aged 15-64.

All the data in this exploratory analysis, the 9 indicators of legal systems and the 10 indicators of other subsystems of society, are cross-sectional. This precludes the possibility of measuring time lags and tracing feedback effects. Hence, I shall follow the general sociological assumption of regarding the indicators of the legal system as *dependent* variables and the other indicators as *independent* variables, without, however, dismissing the possibility of feedback effects occurring over time.

As a first step in the analysis of the data, a matrix of Pearson product-moment correlations is presented in Table 11.1 for a "sample" of nations varying from 20 to 97, depending on

Table 11.1 Pearson Product-Moment Correlation Coefficients of Indicators of Legal and Nonlegal Institutions of Selected Nations†

Variable	Variable No.	1	2	3	4	5	6	7	8	9	10	11	12	13	14	15	16	17
		Law Schools per 1,000 population	Law Professors per 1,000 population	Lawyers per 1,000 population	Legislators per 1,000 population	Divorce rate	Suicide rate	Illegitimacy ratio	Industrialization	Urbanization	Bureaucratization	Professionalization	Level of Education	Date of Political Independence	Age of grooms	% of Christians	% of Moslems	Military as % of population
Law Schools per 1,000 population	1																	
Law Professors per 1,000 population	2	.45***																
Lawyers per 1,000 population	3	.42***	.46***															
Legislators per 1,000 population	4	.74***	.18	.20														
Divorce rate	5	.03	-.09	.24	.04													
Suicide rate	6	-.03	-.19	.06	.03	.61***												
Illegitimacy ratio	7	.00	.06	-.14**	.04*	-.52***	-.44**											
Industrialization	8	.16	.00	.47**	.37	.26	.53**	-.46**										

Variable	Variable No.	Law Schools per 1,000 population	Law Professors per 1,000 population	Lawyers per 1,000 population	Legislators pr 1,000 population	Divorce rate	Suicide rate	Illegitimacy ratio	Industrialization	Urbanization	Bureaucratization	Professionalization	Level of Education	Date of Political Independence	Age of grooms	% of Christians	% of Moslems	Military as % of population
Urbanization	9	.21*	.17	.54***	.25	.26	.35*	-.27	.81***									
Bureaucratization	10	.44*	.07	.45*	-.19	.24	.12	-.27	.59***	.49**								
Professionalization	11	.22	.06	.47***	.37	.36**	.48*	-.44***	.91***	.80***	.60***							
Level of Education	12	.22	.28*	.55***	.22	.43**	.59***	-.48***	.90***	.75***	.61***	.91***						
Date of Political Independence	13	.13	.27*	.30**	.04	-.02	.32*	.06	.49	.40	-.26	-.27	.44***					
Age of grooms	14	-.14	-.14	-.08	.00	-.31	-.19	.60***	-.29	-.12	-.58***	-.50***	-.31*	.06				
% of Christians	15	.35***	.49***	.52**	.24	.08	.23	.33	.52***	.51***	.26	.42	.58***	-.51	.11			
% of Moslems	16	-.24*	-.37***	-.36**	-.08	.02	-.31	-.18	-.54***	-.35*	-.31	-.43*	-.62***	-.35***	.00	-.65***		
Military as % of population	17	-.15	-.11	.16	.28	.37**	.07	-.50	.31	.32	.02	.51	.40	-.12	.39**	.02	.00	

* Significant at the .05 level
** Significant at the .01 level
*** Significant at or lower than the .001 level
† The size of the N varies from one pair of variables to another, the largest being 97 nations and the smallest, 20.

169

the availability of each nation's data for a particular pair of variables. Inasmuch as this is an exploratory analysis, a 2-tail probability test is used to decide which of the correlation coefficients to regard as statistically significant.

To begin with, it should be noted that, of the 136 possible correlation coefficients among the 17 variables (7 quantitative indicators of legal systems and 10 quantitative indicators of nonlegal systems), 61 are statistically significant, whereas, on the basis of chance alone, we would expect only 7 significant coefficients. Of the wealth of information in Table 11.1, a few findings are salient. It is surely not surprising that the variables pertaining to law schools, law professors, and lawyers are mutually interrelated. If they were not, we would have grounds for doubting the validity of the data. It is noteworthy, however, that there is a high positive correlation between the number of law schools and the number of legislators. This is consistent with the findings of several studies of the disproportionate representation of lawyers in legislatures and in other branches of government (Matthews, 1954; Gold, 1961). Also noteworthy is the correlation between bureaucratization and the number of law schools. As the proportion of bureaucratic personnel in the labor force increases, more legally educated personnel are required, thus stimulating the development of law schools. In turn, as the pool of available graduates of law schools increases, the level of bureaucratization of the labor force rises, as is also suggested by the high positive correlation between bureaucratization and the number of lawyers.

Apart from the impact of bureaucratization on the number of law schools and lawyers in a country, the other highly positive correlates are the major social trends of industrialization, urbanization, and professionalization. A scattergram of the correlation coefficient of .47 of industrialization and number of lawyers per 1,000 population in 42 nations is presented in Figure 11.1. This finding is related to Nagel's more inclusive observation that

The disproportionate presence of professional judges, jurors, lawyers, promulgating bodies, and appellate courts

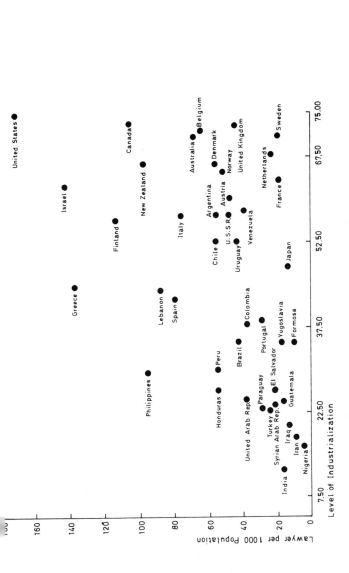

Figure 11.1 Scattergram of Correlation Between Level of Industrialization and Lawyers per 1,000 Population for 42 Nations

171

among manufacturing societies can probably be partially
explained by the fact that increased industrialization
brings increased specialization within the economic system
of a society which carries over into the political and adjudicative systems. (Nagel, 1962:151-152)

The general hypothesis that industrialization has a significant
impact, directly or indirectly, on the legal system appears to be
confirmed by the findings in Figure 11.1 as well as by several
correlations in Table 11.1. Under the circumstances it seemed
reasonable to assume that some of the zero-order correlation
coefficients in Table 11.1 are due to the effects of industrialization. Thus, a partial correlation analysis, controlling for the effects of industrialization, seemed advisable. As shown in Table
11.2, when the effects of industrialization are removed, only 15
of the original 61 zero-order correlation coefficients are statistically significant. Among these are some of the salient findings
noted above.

The impact of industrialization, and attendant social processes, on the legal system is also discernible when we examine
the findings on the role of the policeman in various countries. In
their highly innovative study in comparative social systems,
Banks and Textor categorized the role of police officers in 115
nations as to whether it entails a predominantly law-enforcement function or a political function (Banks and Textor, 1963).
Using their categorization, a statistical comparison was made of
the 10 indicators of nonlegal systems. On 5 of these indicators,
as Table 11.3 shows, the t-tests yielded significant mean differences. As important as statistically significant differences, however, is the pattern of consistency in the results: countries in
which the role of the police officers is predominantly law-enforcement in nature have higher levels of industrialization, urbanization, education, professionalization, and bureaucratization than countries in which the role of the police officers is
principally political in character. Evidently, when the function
of the police officer is confined to law-enforcement, the principles of legality and rationality are prized, and such values appear to be consistent with the five major social processes, listed

in Table 11.3, that differentiate nations in the role their police officers perform.

Thus far, our exploratory analysis of some data on legal systems has probably failed to pique the curiosity of the comparative legal scholar. He is so oriented to the normative content of legal systems that role structures and organizational structures of legal systems (Evan, 1962d), which we have principally dealt with, probably hold little interest for him. Therefore, a modest effort will now be made to meet the comparative lawyer on his own grounds by examining some statistical differences associated with the traditional normative classification of legal systems, namely, civil law, common law, socialist law, and Moslem law.

A review of the interrelations of the various quantitative indicators and the classification of legal systems points to the importance of three variables: level of industrialization, level of education, and number of lawyers per 1,000 population. The largest differences in mean level of industrialization, as shown in Table 11.4, are between Moslem- and civil-law systems, on the one hand, and Moslem- and common-law systems, on the other. Civil- and socialist- law systems are virtually identical in mean level of industrialization. Although common-law systems are noticeably higher than socialist-law systems in their mean level of industrialization, the difference between them is not statistically significant. These findings raise the interesting question of what are the probable long-term effects of a leveling of industrialization on legal systems.

The second variable in Table 11.4, level of education, yields even more significant mean differences among the four types of legal systems. The lowest mean level of education is found among Moslem-law countries and the highest mean among socialist and common-law systems, which have virtually identical mean levels. Thus, the significant mean differences occur between Moslem-law systems and each of the other three types, with the only other significant difference between civil- and socialist-law systems. The import of these differences in level of education for knowledge of the law, compliance with the law, and the development of a "sense of justice" is probably consid-

Table 11.2 Partial Correlation Coefficients of Indicators of Legal and Nonlegal Institutions of Selected Nations, Controlling for the Effects of Industrialization†

Variable	Variable No.	1	2	3	4	5	6	7	8	9	10	11	12	13	14	15	16	17
		Law Schools per 1,000 population	Law Professors per 1,000 population	Lawyers per 1,000 population	Legislators pr 1,000 population	Divorce rate	Suicide rate	Illegitimacy ratio	Industrialization	Urbanization	Bureaucratization	Professionalization	Level of Education	Date of Political Independence	Age of grooms	% of Christians	% of Moslems	Military as % of population
Law Schools per 1,000 population	1	1																
Law Professors per 1,000 population	2	.63 ***																
Lawyers per 1,000 population	3	.42 **	.37															
Legislators per 1,000 population	4	.02	.26	.07														
Divorce rate	5	-.82	-.18	.15	-.13													
Suicide rate	6	-.24	-.25	-.28	-.01	.37												
Illegitimacy ratio	7	-.01	.05	-.13	-.11	-.26	-.10											
Industrialization	8																	

Variable	Variable No.	Law Schools per 1,000 population	Law Professors per 1,000 population	Lawyers per 1,000 population	Legislators pr 1,000 population	Divorce rate	Suicide rate	Illegitimacy ratio	Industrialization	Urbanization	Bureaucratization	Professionalization	Level of Education	Date of Political Independence	Age of grooms	% of Christians	% of Moslems	Military as % of population
Urbanization	9	-.01 *	-.04	.10	-.08	.26	-.02	-.17										
Bureaucratization	10	.41 *	.03	.21	-.63 **	.17	-.18	.01		-.08								
Professionalization	11	.12	.00	.07	.21	.36	.12 *	.07 *		.11	.13							
Level of Education	12	.28	.33	.42 **	.16	.21	.21	.36		.07	.19	.11						
Date of Political Independence	13	.19	.02	-.07	.37	.11	-.29 *	-.25 *		.04	.05	.40	.03					
Age of grooms	14	-.27	-.31	-.07	.13	-.10	-.13	.44 **		.03 **	-.43	-.18 *	-.34	-.13				
% of Christians	15	.25	.38 *	.01	.13	-.33 *	-.21	.49 **		-.41 **	-.13	-.49 *	-.12	-.22	.22			
% of Moslems	16	-.22	-.40 *	-.05	.04	.47 *	-.12	-.51 **		-.31	.06	.27	-.11	-.01	-.02	-.54 ***		
Military as % of population	17	-.18	-.18	.13	.03	.24	-.10	-.39 *		.23	-.37	.29	.11	-.10	-.20	-.26	.33	

* Significant at the .05 level
** Significant at the .01 level
*** Significant at or lower than the .001 level
† The size of the N varies from one pair of variables to another, the largest being 97 nations and the smallest, 20.

175

Table 11.3 Comparison of Means on Five Variables for Selected
Nations Differing in the Role of the Police Officer

Variable	Mean for Nations with a Political Police Role	Mean for Nations with a Law-Enforcement Police Role	d.f.	t-value	Significance Level
Industrialization	32.22 (n=22)	56.70 (n=23)	43	5.56	.0000
Urbanization	16.67 (n=60)	36.53 (n=30)	41	5.08	.0000
Level of Education	43.24 (n=47)	70.66 (n=32)	64	5.03	.0000
Professionalization	3.2 (n=14)	7.50 (n=16)	24	4.88	.0000
Bureaucratization	.68 (n=14)	2.80 (n=16)	17	3.38	.0035

erable. Social science research on these questions is still in its
infancy, though some notable progress has recently been made
by Scandinavian sociologists and legal scholars (Kutschinsky,
1966; Makela, 1966).

The third and last variable of significance for types of legal
systems in Table 11.4 is the number of lawyers per 1,000 population. The highest mean occurs among common-law systems and
the lowest among Moslem-law systems. The significant differences in mean number of lawyers are between Moslem- and
civil-law systems and between Moslem- and common-law systems. The fact that common-law and civil-law systems have a
higher mean number of lawyers than Moslem- or socialist-law
systems suggests a correspondingly higher degree of reliance on
legal institutions as mechanisms for resolving conflicts. More
problems are probably perceived within these legal systems
as likely candidates for judicial decision making for which the
availability of an adequate supply of lawyers is necessary. How
different legal systems are in their institutionalized use of legal
mechanisms for conflict resolution and the sources of these

Table 11.4 Comparison of Means on Three Variables for Selected Nations Differing in Type of Legal System

Variable	Mean for Nations with Moslem Law	Mean for Nations with Civil Law	Mean for Nations with Socialist Law	Mean for Nations with Common Law	t-Test Comparison	d.f.	t-value	Significance Level
Industrialization	24.86 (n=6)	42.69 (n=23)	46.33 (n=2)	61.33 (n=6)	Mos. vs. Civ.	12	3.46	.0046
					Mos. vs. Soc.	2	1.82	
					Mos. vs. Comm.	8	3.48	.0083
					Civ. vs. Soc.	1	.32	.8030
					Civ. vs. Comm.	6	1.87	.1111
					Soc. vs. Comm.	5	1.04	.3467
Level of Education	28.53 (n=11)	57.24 (n=30)	69.87 (n=8)	68.13 (n=10)	Mos. vs. Civ.	22	4.68	.0001
					Mos. vs. Soc.	16	7.11	
					Mos. vs. Comm.	16	4.07	.0008
					Mos. vs. Soc.	32	2.82	.0082
					Civ. vs. Comm.	13	1.21	.2474
					Soc. vs. Comm.	12	.20	.8460
Level per 1,000 population	.18 (n=12)	.44 (n=29)	.38 (n=7)	.57 (n=10)	Mos. vs. Civ.	29	3.03	.0051
					Mos. vs. Soc.	13	1.72	.1082
					Mos. vs. Comm.	13	2.35	.0352
					Civ. vs. Soc.	12	.52	.6115
					Civ. vs. Comm.	12	.81	.4336
					Soc. vs. Comm.	16	1.06	.3101

differences are additional frontier problems for a comparative sociology of law.

SOME UNSOLVED PROBLEMS

Our exploratory analysis of a small body of data may have demonstrated the heuristic value of a data archive of legal systems by identifying some relationships as well as some unsolved problems. Among the unsolved problems pertaining to the development of such an archive, at least three bear mentioning. The first is the general question of the nature of a "legal variable." More particularly, how do we conceptualize the content of legal norms, legal roles and organizational structures of the legal system to make cross-national research possible? The second problem is how do we gather data on legal systems which are currently not routinely collected by either governments or international organizations? The use of mail questionnaires to special informants is one promising technique (Glaser, 1966). The organization of worldwide teams of legal scholars and sociologists is another. To further complicate the data-gathering problems, there is a need to develop time series if we are to make any progress in testing propositions about sources of structural change in legal and nonlegal subsystems of society.

A third unsolved problem is the relevance of some organizational mechanism for accelerating progress in developing a data archive of legal systems. The fact that there is a growing interest in developing a variety of data archives in social science (Merritt and Rokkan, 1966; Bisco, 1966; Glaser and Bisco, 1966; Nasatir, 1967) may well reduce the magnitude of the burden of developing a data archive of legal systems.

CONCLUSION

Mapping the legal systems of the world is a mammoth undertaking that will require the collaboration of sociologists and legal scholars in various countries for many years to come. Such an effort is not unrelated to the extensive work for many years of comparative legal scholars and others to internationalize and unify legal rules and thus contribute to the "common core of legal systems" (Schlesinger, 1961). The very cooperation entailed in implementing the proposal to develop a data archive of legal systems would contribute to the growth of a "global sociology" (Moore, 1966). The intellectual challenge is indeed worthy of the members of the relatively new but fast-growing field of the sociology of law and of the relatively old and well-established field of comparative law.

CHAPTER 12

Human Rights Laws:
Measurement of Compliance

The emergence of what has come to be known as the international movement for human rights (Henkin, 1981a) in the post-World War II period has far-reaching import for international law as well as for the prospects of world order. It also poses a challenge for social indicator research and the sociology of law. I shall argue that an empirically based sociology of law (Evan, 1980) that takes human rights as its subject of inquiry can make a contribution, however small, to the international movement for human rights.

My purpose in this chapter is fourfold: (1) to consider the question of the nature and meaning of human rights; (2) to discuss the concept of legal indicators as it bears on research on human rights; (3) to analyze a number of obstacles to the development of legal indicators of human rights violations; and (4) to illustrate, with some sample data, an approach to research on human rights.

THE CONCEPT OF HUMAN RIGHTS

Notwithstanding the fact that the term "human rights" recurs in the United Nations Charter, such as in Articles 1, 55 and 56, it is nowhere explicitly defined. Phrases such as "reaffirm faith in fundamental human rights," "promoting and encouraging respect for human rights," and "universal respect for, and observance of, human rights" convey the salience of the concept without defining it. This is not a surprising omission; the concept of "human rights" is an intrinsically vague and controversial idea (Kamenka and Ehr-Soon Tay, 1978). At least four issues contribute to the ambiguity of this concept. First, some scholars contend that the idea of human rights is a fundamental element of civilization, that it has its roots in ancient times, and that it is traceable to the Code of Hammurabi, the Old Testament, the New Testament, and to the works of such notable canonists as St. Thomas Aquinas. This notion has been refuted by various scholars (Pagels, 1979; Wyzanski, 1979; Berlin, 1969; Henkin, 1976; Kamenka, 1978) who claim that the idea of human rights emerged in the West during the period of the Enlightenment. These rights were attributed to the individual in his relation to society. "The story of the growing belief in . . . human rights as the eighteenth century saw them is the story of the rise of individualism in the theory and practice of society" (Kamenka, 1978:6).

Second is the philosophical assumption that the concept of human rights presupposes a theory of "natural law," "natural rights" and "inalienable rights"—as inspired by John Locke—all of which are counterposed to the positive law of any given society. In other words, human rights refer to rights attributable to all human beings by virtue of the fact they are human and not because they are members or citizens of this or that society. This is an understandable perspective on the part of those who wish to challenge the moral as well as legal legitimacy of a legal order by arguing for the universality and intrinsic character of human rights.

Third is the legal or jurisprudential view that human rights are legal norms embodied in an expanding corpus of international law which all sovereign states should obey and incorporate into their system of municipal or national law. A provocative variation on this theme is the theory of international law advanced by Lasswell and McDougal, to wit, that it is possible to avoid "trans-empirical" assumptions by focusing on a set of "basic values" of general and universal relevance, namely, power, respect, rectitude, affection, wealth, well-being, skill, and enlightenment (Lasswell, 1963, 1971; McDougal and Feliciano, 1961:302-309). An alternative schema of global values, having some kinship to the work of Lasswell and McDougal and incorporated into the World Order Models Project, is as follows: peace, economic well-being, social and political justice, ecological balance, and human governance (Falk, 1975, 1983:306-307). The latter scheme is more closely linked with the legal aspect of the concept of human rights.

The fourth issue which contributes to the confusion surrounding the concepts of human rights is anthropological in nature. If the concept of human rights has its origins in Western civilization, aren't we guilty of ethnocentrism and political bias in claiming universality for a given set of rights? The underlying assumption of this perspective is that cultural values of societies around the world are very diverse and, hence, the only defensible anthropological theory is cultural relativism or cultural pluralism. The counter argument, however, is that we are witnessing an evolutionary process whereby the values and norms of human rights, viz., the rights of the individual human being vis-à-vis society and the state, are becoming internationalized and universalized.

THE PROCESS OF UNIVERSALIZATION
OF HUMAN RIGHTS

It is the last point that bears closer scrutiny, especially from the viewpoint of developments since World War II. Although some international lawyers in the nineteenth century considered the need for rules of international law to protect human rights, two theories precluded any developments in this direction:

First, there was the so-called "dualist theory," according to which only states were the subjects of international law. Individuals, on this theory, were objects but not subjects of international law, and without standing to enforce their rights before, or be heard by, an international tribunal. Accordingly, this theory precluded the recognition at international law of individual human rights. Secondly, there was the doctrine that a state has complete sovereignty over its own nationals to the extent that such sovereignty constitutes a sphere of reserved jurisdiction into which international law is not permitted to reach. (Starke, 1978:114)

Consequently, prior to World War II, "human rights was not a subject of international concern and was treated as being exclusively within the domestic jurisdiction of individual states" (Buergenthal, 1979:15). With the founding of the United Nations in 1945 there was a great impetus to develop an "international bill of rights" (Henkin, 1981a:ix). The task of drawing up the first instrument to protect human rights was assumed by the Human Rights Commission, a subordinate component of the Economic and Social Council of the United Nations. After three years of successive drafts and numerous controversies the Commission produced the Universal Declaration of Human Rights, which the General Assembly adopted in 1948 as "a common standard of achievement for all peoples and all nations" (United Nations, 1980:9).

The 30 articles comprising this historic document are a blend of philosophical and legal norms of an individual and collective character. Articles 1-3 are statements of ideals: right to life, liberty, equality, and security of persons. Articles 4-27 set forth civil and political rights for everyone, such as freedom from slavery and servitude, freedom from torture, right to an effective judicial remedy, freedom of movement, right to asylum, and so on. Article 22 introduces Articles 23-27 pertaining to economic, social, and cultural rights, viz., entitlements as a "member of society," such as the right to work, right to rest and leisure, right to education, etc. The concluding Articles 28-30 underscore that everyone is entitled to an international and social order in which all human rights can be fully realized.

Although the Universal Declaration of Human Rights is not legally binding on the member states of the United Nations, its impact—legal, moral, and symbolic—has been extensive (Humphrey, 1979; United Nations, 1980). The resolutions of the General Assembly, the treaties of regional communities, the constitutions of many nation-states, and the decisions of the International Court of Justice, all reflect the influence of the Universal Declaration of Human Rights. In addition, and of considerable import, it paved the way for the drafting of two legally-binding covenants: the International Covenant of Civil and Political Rights and the International Covenant on Economic, Social, and Cultural Rights.

These two controversial covenants, along with the Optional Protocol to the Covenant on Civil and Political Rights—permitting individual citizens whose rights have been violated to send a written communication to the Human Rights Committee—were submitted to a vote in the General Assembly in 1966. Although adopted by the General Assembly in 1966, it took 10 years before the requisite number of ratifications brought them into force.

While these human rights laws were being fashioned, other significant multilateral treaties in the field of human rights were being created, notably, the Genocide Convention, the Convention on the Elimination of all Forms of Racial Discrimination, the Convention on the Political Rights of Women, the European Convention on Human Rights, etc. (Bilder, 1978). Clearly, the process of universalizing human rights norms has been a continuous challenge from the time of the founding of the United Nations to the present. Opposition to such legal norms is bound to be endemic in a world comprised of sovereign states struggling to maintain themselves in power against threats from within as well as from without.

THE PROBLEM OF IMPLEMENTATION OF HUMAN RIGHTS LAWS

Few scholars would deny that the two International Covenants on Human Rights are landmarks in the evolution of international law. On the other hand, the fact that only about two-fifths of the member states of the United Nations have thus far ratified these treaties points to a rather modest level of consensus in the community of nations with respect to these covenants. In large measure, opposition to the covenants come from socialist and Third World countries (see Tables 12.1 and 12.2). These states, many of which have authoritarian or totalitarian political systems, evidently wish to retain a maximum of autonomy in enacting their domestic laws and exercise a maximum of political control over dissident and disloyal social groups.

In the unlikely event that the two covenants and related human rights laws were ratified by all 158 member states of the United Nations, would that in itself constitute evidence for the triumph of the international movement for human rights? Obviously not, unless all 158 states faithfully implemented the human rights laws. This points to the Achilles' heel of human rights laws. To date, the record of implementation of human rights laws by the various organs of the United Nations is decidedly unimpressive. There is virtual agreement among scholars in international law that the present enforcement machinery is inadequate (Starke, 1978; Buergenthal, 1979; Ramcharan, 1979; Singh, 1982). Thus, for example, Buergenthal (1979:8) states: "While the codification effort of international human rights norms has been quite successful, the opposite is true with regard to implementation. Various international institutions exist and some have done better than others, but on the whole the record is not a very good one." Likewise, Starke (1978:128) asserts that "The impression remains that despite the accumulation of declarations, resolutions, rules, standards, and guidelines within the framework of the United Nations, the abiding weakness is that of implementation."

Early in its history, the Human Rights Commission declared, with the approval of its parent body, that it lacks the authority to take action on individual human rights complaints (Starke, 1978:123-124). The situation changed in 1967 when the Human Rights Commission was granted authority to inquire into "a consistent pattern of violation of human rights." Notwithstanding overt and covert political pressures by member states, the Human Rights Commission does have a number of remedial

mechanisms at its disposal, ranging from fact-finding, negotiation, conciliation, and publicity, to the dissemination of information. For example, this commission's "Point 13 of the Agenda" is
devoted to "violations of human rights anywhere in the World";
members of this commission can express themselves on any
serious problem, as they did in cases involving Chile, South
Africa, and occupied Arab territory. However, though it does
not have the authority to take action with respect to any violation, it does have "the ability to point to an incident, draw
attention to it, and give it publicity to at least embarrass the
wrongdoer if nothing more" (Singh, 1982:38).

In accordance with Articles 28 and 41 of the International
Covenant on Civil and Political Rights, a Human Rights Committee was established with authority to "receive and consider
communications to the effect that a State Party claims that another State Party is not fulfilling its obligation under the present
Covenant." The Committee's closed meetings and other proceedings are carefully designed to protect the state parties from
adverse publicity. The Committee may not, however, receive
any communications from individuals complaining that their
human rights have been infringed upon unless their governments have signed the Optional Protocol to the International
Covenant on Civil and Political Rights. Thus far, only 10 nations
have signed this optional protocol. This fact highlights the resistance of member states to permit their citizens to seek to vindicate their human rights in an international forum.

The barriers to implementing human rights laws pose a serious dilemma for international law. If a sovereign state chooses
to violate a legally binding norm, ostensibly in order to protect
and promote its self-interest, what recourse is there within the
community of sovereign states, as it is presently constituted, to
bring pressure on the transgressor? The answer, clearly, is relatively little. Apart from moral suasion, trade sanctions can be
imposed and resolutions deploring the action of the transgressor can be passed. These sanctions, however, are likely to have
limited effectiveness. Given the transcendent principle of national sovereignty, no effective system of enforcement is likely to
emerge. Short of transforming the present international system

in the direction of a transnational or a supranational system of world order, the problem appears to be insoluble (Evan, 1962a; Kothari, 1974; Falk, 1975, 1983). To promote the transformation of the international system, international nongovernmental organizations, especially but not exclusively in the field of human rights, can perform a salutary function (Evan, 1981; Scoble and Wiseberg, 1981). Apart from publicizing human rights violations, international nongovernmental organizations can develop knowledge-based proposals for institutional innovations. As regards human rights violations, a creative proposal, for example, advanced by a number of scholars and groups as long ago as 1954, deals with the establishment of an international court of criminal justice (Gross, 1973; Murphy, 1974; Woetzel, 1974).

LEGAL INDICATORS AND THE MEASUREMENT OF HUMAN RIGHTS LAWS

As with any law, national or international, the measuring of compliance is a daunting problem. The making and interpreting of laws involve a complex process that generates a voluminous record. Therefore, it is not surprising that legal scholarship traditionally tends to be qualitative in its mode of analysis. It is also not surprising that the so-called social indicator research movement (Bauer, 1966; Sheldon and Moore, 1968; Sheldon and Land, 1972; Johnston and Carley, 1981) has thus far virtually bypassed legal scholarship, notwithstanding the fact that Durkheim, the father of modern sociology, was, to my knowledge, the originator of the concept of an "index"—an indirect and external measure of a complex dimension of social structure— which he developed in connection with an analysis of "juridical rules" (Durkheim, 1933:64-65; Evan, 1984:28-29).

This movement has spawned a number of invaluable compendia of social indicators, such as those of Banks and Textor (1963), Russett et al. (1964), Taylor and Hudson (1972), and a publication by the U.S. Department of Commerce (1980). The bulk of the indicators contained in these compendia are objective measures of social systems pertaining to demographic, economic, educational, political, and communication variables. Conspicuously lacking in these handbooks, however, are measures of attributes of legal systems—except for some criminal statistics. An observation by Merryman, a comparative law scholar, goes a long way to explain this lacuna: "The general unconcern about quantitative legal information among lawyers both explains and perpetuates the relative unavailability of legal measurements" (Merryman, Clark, and Friedman, 1979:14). Transforming the masses of qualitative data lawyers deal with— for instance, statutes, judicial decisions, and administrative actions—requires special social science research methods with which legal scholars are generally unfamiliar.

The field of human rights laws is patently an area which, from the viewpoint of the development of theory as well as public policy, warrants research attention by a number of disciplines. Theoretically, analyzing the differential responses—and changes in responsiveness over time—of 158 member states of the United Nations, to human rights laws, poses a challenge to at least three disciplines: international law, comparative law, and the sociology of law. What factors in the social structure of a society are conducive, on the one hand, to the legislative enactment of domestic human rights laws, and on the other hand, to the ratification and implementation of international human rights laws? An equally challenging problem, from a public policy standpoint, is how to overcome some barriers to the implementation of international human rights laws.

Several researchers have already responded to this challenge. Before appraising their work, some observations on obstacles encountered in measuring compliance with human rights laws are in order. First, access to relevant data is difficult, especially if it requires the cooperation of nation-states whose public image may be adversely affected by the findings of objective inquiry (Merryman, Clark, and Friedman, 1979:24). Second, and closely related to the first observation, data collection on compliance with human rights laws is obviously not a value-neutral activity. It directly involves political considerations of a positive or a negative variety. Third, a global monitoring system to record compliance and changes in compliance with human rights laws is required. This system would resemble the worldwide data gathering operations by specialized U.N. agencies such as the Food and Agricultural Organization, the World Health Organization, and the World Meteorological Organization, which study, respectively, locust plagues, epidemic diseases, hurricanes, and tornadoes. Although the U.N. Human Rights Commission or UNESCO are obvious candidates for establishing such a global monitoring system, the potential political ramifications are such that it is unlikely that either would be able to undertake such a project in the foreseeable future. Fourth, any type of global monitoring system of compliance with human rights laws would necessitate a substantial allocation of financial and human resources.

Under these circumstances, nongovernmental organizations have stepped in to fill the vacuum. The first and perhaps most impressive and useful undertaking was initiated in 1961 by Amnesty International. In preparing its annual reports, Amnesty International seeks to record evidence of arbitrary arrests, detention, torture, and murder of political dissidents or "prisoners of conscience" who have not committed acts of violence. The annual narrative reports from 1961 to the present for a large number of nation-states, are a rich source of data (Scoble and Wiseberg, 1981:148-152). With the application of content analysis techniques to the annual reports, it would be possible to generate comparative and longitudinal quantitative measures of compliance with several provisions of the International Covenant of Civil and Political Rights, such as Articles 6 (right to seek a pardon or commutation of death sentence), 7 (torture), 9 (arbitrary arrest and detention without charges), and 14 (due process rights for anyone charged with a criminal offense).

A second source of data of some relevance to human rights laws is the "Comparative Survey of Freedom" produced by Freedom House, an American nongovernmental organization (Gastil, 1981). Since 1973, these surveys have conceptualized freedom in terms of political and civil rights and have rated each nation on two 7-point scales of "political rights" and "civil rights." To the extent that the dimensions of each scale are identified, no effort is made explicitly to relate them to the provisions of any human rights law (Gastil, 1981:3). Nor is it clear from the published reports of the surveys how the two 7-point ratings are arrived at; nor are any coefficients of reliability presented to demonstrate the reliability of the ratings. In the course of an extensive substantive and methodological critique of the Freedom House surveys, Scoble and Wiseberg state:

> In summary, Freedom House's conceptualization of freedom draws on two underlying dimensions of political rights and civil liberties that, when illustrations and emphases are examined, contain hints that it is really "the American democracy" that is held as the model and metric. The Freedom House/Gastil comparative survey exposes itself to far more important criticisms when one asks *how* one gets from such broad concepts of Western political philosophy to actual ratings of specific nations . . . one must question the reliability, validity, and replicability of the annual comparative surveys of freedom. (Scoble and Wiseberg, 1981:155)

At the same time, Scoble and Wiseberg point out that because of the widespread assumption that "some data are better than no data," the Freedom House survey ratings "because they exist and are in quantified form . . . are readily available to be appropriated by social scientists for their secondary analysis" (Scoble and Wiseberg, 1981:148-152).

A third source of data, allegedly bearing on human rights laws, is the Physical Quality of Life Index developed by economists working for the Overseas Development Council, a nongovernmental organization seeking to increase the understanding of Third World countries by Americans (Scoble and Wiseberg, 1981:164-167, n. 35). Seeking to avoid a culture-bound ethnocentric index that presupposes Third World countries will pass through "stages of growth" of developed countries, the economists selected three measures (infant mortality, life expectancy at age one, and literacy), and combined them into one index. Rather than yielding a measure of economic, social, and cultural rights, which Scoble and Wiseberg imply, this index, in my view, taps available public health and educational resources which are essential for a country's economic and social development. Hence, this index, as we shall presently see, may be viewed as a *predictor* rather than as a *measure* of compliance with human rights laws.

The fourth source of data on human rights laws are the "Country Reports on Human Rights Practices" produced by the U.S. Department of State in accordance with provisions of the Foreign Assistance Act of 1961, as amended. The 1980 report on 153 countries, for example, states that it "draws on information furnished by United States Missions abroad, Congressional studies, nongovernmental organizations, and human rights bodies of international organizations" (U.S. Department of State, 1981:2). Owing to a 1979 amendment to the Foreign Assistance Act, the coverage of this report was expanded to include all members of the United Nations instead of only those countries receiving economic or security assistance from the United States. Each country's report was organized under clusters of civil, political, social, and economic rights. In principle, therefore, it would be possible to relate some of these rights to specific provisions in the International Covenant on Civil and Political Rights (ICCPR) and the International Covenant on Economic, Social and Cultural Rights (ICESCR). Assuming this were done, it would be possible, as in the case of Amnesty International reports, to apply content analysis techniques so as to produce an array of quantitative measures of compliance with human rights laws. In short, the State Department's Country Reports, like Amnesty International reports, are a valuable source of data for researchers interested in developing measures of compliance with human rights laws.

The last source of data on human rights laws is a country-by-country handbook titled *World Human Rights Guide* (Humana, 1983). Originated and compiled by Charles Humana, this handbook has the unique feature of presenting ratings based in part on a country's compliance with provisions of the ICCPR. For each country, Humana presents a checklist of 50 items, 27 of which deal explicitly with provisions of the ICCPR and 23 with rights not presently incorporated in international human rights laws, such as those pertaining to abortion, divorce, capital punishment, and so on. For each of the 50 rights, a 1 to 4 rating scale is used ranging from "most free" to "most severe" or "most restrictive." Humana eventually sums the scores to produce a percentage score for each country.

There are a number of obvious difficulties with Humana's ratings. First, he is perhaps understandably vague as to the sources of his data:

> Many Embassies and High Commissions were equally helpful and I am indebted to their legal, press or information attaches. Not all, however, were cooperative and it is to correspondents in countries intent on suppressing the truth that I must offer a special word of thanks. At great physical risk to themselves, these courageous, unnamed individuals have regularly supplied me with facts and information. . . . In most instances information has come from the most authoritative sources and is the latest available at the time of compilation. Many countries, however, are reluctant to make public facts or documents that are usually obtainable by the researcher, in some cases even their penal codes and constitutions. In these cases, where official documents or information has been withheld or should be regarded as dubious, the Guide has used facts from unofficial but authoritative sources. These have always been subject to further scrutiny. (Humana, 1983:5, 9)

Second, Humana does not disclose how he converted the information he received into 1-4 ratings for each of the 50 items in his checklist. Third, as in the case of the "Comparative Survey of Freedom," Humana does not present any evidence as to the reliability of his ratings. Finally, Humana's inclusion of 23 items in his 50 item checklist of rights, which are not presently institutionalized as international human rights laws, introduces an unnecessary element of subjectivity in the country ratings. Fortunately, given his mode of data presentation, it is possible to recalculate a score for each country's compliance with the 27 articles of the ICCPR. Notwithstanding the obvious deficiencies,

Humana's handbook—a veritable tour de force—is a distinctive contribution to the literature.

A MINIMAL SET OF LEGAL INDICATORS FOR MEASURING COMPLIANCE WITH HUMAN RIGHTS LAWS

In light of the foregoing substantive and methodological considerations concerning the definition of human rights and the measurement of compliance with human rights laws, I shall venture to formulate a minimal set of legal indicators that, given the requisite resources, could become the basis for a research agenda (see Figure 12.1).

First, notwithstanding the controversies surrounding the concept of human rights, an institutionalized standard defining human rights can be adopted, viz., a legal norm pertaining to the rights of individuals or collectivities vis-à-vis a society that is included in a legally binding international instrument such as a covenant, convention, treaty, etc. Inasmuch as any international human rights law is a composite of a number of norms, it is important to itemize the norms comprising the law in question. In the first column in Figure 12.1 I have listed, as an example of an international law, the ICCPR. Of the 53 articles comprising the covenant, only 27 pertain to rights of citizens of all countries. Hence these 27 norms can be enumerated in the table, as Humana does in his handbook.

The second column of Figure 12.1 deals with whether a country has ratified the given human rights law. Although there is frequently a sharp disjunction between ratification of a law and implementation of a law, ratification is clearly an example of a minimal standard of support on the part of a member state of the United Nations.

Third, how many of the provisions of the human rights law in question have been incorporated, per year, in the domestic law of a country, whether in a constitution, statute, etc.? Such a legislative endorsement of a human rights norm can precede as

Human Rights Law	Ratification of a Given Law	No. of Provisions Legislatively Incorporated per Year in Domestic Law	No. of Provisions Invoked in Litigation per Year in Domestic Courts	No. of Victims of Violation of Provisions per Year	Percentage of Total Population Who are Victims of Violation of Provisions per Year	Scope of Violations: No. of Provisions Violated per Year
E.G.						
International Covenant on Civil and Political Rights						
PROVISIONS						
Article 1						
↓						
Article 27						

Figure 12.1 A Minimal Set of Legal Indicators for Measuring a Country's Compliance with Human Rights Laws

well as follow its official incorporation in the body of international law.

Fourth, how many of the provisions of the human rights law have been invoked in litigation in domestic courts? Whether such efforts are successful in domestic courts is less important than the fact that individuals and organizations have sought to use international human rights norms in pressing their claims in domestic courts (Lillich, 1978).

Fifth, how many victims are there, per year, of a violation of a given provision of a human rights law? Admittedly, in a totalitarian country in which the press is rigidly controlled, this statistic may be difficult to ascertain. In such circumstances subjective estimates by experts may have to suffice.

Sixth, what percentage of the total population of a country are victims, per year, of a violation of a specific provision of a human rights law? Again expert judgment may be necessary in the absence of available statistics.

Finally, how many provisions, of the total number of provisions comprising a given human rights law, are violated per year? In other words, what is the scope of violations of a given law—is it very narrow or very wide?

ANALYSIS OF A SAMPLE DATA SET ON HUMAN RIGHTS LAWS

Ideally, I would have preferred to illustrate the applicability and utility of the minimal set of legal indicators, presented in Figure 12.1, by analyzing a relevant sample data set. Since such a data set is, unfortunately, not available, I have constructed a considerably more simplified data set for illustrative purposes.

Beginning with the elementary variable of ratification of a human rights law, which, of course, is dichotomous in nature, a nominal or categorical variable was sought that might be used to test an association and throw light on the differential behavior of the member states of the United Nations. This question suggested a basic macrosociological hypothesis, viz., that political-economic differences are associated with the ratification of

Table 12.1 Relationship between Membership in First, Second and
Third World Countries and Ratification of the International
Covenant on Civil and Political Rights

| | Membership | | |
Ratification	First World Countries	Second World Countries	Third World Countries
No	20% (4)	52% (12)	67% (78)
Yes	80% (16)	48% (11)	33% (38)
	100% (20)	100% (23)	100% (116)

$\chi^2 = 16.28914$ $p = < 0.0003$

human rights laws by different countries. Western or "First
World" countries, with their long tradition of civil liberties, have
developed an infrastructure of economic, political, and cultural
institutions that makes it possible for them to subscribe to, as
well as to incorporate, international human rights norms. This is
much less true of socialist or "Second World" countries in which
there is an ideological opposition to individual human rights
and practices. In developing or "Third World" countries, the
economic, political, and cultural institutions are so precarious
that the political elites tend to perceive international human
rights laws as a threat to their power (Strouse and Claude, 1976;
Espiell, 1979).

Data pertaining to ratification of human rights laws were
readily available in Appendix C of the Department of State's
publication *Country Reports on Human Rights Practices* (U.S. Department of State, 1984). This appendix lists 165 nation-states
and tabulates whether or not each state has ratified 12 selected
human rights laws. Three of these laws were selected for analysis: the ICCPR, the ICESCR, and the Genocide Convention. After
categorizing each of the 165 nation-states as to membership in
the three worlds, the cross-tabulations were run. In Table 12.1,
the hypothesis of the differential response of the countries of the
three worlds to the ICCPR was clearly borne out, with 80%
ratification in the First World, 48% in the Second World and 33%

Table 12.2 Relationship between Membership in First, Second and Third World Countries and Ratification of the International Covenant on Economic, Social and Cultural Rights

	Membership		
Ratification	First World Countries	Second World Countries	Third World Countries
No	20% (4)	35% (8)	63% (74)
Yes	80% (16)	65% (15)	37% (42)
	100% (20)	100% (23)	100% (116)

$\chi^2 = 17.21018$ $p = < 0.0002$

in the Third World. The Chi-square value is statistically significant to four decimal points.

In Table 12.2, we note a similar finding with respect to the ratification of the ICESCR. And in Table 12.3, the association between the countries of the three worlds and ratification of the Genocide Convention is virtually identical, with an even larger Chi-square value than those in Tables 12.1 and 12.2.

Humana's new human rights index, notwithstanding its shortcomings, was a great inducement for statistical exploration. Since his ratings are at least ordinal and possibly even interval in level of measurement, it suggested the feasibility of undertaking a multiple regression analysis to explore not only the effect of membership in the three worlds but also the effects of two measures of economic development: the Physical Quality of Life Index and GNP/Capita growth. Both measures of economic development were obtained from Appendix II of the Department of State's *Country Reports* (U.S. Department of State, 1979). In the regression analysis, the nominal variable of membership in the three worlds was treated as a dummy variable.

In light of the findings in Tables 12.1-12.3, the results of the stepwise regression on Humana's human rights index, presented in Table 12.4, will not strike the reader as very surprising. The Western countries variable has the highest beta coefficient and yields an R^2 of .48326; and the Physical Quality of Life Index also produces a significant beta coefficient, but adds only

Table 12.3 Relationship between Membership in First, Second and Third World Countries and Ratification of the Convention on the Prevention and Punishment of the Crime of Genocide

Ratification	First World Countries	Membership Second World Countries	Third World Countries
No	10% (2)	26% (6)	57% (68)
Yes	80% (18)	74% (17)	43% (48)
	100% (20)	100% (23)	100% (116)

$\chi^2 = 17.21018$ $p = < 0.0002$

a modest amount to the R^2. The GNP/Capita growth, possibly because of its interrelationship with the Physical Quality of Life Index, has no significant effect on Humana's human rights index; nor do the two dummy variables of communist and developing countries.

In short, the findings in Tables 12.1-12.4 bear out the proposition that political-economic factors have a significant effect in differentiating and dividing the nation-states of the world with respect to compliance with human rights laws.

Table 12.4 Stepwise Regression on Humana's Human Rights Index for Countries

Independent Variables	Beta Coefficient	R^2	F Value	Significance F
Western Countries	.46064	.48326	82.2936	.0000
Physical Quality of Life Index	.35757	.55757	54.49743	.0000
GNP/Capita Growth 1970–1976	.12307	—	—	NS
Communist Countries	.02124	—	—	NS
Developing Countries	.03383	—	—	NS

CONCLUSION

The thrust of this chapter has been on both substantive and methodological issues bearing on human rights laws. Substantively, the ongoing evolution of human rights, and the barriers to their implementation, provide ample challenge simultaneously to students of international law, comparative law, and the sociology of law. By focusing on variations over time in rates of compliance of nation-states with human rights laws, we will very likely discover significant trends in social, political, and economic development in the international system.

Methodologically, the appraisal of alternative methods of measuring human rights and the formulation of a minimal set of legal indicators for measuring compliance with human rights laws point to the need for a collaborative, multidisciplinary effort to establish a global monitoring system. Because of the politicization of human rights issues in the organs of the United Nations and among the nations of the world, there is much to be said for organizing a global monitoring system under private auspices, preferably with the aid of a number of nongovernmental human rights organizations and several international scientific and professional associations (Evan, 1981). What David Rockefeller once said of the Trilateral Commission may apply as well in the present context: "Private citizens are often able to act with greater flexibility than governments in search for new and better forms of cooperation" (Falk, 1975:1004).

If an objective, empirically based approach to human rights laws can be mounted on a global scale, socio-legal research may contribute to the strengthening of the international movement of human rights which can potentially have a profoundly civilizing effect on relations within and among the nations of the world.

CHAPTER 13

Human Rights, the Nation-State and Transnational Law

Human rights pose many practical as well as theoretical problems. First and foremost is the extraordinary phenomenon of the
systematic and pervasive violations of the human rights of millions of people by the governments under which they live. This
depressing predicament has been annually and grimly documented by Amnesty International since this organization was
founded in 1961. By contrast, the theoretical concerns of a variety
of disciplines seeking to throw light on problems of human
rights are indeed remote from the realities of human rights
around the world. Thus, philosophers wonder about the nature
of human rights and the theoretical justification for advocating
any one or more human rights. Legal scholars, pondering the
marked growth of legal norms that promote human rights since
World War II, are baffled by the continuing problems of their
enforcement. And social scientists, whether political scientists,
anthropologists or sociologists, take into account political, cultural, and social context factors in order to explain the emergence of human rights and the obstacles to their enforcement.

As the title of this chapter suggests, I shall examine some
problems of human rights as they relate to (a) the nation-state
and (b) transnational law. Anticipating the conclusion, the thesis
is advanced that there is an incipient paradigmatic transition

occurring from international law, which may facilitate the further institutionalization and universalization of human rights.

PHILOSOPHICAL AND SOCIAL SCIENCE ISSUES

Philosophers and legal scholars have long wrestled with questions pertaining to human rights. Within the framework of scholastic theories of natural law, human beings, by virtue of reason and faith, are assumed to have "natural rights" over and above those grounded in positive law. According to Locke, these rights are "inalienable," a concept Jefferson adopted in formulating the Declaration of Independence. For Kant, the Categorical Imperative is a universalistic maxim mandating that all persons are to be treated as ends in themselves and never as means. This sweeping, idealistic concept can provide the foundation for articulating a set of human rights; and it has indeed inspired a number of such efforts. For example, Henry Shue[1] posits three "basic rights: subsistence, security, and liberty" (Shue, 1980). "Basic rights," according to Shue, "are everyone's minimum reasonable demands on the rest of humanity" (Shue, 1980:19). Similarly, Milne, in the course of interpreting Kant's Categorical Imperative, focuses on a substantive moral principle, which he calls the "humanity principle":

> To treat a human being merely as a means is to treat him as lacking all intrinsic value. If he has any value at all, it is only extrinsic or instrumental. To treat him always as an end is always to treat him as having intrinsic value, irrespective of any extrinsic value he may happen to have. But what is it to treat him as always having intrinsic value? . . . According to Kant, it requires that a human being must always be respected as an autonomous agent: that is, as a person capable of formulating and pursuing progress of his own. (Milne, 1986:82)

This analysis of the Categorical Imperative leads Milne to analyze human rights in terms of a set of "universal minimum moral rights." Universal morality, says Milne, is "the source of seven main rights and it is these which are human rights properly so-called. They are the rights to life, to justice in the form of fair treatment, to aid, to freedom in the negative sense of freedom from arbitrary interference, to honourable treatment, to civility and, in the case of children, to care" (Milne, 1986:139).

Legal philosophers, whether advocates of positivism or natural law, have addressed the thorny problem of the relation between law and morality. Not all of these philosophers, however, have dealt with the issue of human rights. Of special note, in this context, are the views of H. L. A. Hart. His positivism notwithstanding, Hart sets forth five basic rules of law and morals which he asserts comprise the "minimum content of natural law": human vulnerability, approximate equality, limited altruism, limited resources and limited understanding and strength of will (Hart, 1961:189-193). Fuller, on the other hand, in *The Morality of Law,* develops an argument for a theory of procedural natural law. His eight principles of the law's inner morality are as follows: generality of law, promulgation, retroactive laws, the clarity of laws, contradictions in the laws, laws requiring the impossible, constancy of the law through time, congruence between official action and declared rule (Fuller, 1964:46-91). Although the components of procedural natural law have implications for formulating a set of human rights, Fuller does not explicitly deal with any specific human rights, any more than Hart does. Nor does Fuller's single principle of substantive natural law—"open channel of communication"—directly grapple with any human rights issues. However, in addressing questions about a modern natural law theory, Hart and Fuller in effect direct our attention to a jurisprudential rationale for human rights.

Unlike philosophers and legal scholars, social scientists who have given some thought to problems of human rights have been wary about generalizing them across time and space. Ever since Sumner's seminal work *Folkways* appeared, social scientists have been sensitized to multiple manifestations of ethnocentrism (Sumner, 1906). The idea of human rights which many social scientists and philosophers are eager to universalize—

especially since the promulgation of the Universal Declaration of Human Rights—has its origin in the West. For example, Pollis and Schwab, two political scientists, conceive of human rights as a Western construct.

> It is becoming increasingly evident that the Western political philosophy upon which the [United Nations] Charter and the Declaration are based provides only one particular interpretation of human rights, and that this Western notion may not be successfully applicable to non-Western areas for several reasons: ideological differences whereby economic rights are given priority over individual civil and political rights and cultural differences whereby the philosophic underpinnings defining human nature and the relationship of individuals to others and to society are markedly at variance with Western individualism. (Pollis and Schwab, 1974:1)

The sociologist Boli-Bennett, in a content analysis of constitutional rights, observes substantial variation in definitions of citizen rights between Latin American, Moslem-Middle Eastern, Asian, and European Protestant countries. Boli-Bennett concludes that "countries having a Catholic heritage define constitutional citizen rights much more extensively than do countries having a Protestant heritage" (Boli-Bennett, 1981:182).

The anthropologist Naroll, in his ambitious analysis of the human situation entitled *The Moral Order*, lays bare his own value premises by enumerating four clusters of values which he acknowledges are the "chief values of European humanism," viz., peace, humanism, decency, and progress (Naroll, 1983:46-48). Naroll does not derive any specific rights from these value clusters, nor does he claim that they are "cultural universals." Nevertheless, he asserts that these values are in the process of diffusing, notwithstanding the existence of a diversity of cultures.

On the other hand, acknowledging cultural diversity leads many social scientists, unlike Naroll and others, to adopt a philosophy of cultural and ethical relativism—differences in cultural values and patterns of behavior are incommensurable

from a moral perspective. By contrast, philosophers such as
Milne and Shue, although cognizant of cultural diversity, reject
moral relativism and seek to justify a set of minimal moral rights
for human beings everywhere, viz., by formulating a theory of
ethical universalism.

NATION-STATES AND THE INSTITUTIONALIZATION OF HUMAN RIGHTS

The process of institutionalizing human rights began with the
establishment of the United Nations in 1945. Articulating the
purposes of the United Nations, Article 1 of the Charter calls for
"promoting and encouraging respect for human rights and for
fundamental freedoms for all without distinction as to race, sex,
language or religion." And again in Article 55, the United Nations pledges to promote "universal respect for and observance
of human rights and fundamental freedom for all without distinction as to race, sex, language, or religions." These historic
provisions facilitated the formulation and adoption by the General Assembly of the "Universal Declaration of Human Rights"
in 1948. In the 30 articles comprising this Declaration there is
an admixture of unattainable ideals such as "all human beings
are born free and equal in dignity and rights" and specific im-
plementable rights such as "No one shall be held in slavery."

As a declaration, this document is not legally binding on the
member states of the United Nations. Nevertheless, its impact—
legal, moral, and symbolic—has been extensive (Humphrey,
1979; United Nations, 1980). In many of the resolutions of the
General Assembly, the Security Council, and the Economic and
Social Council, there are repeated references to the Universal
Declaration of Human Rights. In addition, many national constitutions adopted after 1948 reflect the influence of the Universal Declaration of Human Rights; and in a number of decisions
of the International Court of Justice, the judges have taken judicial notice of the Universal Declaration of Human Rights. But by
far the most significant contribution of the Declaration is that it

has paved the way for the drafting of two legally binding covenants, viz., the International Covenant on Civil and Political Rights and the International Covenant on Economic, Social, and Cultural Rights.

The fact that it took 18 years for the two covenants to be drafted before they came to a vote in the General Assembly in 1966 attests to the level of manifest and latent conflicts surrounding these two human rights instruments (Henkin, 1981: 9-10). Even more controversial was the third instrument, the Optional Protocol to the International Covenant on Civil and Political Rights, which was submitted and adopted by the General Assembly in 1966. The Optional Protocol enables an individual who claims to be a victim of violations of any right set forth in the covenant, to submit a written communication to the Human Rights Committee—established under the terms of the Covenant. This right of individual petition can only be exercised after exhausting all available domestic remedies. Further reflecting the controversy regarding human rights innovations, almost 10 years elapsed before the minimum number of ratifications or accessions brought the two covenants into force. Thus, as of 1976, the International Bill of Rights consisting of the two covenants and the Optional Protocol, together with the Universal Declaration of Human Rights, was brought into being (Henkin, 1981).

To what extent do nation-states comply with the provisions of these two covenants on human rights? No definitive answer can be given because of the absence of a comprehensive international, impartial monitoring and reporting service that systematically and periodically collects comparable data on nation-state compliance with the gamut of human rights laws (McCamant, 1981). However, based on at least two annual reporting services, namely the U.S. Department of State "Country Reports on Human Rights Practices" and Amnesty International (AI) annual reports, it is safe to conclude that the level of violation of human rights laws throughout the world is very high indeed. If, in the interest of avoiding controversy over the impartiality of the data, we limit our attention to AI annual reports, we are automatically restricted to data on the treatment of political dissidents and "prisoners of conscience." An examination of AI reports for the past decade, from 1978-1987, discloses that the number of countries cited as violating the human rights of their citizens ranges from a low of 96 countries in 1979 to a high of 128 countries in 1987.

A number of statements from AI's annual reports capture something of the mission and findings of AI:

> The [1978] *Report* give[s] a depressing picture of systematic violations of basic human rights in most of the countries of the world. People are imprisoned because of their opinions, prisoners are tortured and even executed. (Amnesty International Report, 1978:3)

> Amnesty International seeks . . . the immediate and unconditional release of men and women detained anywhere because of their beliefs, colour, sex, ethnic origin, language or religious creed, provided they have not used or advocated violence. These are termed prisoners of conscience. It works for fair and prompt trials for all political prisoners, and works on behalf of such people detained without charge or trial. It opposes the death penalty and torture or other cruel, inhuman or degrading treatment or punishment of all prisoners without reservation. (Amnesty International Report, 1982:1)

> Prisoners of conscience are held by governments in all the geographical regions of the world, in countries with the most diverse political, social and economic systems. . . . During the year Amnesty International worked for the release of prisoners of conscience in more than 60 countries. (Amnesty International Report, 1981:4)

The mission of AI unavoidably brings it into direct conflict with nation-states, the principal violators of human rights:

> Amnesty International regards any violation of the fundamental human rights within its mandate as a threat to the rights and dignity of all people. It concentrates on trying to halt violations committed or tolerated by governments, because it is they who are responsible for upholding the

standards agreed by the international community. (Amnesty International, 1981:3)

Amnesty International is founded on the twin propositions that just as human rights transcend the boundaries of nation, race and belief, so does the international responsibility for the protection of these rights. (Amnesty International, 1980:4)

AI, it should be noted, refrains from ranking or grading countries according to levels of violation of human rights, claiming that "such comparisons would never be meaningful because of the suppression of information but also because of the incommensurability of forms of repression" (Amnesty International, 1983:3-4). Nevertheless, there is a general perception, as well as some evidence, that the level of human rights violations does vary among countries, to wit, that Third World countries and socialist countries have a higher level of violation than Western countries (Evan, 1986). Assuming, for present purposes, that this perception is valid, there are at least four possible explanations for variations in the incidence of human rights violations. First, the International Bill of Human Rights is indeed imbued with Western values; hence it should come as no surprise that Third World and socialist countries, guided by different values, would have a higher incidence of violations of human rights than Western countries. Second, socialist countries tend to have a single-party and an authoritarian political system, unlike the multiparty and pluralistic political system in Western countries. Hence, again, it is reasonable to expect that socialist countries would have a lower threshold of tolerance for political dissent. Third, less developed countries, with a legacy of colonial domination and confronted with a complex array of pressing economic and political problems, tend to place much less value on human rights than Western countries (Wai, 1979). Finally, in light of the foregoing considerations, socialist and Third World countries very likely experience a higher level of political insecurity than Western countries. If these assertions are true, the tendency of these countries to repress political dissidents is not surprising at all—though indefensible nonetheless.

EMERGENT TRANSFORMATION
OF THE INTERNATIONAL SYSTEM

The nation-state, as the principal culprit of human rights violations, is viewed by most social scientists as the most durable
and significant social system in world affairs. As Deutsch puts
it, "The nation-state is the most powerful instrumentality de-
vised by man for getting things done, and it is the only such
effective general purpose instrumentality above the level of the
family" (Deutsch, 1968:59-60). Since the seventeenth century, the
nation-state has been the principal actor in world politics, so
much so that "modern international law arose to give juridical
expression to this political reality" (Falk, 1975:655). However,
since World War II, the international system has undergone significant changes such that the "state-centric paradigm" (Keohane and Nye, 1972) is no longer deemed adequate for understanding world events. New *nonstate actors* have appeared in the
international arena. These nonstate actors may, in due course,
diminish the sovereignty of nation-states (Evan, 1962a, 1976a;
Burton et al., 1974; Inkeles, 1975). With the establishment of
the United Nations over 200 specialized agencies or international governmental organizations have emerged. In the intervening decades, three additional significant developments have
occurred in the international system: the proliferation of international nongovernmental organizations such as international
scientific and professional associations (Skjelsbaek, 1972; Evan,
1974); the emergence of various regional organizations, notably
the European Economic Community; and the marked growth of
multinational corporations. Many multinational corporations
have at their command larger resources than do nation-states.
For example, in 1973 General Motor's total sales were higher
than the GNP of Switzerland, Pakistan, and South Africa combined (Barnet and Muller, 1974).

Will the emergence of these nonstate actors exert countervailing pressures on nation-states such that the latter's record with
respect to the implementation of human rights laws will im-
prove? Or will nonstate actors, especially multinational corporations, because of their preoccupation with increasing profits,

seek to exploit their employees in host countries, thus undermining their social and economic rights? Several codes of conduct—the Sullivan Principles, the British Code, and the European Code—have sought to insure that multinational corporations with operations in South Africa would act as agents of social change against the apartheid system (Paul, 1987; Weedon, 1987). Although the controversy over corporate divestment continues, the decision on the part of many multinational corporations, especially American, to divest points to a failure on their part to effect social change in support of the human rights of South African blacks (Buthelezi, 1987; Wilking, 1987).

Notwithstanding the limited success of multinational corporations in transforming South Africa's apartheid laws, the ongoing changes in the international system suggest an incipient shift in the legal paradigm (Kuhn, 1970) from an *international* to a *transnational* system. Non-state actors are the principal mechanisms for effecting this evolution. When this evolution is completed, it could have a salutary effect on the human rights movement.

A MODEL OF TRANSNATIONAL LAW AND HUMAN RIGHTS

To convey what is meant by a paradigm shift, we will discuss the model presented in Figure 13.1. Undergirding the prevailing system of national laws of nation-states is a jurisprudential theory of legal positivism. The domestic laws of each nation have a claim to validity and demand compliance from its citizens. Positive law and legal positivism postulate that whatever laws are promulgated by a state are valid without regard to their moral underpinnings—extreme examples of this being the Nazi laws and the apartheid laws of South Africa. Furthermore, associated with the laws of each nation are sanctions enforcing compliance.

The principal status, under a system of national sovereignty, is the citizen whose rights and duties, regardless of the political system, are typically articulated in a constitution. In Western nations the rights of citizenship have evolved over the past three

Legal Paradigm	Jurisprudential Paradigm	Principal Status	Type of Rights	Duties
National Law (Positive Law)	Legal Positivism	Citizen	Civil, Political, Social, Economic Rights	Nation-State
Transnational Law	Modern Natural Law Theory	Person	Human Rights	Transnational Institutions, other persons generally (humanity)

Figure 13.1 A Model of Transnational Law and Human Rights

centuries. In a masterly essay tracing the evolution of citizenship, T. H. Marshall (1964) argues that in the eighteenth century the civil rights of citizens such as freedom of speech and equality before the law, were institutionalized; in the nineteenth century, political rights, such as the right to vote, were established; and in the twentieth century various social and economic rights, such as the right to work and protection against unemployment, were added with the rise of the welfare state. The nation-state's correlative duties to its citizens include safeguarding these institutionalized rights. In socialist countries, as we have seen, there is a preponderance of weight attached to social and economic rights rather than to civil and political rights. In Third World countries, because of large-scale economic deprivation, the rights of citizenship tend to get short shrift. While nation-states—as the objects of international law—can incorporate the human rights Covenants into their national laws, relatively few states have in fact done this, thus underscoring the strength of the ideological commitment to national sovereignty and positive law.

By contrast, the emergent legal paradigm, following Jessup's usage, may be designated as "transnational law." In Jessup's (1956:2) words, transnational law includes "all law which regulates actions or events that transcend national frontiers. Both public and private international law are included, as are other rules which do not wholly fit into such standard categories."

Unlike the term "international law" which suggests "law of, by, and for, nations" (D'Amato, 1987:91), the term "transnational law" acknowledges a multiplicity of objects of laws, either within or outside the borders of nation-states. A great variety of transnational situations arise which may involve individuals, corporations, organizations of states, intergovernmental organizations as well as nongovernmental organizations.

The jurisprudential basis of this paradigm is a modern natural law theory, namely a secular conception of a body of law based on values appropriate for human beings, regardless of national, racial, religious or other distinctions. In an essay in honor of Jessup, Friedmann observes: "The seat of human rights is not any positive law, not in the public authorities, but in 'the conscience of mankind' and 'moral law,' which are nothing else but natural law. In regard to such matters public authorities of any state play only a declaratory role" (Friedmann, 1972:254).

The principal status under this type of legal paradigm is the person, not the citizen. In many constitutions the concept of person is frequently used, though not defined. In the preamble to the United Nations Charter, there is a reaffirmation of faith in "fundamental human rights, in the dignity and worth of the human person. " A suggestive definition of the concept of person is offered by Dennett in his essay on the "Conditions of Personhood." From a moral perspective, according to Dennett, a person is a being "who is accountable, who has both rights and responsibilities" (Dennett, 1978:268). Associated with personhood are a set of generic human rights such as those formulated by Shue and Milne in philosophy and by McDougal and Lasswell (1966), Wright (1966), Falk (1975), and D'Amato (1987) in international law: namely, universal demands to protect the right to life and dignity of all human beings.

D'Amato, an authority on international law, conceives of human rights as a set of international entitlements. This leads

D'Amato to question the positivist theory that individual citizens do not have claims against their own governments for violating their entitlements. By claiming that human rights norms are part of international law, D'Amato argues that they become universally held entitlements:

> The idea of international human rights is so explosive, so revolutionary, that even as an idea it has yet to be assimilated into the collective consciousness. For, ultimately, human rights in international law means that the state is not the sole entity that possesses rights, it is not the alpha and omega of international law. Instead, individual persons have direct claims under international law. And more revolutionary than that, individuals under international law may have direct claims against their own states. (D'Amato, 1987:89)

Transnational institutions, rather than nation-states, may eventually become the guarantors of such rights as well as the object of duties by persons regardless of membership in nation-states. Real-world approximations to this ideal system are the Inter-American Court of Human Rights and the European Court of Human Rights. All 21 member states of the Council of Europe are parties to the European Convention on Human Rights. Article 25 of this convention provides for the right of individual petition, via a commission, to the European Court of Human Rights to vindicate rights transgressed by his or her own government. All but a few of the member states of the Council of Europe have accepted Article 25 (Amnesty International Report, 1987:19). Granting standing to individuals in human rights cases, in the European Court of Human Rights as well as in the Inter-American Court of Human Rights, is an innovation of singular importance. It may indicate, as D'Amato has observed, that "as the notion of human rights becomes increasingly perfected, it requires giving standing to individuals and groups to claim entitlement under international law" (D'Amato, 1987:199).

CONCLUSION

Admittedly, the transnational law model presented in Figure 13.1 purports to be a representation of emergent trends as well as a vision of the possible direction of change of the international system in the years ahead. In this respect it bears a strong resemblance to Falk's World Order Models (1975). This model combines descriptive and normative elements. It also presupposes that (a) the legal elite will participate in promoting the development of transnational law, and (b) that the worldwide human rights movement will continue to grow in strength. According to AI, as of 1986 there were over a thousand human rights organizations—national, regional, and international—campaigning for human rights (Amnesty International Report, 1986:1). If these organizations, in cooperation with others, succeed in institutionalizing and universalizing perhaps the *most fundamental* human right (Ferencz, 1988)—the right to life—mankind may yet succeed in averting nuclear war, and thus human history may yet continue into the twenty-first century.

NOTE

1. I am grateful to Thomas Donaldson's "Rights in the Global Market," presented as one of the Ruffin Lectures in Business Ethics, April 7-9, 1988, at the Darden School, University of Virginia, for bringing to my attention the work of Henry Shue.

Part IV

Systems Theory and the Experimenting Society

CHAPTER 14

Toward a Systems Model of Law and Society

In Chapter 2, a social-structure model of law was outlined. With the aid of some concepts and propositions of systems theory, I shall elaborate upon this model in the present chapter.

For several decades, researchers from a number of fields—biology, engineering and the social sciences—have been developing systems-theoretic concepts and principles which have been applied to diverse phenomena. Thus far, this meta-theory has not been applied to an entire social institution or societal subsystem, let alone to an entire society. Nor is it clear whether this meta-theory can be applied and, if it can, how it might be done. Buckley (1967) has explored this question, and Miller (1978) has attempted to apply one version of a systems theory—referred to as general systems theory—to different levels of complexity ranging from the cell system to the supranational system. Forrester (1969, 1971) has applied a quite different version of systems theory in modeling urban problems and world problems. Vanyo (1971) has assayed the application of systems theory to the field of environmental law and Evan (1976a, 1976c, 1977) has explored the applicability of systems-theoretic ideas to organization theory, problems of organizational effectiveness, and administrative law. What systems concepts and principles are potentially applicable to the complex dynamic relationship between law and society?

The first and fundamental concept relates to the distinction between open versus closed systems. All living systems, including social systems and subsystems, are open, that is, they are involved in a continual exchange of matter, energy and information between themselves and their environments. Second, a system is decomposable into a number of parts, entities or components. Third, mechanisms develop through natural evolutionary processes or are artificially designed to maintain relations among the parts of a system. Fourth, any system exhibits four fundamental processes: input of resources from the environment, transformation of resources, output of a product or a service to one or more environing systems, and feedback, that is, a part of the output is returned to the system either through a negative feedback loop or through a positive feedback loop. The concept of feedback, in turn, presupposes three other concepts: (a) goal parameters of a system that are either given in a system by virtue of an evolutionary process or are artificially designed by systems planners, legislators, executives, etc.; (b) communication, a process of transmission of information from one component of a system to another and from the system to its environment and vice versa; and (c) control or an effort to adapt the system to its environment in order to achieve a steady state, either through deliberate planning and design or as a result of a natural evolutionary process. Negative feedback, in light of these concepts, involves a reduction of deviation from the system's goal parameters, whereas positive feedback involves an increase in deviation which can either be detrimental, leading to the system's demise, or beneficial, leading to its continued viability and possible growth (Maruyama, 1963).

The foregoing concepts have led to the formulation of various systems principles, several of which are of particular relevance for our study of law and society. First, open systems, in their effort to survive, seek to maintain a steady state. Second, open systems tend toward internal differentiation in an effort to achieve a steady state. Ashby's "law of requisite variety" may provide an explanation for the tendency toward internal differentiation (Ashby, 1968). Third, taking into account von Berta-lanffy's (1968) principle of equifinality, open systems can reach the same final state from different initial conditions and by different means.

Can these very general systems concepts and principles help us illuminate the complex, dynamic relations between law and society? Clearly, society is an open system that seeks to achieve a steady state by means of a progressive process of adaptation to its environment. Furthermore, the legal system seeks to perform a regulatory or social control function for society. This regulatory function is hampered by intrasystem and intersubsystem problems, including communication blockages and information flow bottlenecks. Inadequate societal monitoring mechanisms— in part due to the absence of sensitive social and legal indicators—make it difficult to assess the multiple feedback loops, interrelating the legal system with the nonlegal subsystems of a society.

With these elementary systems concepts and principles as given, we now turn our attention to outlining a systems model of law and society.

A SYSTEMS MODEL OF LAW AND SOCIETY

If one undertakes to model the relationships between law and society, one of the first decisions is to identify the relevant systems and their relationships. This is tantamount to developing a model of a total society from the vantage point of law. Since social science terminology varies from one discipline to another, some clarification of the basic terms in the model is essential.

We shall retain the expression "legal system" since it is widely used, although, from a systems point of view, the legal system is a "subsystem" of the environing system of a society— or more briefly a "societal subsystem." Similarly, we shall refer to six other systems, each of which, in varying forms, is found in all societies: economic system, family system, religious system, educational system, political system, and scientific-technological system. The last two systems warrant a word of explanation.

By political system, in this context, is meant the type of power—including control over the instruments of coercion—exercised by the state, whether it involves a high level of participation of the citizenry or a high level of concentration of control in the hands of relatively few officials. By scientific-technological system, I refer to the knowledge about nature and applications of such knowledge, whether it is based on naturalistic or supernaturalistic foundations. In traditional and nonliterate societies this system consists largely of supernatural beliefs and magic.

Each of the seven systems comprising a societal system consists of four building blocks or components: values, norms, roles, and organizations (Parsons, 1961; Evan, 1975). Values refer to a concept of that which is desirable, whether couched in terms of assumptions, beliefs, or goals; norms refer to rules, prescriptions or proscriptions of behavior; roles refer to expectations, orientations or behavior associated with various positions in a given system; and organizations refer to formally created entities which consist of three basic elements: a set of values and goals, a set of norms, and a set of roles. All members of a society are directly or indirectly involved in each of the seven systems by virtue of the fact that they occupy a status or position and perform a role with respect to each system.

With these terms in mind, I shall now consider in some detail the flow diagram of our systems model of law and society as shown in Figure 14.1. This model is admittedly crude and complex. It is crude in that the parameters and variables need to be more precisely defined and refined before it would lend itself to computer simulation; it is complex in that the mechanisms relating the various components of the model are too diverse to be readily operationalized.

Underlying our model are the following general questions:

1. What is the impact of nonlegal subsystems on the legal system?
2. To what extent do noneconomic subsystems affect the legal system?
3. What is the nature of the feedback effects (i.e., negative vs. positive) from the legal system to the nonlegal subsystems?

4. To what extent and under what conditions does the legal system exhibit a level of "relative autonomy" from the nonlegal subsystems?

5. Do legal system "lags" in relation to nonlegal subsystems reflect "relative autonomy" and not merely inertia?

6. a) To what degree is legal system stability (or legal equilibrium) achieved?

   b) To what degree does legal system stability contribute to the stability of the nonlegal subsystems?

7. How do variations in the values of the parameters affect the functional relationships of the variables in the model?

I shall begin with four parameters: time horizon, population heterogeneity, population size, and structural configuration of the nonlegal institutions or subsystems of a society.

The first parameter is the time horizon (1).[1] For purposes of this model, I shall distinguish four time periods or time cycles: short-term (1-10 years), intermediate period (11-25 years), long term (26-100 years), and historical period (over a century). Legal systems register minor changes in the short term, substantial changes in the intermediate period, significant changes in the long term, and fundamental changes in the course of an historical period.

The second parameter is population heterogeneity (2). Societies vary greatly in the degree of homogeneity of their population as regards ethnicity, language, religion, race, etc. Such differentiations may become the bases for the stratification of a society and may also lead to intrasocietal as well as intersocietal conflicts (Taylor and Hudson, 1972:214-218).

The third parameter is population size (2a). Societies also vary greatly in size—from much less than one million to over one billion. This parameter has profound implications for the type of social order that emerges in a society as well as its capacity to adapt to its environment.

The fourth parameter is the structural configuration of the nonlegal institutions or subsystems of a society (3). The six nonlegal institutions of a society can be compared to one another in terms of four structural components, viz., values, norms, roles

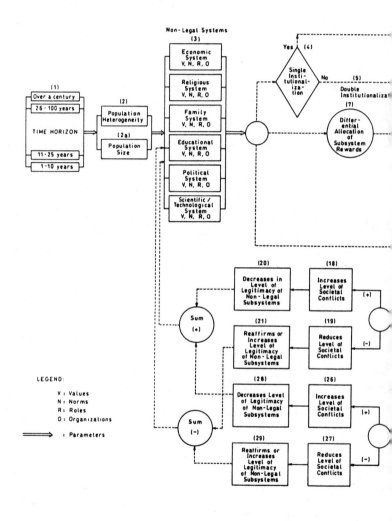

Figure 14.1 A Systems Model of the Interaction of Legal and Nonlegal Subsystems of a Society

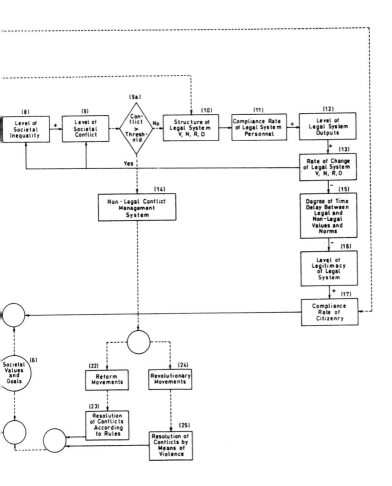

and organizations. For example, the values associated with the economy, religion, education and family can be rank-ordered yielding a "coefficient of importance" for each institution. A similar comparative evaluation could be undertaken for the degree of differentiation of the norms, roles and organizations associated with each of the six institutions. Such a comparison process would no doubt demonstrate that the institutional or subsystem configuration differs appreciably from one society to another.

Several examples of nonlegal institutional configurations might be in order. A traditional Moslem society such as Saudi Arabia has a nonlegal institutional configuration in which religious values pervade each of the other five nonlegal subsystems. In this respect, a Moslem society differs fundamentally from, say, the Soviet Union where political values of socialism, as mediated by the Communist Party, dominate the other five subsystems. Saudi Arabia as well as the Soviet Union, in turn, differ in basic ways from the United States in which political/economic values of democracy, pluralism and capitalism are diffused throughout the other nonlegal institutions.

With the foregoing four parameters as a point of departure, we now turn to the variables of the model. The first variable is the stratification of the nonlegal subsystems (7). Based on anthropological, sociological and historical studies, social institutions have been observed to differ substantially in relative dominance in a society. Any one social institution, or a combination of social institutions, can achieve functional primacy in a society and determine the functioning of the other social institutions (Tumin, 1956). Thus, in preliterate societies, family and kinship are primary in relative institutional importance; in traditional societies family and religion may both be the dominant institutions; in modern societies, by contrast, economic and/or political institutions can assume this dominant role. Although education, science and technology can individually, or in combination, replace the hegemony of economic and political institutions, no modern society has yet developed into a full-fledged meritocratic or technocratic direction. Nor, for that matter, has any society achieved an undifferentiated or equally weighted set of institutions or subsystems. In other words, there is a tendency for a stratification or ranking of subsystems to occur such that, in a given society, at a particular point in time, one of the nonlegal systems, or a combination of two or three nonlegal systems, may be dominant and the others subordinate in ranking; at an earlier or a later period of time in the same society, the ranking of the subsystems may be substantially different. In another society, at a comparable time period, the ranking of the nonlegal systems may be radically different. Thus, for example, the stratification of the nonlegal subsystems in the United States and the Soviet Union is very likely to be quite different: the economy, religion and the family probably rank higher in the United States than in the Soviet Union; the political system is probably more dominant in the Soviet Union than in the United States; and education, science and technology are probably accorded a similar ranking in both societies.

As the nonlegal subsystems become stratified, the societal values and goals become correspondingly rank-ordered (6). In addition, the nonlegal subsystems reflect, over time, varying degrees of value consistency. The stratification of the nonlegal subsystems may be so salient as to have a direct impact on the compliance rate of the members of a society (17), in which case a "single institutionalization" process occurs (4) instead of the "double institutionalization" process (5) (Bohannan, 1968) mediated by the legal system (10). Double institutionalization occurs because of several intervening societal processes: differential allocation of rewards to the members of a society, which gives rise to a "class structure" (7); level of societal inequality (8) due to the differential allocation of subsystem rewards (7); and level of societal conflict (9) which is largely a function of the level of inequality in a society (8).

When societal conflict is at low or moderate levels, double institutionalization occurs through the instrumentality of the legal system (10). The values and norms articulated by the legal system largely derive from the nonlegal subsystems. On the other hand, the roles and organizations of legal systems are relatively unique. The structural configuration within the legal system of values, norms, roles and organizations directly affects the compliance rate of legal personnel (11) and indirectly affects the outputs of the legal system (12). In turn, legal system outputs result in changes in the values, norms, roles and organizations comprising the legal system (13). These changes not only influence the functioning of the legal system (10) but also the level of societal conflict (9) and the level of societal inequality (8). These changes can increase societal conflict (9) and, in turn, societal inequality (8) if "vested interests" succeed in imposing their will on rank-and-file citizenry through the instrumentality of the legal system; alternatively, the changes can decrease the level of societal conflict and societal inequality by legally redefining statuses and by redistributing wealth and resources, as is evident in the movement for increasing entitlements in Western societies. There are innumerable examples of both types of processes. The Enclosure and Combinations Acts in England, towards the end of the eighteenth century, had the manifest effect of increasing societal conflict and the societal inequality; on the other hand, the Civil Rights Act of 1964 in the United States had the effect of increasing societal conflict and eventually decreasing societal inequality.

The nonlegal subsystems (3) also change at different rates relative to each other, with the economic system, in modern industrialized societies, for example, changing at a faster rate than, say, the religious or family systems. The legal system, on the other hand, because it is generally *reacting*—rather than *proacting*—to the differing rates of change of the other subsystems, tends to exhibit a lower rate of change than most of the other subsystems. The rate at which changes occur in the values, norms, roles and organizations of the legal system influences the degree of time-delay between legal and nonlegal system values and norms (15). To the extent that the rate of change of legal system values and norms is out-of-phase with the rates of change of other subsystems, significant maladaptive consequences are generated: a decrease in the level of perceived legitimacy of the legal system is likely to result in a decrease in the rate of compliance of the citizenry to legal norms (17).

If the rate of change within the legal system (13) and the level of societal conflict (9) reach a threshold value (9a), a significant societal process will develop: conflicts resulting from societal inequalities tend to bypass the legal system and are managed by a nonlegal, conflict management system (4) such as labor or commercial arbitration. Such conflicts, which stimulate the rise of reform movements (22), tend to be resolved according to rules (23), albeit outside the formal boundaries of the legal system. In the absence of such a resolution, societal conflicts tend to stimulate the growth of revolutionary movements (24) which will lead to violence, whether in the form of strikes, riots, assassinations, revolts, etc. (25). Examples of recourse to violence (25) and revolutionary movements (24) are the slave riots in Colonial America, Luddism in early nineteenth-century England, and the 1968 revolt in France. In each of these instances, there was a challenge to the institutional foundations of the society. By contrast, reform movements such as the Anti-Slavery Movement, the civil rights movement in the United States, the women's rights movement in various countries, and the ecology movement basically accept the status quo and seek to resolve conflicts according to rules, whether within the framework of the legal system or within the nonlegal conflict management system.

The compliance rate of the citizenry (17), the rate of resolution of conflict according to rules (23), and the rate of recourse to violence (25)—emergent trends of the nonlegal conflict management system—when compared with societal values and goals (6), generate two types of feedback: positive and negative. Positive feedback involves an increase in the level of societal conflict (18 and 26), which, in turn, decreases the legitimacy of the nonlegal subsystems (20 and 28). Negative feedback, on the other hand, involves a reduction in the level of societal conflict (19 and 27), which in turn reaffirms or increases the legitimacy of nonlegal subsystems (21 and 29). The cumulative feedback processes affect the configuration of the nonlegal subsystems (3) of a society for a given period of time.

In constructing the model, the following hypothesized functional relationships were formulated:

1. The level of societal inequality (8) is positively related to the level of societal conflict (9).

2. The structure of a legal system (10) is associated with the compliance rate of legal system personnel (11), without specifying whether this relationship is positive or negative.

3. The compliance rate of legal system personnel (11) is positively associated with the level of legal system outputs (12).

4. The level of legal system outputs (12) is positively associated with the rate of change of legal system, values, norms, roles, and organizations (VNRO) (13).

5. The rate of change of legal system VNRO (13) is associated with the level of societal conflict (8).

6. The rate of change of legal system VNRO (13) is associated with the level of societal inequality (8).

7. The rate of change of legal system VNRO (13) is inversely related to the degree of time delay between legal and nonlegal values and norms (15).

8. The degree of time delay between legal and nonlegal values and norms (15) is inversely related to the level of legitimacy of the legal system (16).

9. The level of legitimacy of the legal system (16) is positively related to the rate of compliance of the citizenry to law (17).

10. A high rate of compliance of the citizenry to law (17) reduces the level of societal conflicts (19), whereas a low rate of compliance increases the level of societal conflicts (18).

11. The level of societal conflicts (18, 19, 26, 27) is negatively related to the level of legitimacy of the nonlegal subsystems of a society (20, 21, 28, 29).

12. The type of output of the nonlegal conflict management system (14) is associated with the level of societal conflict (26, 27) and with the level of legitimacy of the nonlegal subsystems of a society (28, 29): resolution of conflicts according to rules (23) reduces the level of societal conflict (27) and increases the level of legitimacy of the nonlegal subsystems of a society (29), whereas the resolution of conflicts by means of violence (25) increases the level of societal conflict (26) and reduces the level of legitimacy of the nonlegal subsystems of a society (28).

This model can be used to explain stability as well as instability of the legal and nonlegal subsystems of a society. An institutional configuration that increases societal inequality

and, in turn, the level of societal conflict, will place an un-
due burden on its legal system. Failure to resolve the growing
accumulation of conflicts within the framework of the legal system will eventually lead to a process of circumventing the
system through an auxiliary conflict-management system and
through reform and/or revolutionary movements. Depending
on which type of legal system bypass occurs, the level of legitimacy of the nonlegal subsystems will be either increased or
decreased.

The model sketched above can, in principle, be disaggregated
to components within a legal system such as tort law, contract
law, criminal law, tax law, family law, etc. Implicit in this model
is an assumption that exogenous variables pertaining to the
international system do not have a significant impact on the
interaction between the legal and nonlegal institutions of a
given society. This is obviously untrue. However, if this assumption were relinquished, it would, in effect, necessitate transforming the model presented above into a global societal model,
which at the present stage of social science knowledge would be
impossible. In short, our systems model, though founded on
open systems theory (complemented by concepts and propositions from structural-functionalism), is of necessity and para-
doxically a closed systems model which seeks to represent the
social system of a given society that is, in fact, functionally open.

TESTING THE MODEL

Our social systems model is admittedly much too complicated in its array of variables and functional relationships for
any direct empirical test. What is more, the necessary data for a
comparison of even two societies, let alone a sample of societies,
is not presently available for the purpose of conducting an empirical test of the model. Nevertheless, when the model is appro-
priately refined and simplified, it may serve as a heuristic device
which would lend itself to computer simulation experiments. By

systematically varying the parameters of the model, viz., time horizon, population heterogeneity, population size and the configuration of nonlegal subsystems, the model could be formally tested with the aid of computer simulation methodology. The potential value of such computer simulation experimentation is three-fold: (1) it is a vehicle for formalization or the deductive development of hypotheses, (2) it generates new insights into the functioning of legal systems, and (3) it clarifies the kind of empirical data that would ideally be necessary for a proper empirical test of the model.

To design a computer simulation experiment would in itself require a considerable expenditure of time and treasure. However, it is not unreasonable to expect that a computer simulation experiment on this model would yield insights and hypotheses that could eventually be tested by traditional research methods using real data rather than simulated data. Although the entire systems model may not lend itself to a direct or even to an indirect empirical test, those parts of it that are articulated in sufficient detail may point to the kind of real world data that would be needed for an empirical validation.

Short of compiling a set of comparative social indicators such as envisioned by Gross (1966), Biderman (1966), Evan (1968) and others, for our systems model of law, which would be a vast undertaking, a quite different research strategy might also be explored. The time parameter of our model suggests the importance of tracing changes over time in the interactions between legal and nonlegal institutions. In the absence of relevant time series data, it might be fruitful to reanalyze legal historical monographs covering comparable periods of time in two or more countries. Such a reanalysis, designed to test parts of our model or its entirety, would have to be guided by a logic of categorization akin to that used by Murdock (1963) in developing the Human Relations Area File. For example, starting with a monograph such as Horwitz' (1977) on the development of commercial law in the United States from 1780 to 1860, it would probably be possible to discover comparable studies in other countries as sources of data for a test of part of our model.

CONCLUSION

As an interdisciplinary field, sociology of law is obviously fraught with great difficulties because of the inadequacies of its theory and of the available data. The prevailing theoretical foundations of both law and sociology are deficient in either illuminating the relationships between law and society or in formulating propositions that are empirically testable.

The data problems are no less serious. Although the volume of information on the functioning of legal systems is immense, it is enormously difficult to transform the morass of information on judicial decisions, administrative actions and legislative enactments into data usable for sociological research. Sociologists of law, in failing to develop a system of legal indicators, have not found a way of converting the massive volume of information on legal systems, especially of a quantitative nature, into data that would permit the testing of hypotheses (Evan, 1984).

In short, paraphrasing Pool's (1967) observation about computer simulation of total societies, the sociology of law is both theory poor and data poor. If this field is to extricate itself from its condition of poverty, new theoretical and methodological strategies are essential. The systems model presented in this chapter, along with its implications for computer simulation experimentation, on the one hand, and for reanalysis of legal historical monographs on the other, represents one such new departure. Only time and further research will tell whether it will eventually contribute to the intellectual enrichment of the sociology of law. At least one researcher confidently predicted that "in ten years' time [1984] people will have modeled the legal system with a considerable degree of accuracy" (Vanyo, 1974:62).

NOTE

1. Each of the parameters and variables of the model is designated by a number in parentheses in Figure 14.1.

CHAPTER 15

Law and the Experimenting Society

The enactment of law, whether in the course of legislation, judicial decision making, administrative action, or executive decision making, can be guided by scientific knowledge. Typically, however, it is not; "conventional wisdom" and intuition are all too often the bases of policy decisions. For example, Cohen, Robson, and Bates have pointedly drawn attention to the court's frequent reliance on the "moral sense" or "common conscience" without any systematic scientific inquiry into its content:

Despite lip service to the need to treat the moral sense as an observable datum; and despite exhortations to employ "the spirit of science" in the task of observation, judicial law-makers have relied mainly upon intuitive hunch, on the vagaries of "judicial notice," on the predilections of the groups identified with the social origin of the law-makers, on crude personal observation, on a "best guess," or some such other esoteric method for divining the *Zeitgeist*. It is not that there is an unawareness of the unreliability of these methods. Mr. Justice Cardozo's observation that "In every court there are more likely to be as many estimates of the *'Zeitgeist'* as there are judges on its bench," and Judge Frank's wry remark that "Usually a person who talks of 'opinion of the world at large' is really referring to the 'few people with whom I happened to converse,' " evidence a lively alertness to the problem. (Cohen, Robson, and Bates, 1958:7-8)

Almost as uncommon is an appreciation of the importance of empirically assessing the consequences of a legal enactment in order to discover whether the implicit or explicit purposes of a law have been fulfilled.

Small wonder that many laws fail to achieve their avowed objectives and that legal systems, as a whole, are subject to many failures. A legal system, whether of a given society or of the international system as a whole, can fail to achieve its purposes because of internal as well as external structural features. Internally, a legal system may suffer from various defects in its configuration of values, norms, roles, and organizations; its norms may be inconsistent, imprecise, and unsupported by any relevant sanctions; its structure of roles of legal personnel may be inappropriate; its role occupants may not be adequately socialized into pertinent values, and hence, highly vulnerable to corruption; its organizations may be ineffectively designed; and so on. Externally, a legal system may be constrained to such a degree, by one or more nonlegal social institutions in a society, as to lose any semblance of an institution seeking to generate universalistic norms and to apply these norms in a disinterested manner in regulating the behavior of the citizenry.

More specifically, there are many ways in which a legal system can fail—through its inability to cope with dysfunctional and unanticipated consequences of legal decisions, through the exercise of uncontrolled discretion on the part of judges, and administrative and law enforcement officials; and through its unresponsiveness to a society's urgent problems. Other examples of legal system failures include a tendency for law to lag behind changes in nonlegal institutions, which results in maladjustments that entail considerable social costs; a tendency for "group-interest" laws to be enacted instead of "social-interest" laws, which may eventually undermine the confidence of the citizenry in the impartiality, legality, and independence of the law; inefficiency in enforcing some laws because of limited resources; and the failure of a legal system to promote the "double institutionalization" of some beneficial customs that have low normative salience among the citizenry.

The cumulative effect of legal system failures over time is a progressive decline in the perceived legitimacy of the legal system, viz., it leads to a withdrawal of support from the legal system. Short of a total collapse caused by a multitude of failures, a legal system may be progressively bypassed by subgroups in society through the use of two contrasting strategies: (1) extra-legal mechanisms to manage societal conflicts, such as the use of labor and commercial arbitration in the United States; and (2) recourse to violence, either by legal personnel, rank-and-file citizenry, or both (Evan, 1978).

To what extent does a legal system make use of relevant scientific knowledge *prior* to making new legal policies or *after* making policy decisions, in order to assess its impact? Public policies, whether resulting from legislative decision making, judicial decision making, or administrative or executive decision making, presuppose an accurate diagnosis of a societal problem for which they propose a workable solution. With some exceptions (Evan, 1980:608-633), legislators, judges, and administrators of government agencies do not, as a rule, acknowledge that the public policies they generate are in need of systematic empirical evaluation.

A case in point is the Civil Rights Act of 1964. Section 402 of Title VI of this act requires a postpolicy study to be reported to the president and the Congress "within two years of the enactment of this title, concerning the lack of availability of equal educational opportunities for individuals by reason of race, color, religion, or national origin in public educational institutions at all levels in the United States, its territories and possessions and the district of Columbia." This provision paved the way for the evaluation study titled *Equality of Educational Opportunity* (Coleman et al., 1966).

The 1978 amendment to the Age Discrimination Act of 1967, extending involuntary retirement from 65 to 70 years of age, stipulates that the Secretary of the Department of Labor shall undertake a study of the consequences of this policy for executives in industry and officials in government.

Unlike the two foregoing laws, the Technology Assessment Act of 1972 is concerned with providing Congress with relevant knowledge *prior* to the enactment of laws involving the application of new technology. Acknowledging the possibility that technological applications can have beneficial as well as detrimental effects, Congress recognized the need for prepolicy studies as an aid to the legislative process. With the passage of this law, the Office of Technology Assessment was established with a mission "to provide early indications of the probable beneficial and adverse impacts of the applications of technology and to develop other coordinate information which may assist Congress." The underlying assumption of this act is that the legislative branch can channel technology for the benefit of society instead of assuming that law can only perform a reactive function with respect to technology.

Perhaps the clearest example of prepolicy research in federal administrative agencies is the institutionalization of environmental impact analysis; and the resulting document is known as an "environmental impact statement" (EIS). The National Environmental Policy Act (NEPA), which was signed into law in 1970, requires that each federal agency, before proceeding with any major action, recommendation, or report on proposals for legislation, undertake a study of the probable changes in the various socioeconomic and biophysical characteristics of the environment which may result from the proposed action. To develop guidelines for the preparation of environmental impact statements, and to review and appraise the environmental impact statements of the various agencies, NEPA created the Council on Environmental Quality.

Since environmental impact analysis is a complex undertaking which deals with problems that fall into the domain of different disciplines, Section 102(2)A of NEPA requires that a "systematic and interdisciplinary approach" be used to ensure the integrated use of social, natural, and environmental sciences in planning and decision making.

The foregoing examples of the acknowledgement of the need for making prepolicy and postpolicy studies implies an emerging function for law, viz., the process of enacting law can be conceived of as engaging in "legal experiments" (Cowan, 1954a, 1954b). Cowan, a legal scholar, presented one of the earliest arguments in favor of the proposition that law provides the basis for an application of experimental method to social problems. This proposition was further spelled out by Campbell in "Legal Reforms as Experiments" (1970). Applying his concept of "quasi-experimental" design and his perceptive analysis of the threats to internal and external validity, Campbell argues that it is possible and desirable to undertake quasi-experiments with any legal reform.

Several such experiments have in fact been undertaken, some with and some without the inspiration of Campbell's work. An impressive study is Ross's application of interrupted time series analysis to an experiment in the enforcement of a drunk-driving law in Britain. Anteceding this experiment was the Chicago jury project which entailed the use of experimental and control groups to test the difference between the conduct of a bench trial versus a jury trial (Zeisel, Kalven, and Bucholz, 1959). Partly inspired by the Chicago court delay project, Rosenberg undertook an experiment in New Jersey on the impact of pretrial hearings on the settlement ratio of personal injury cases (1964). In recent years, researchers have designed mock jury experiments with simulated legal trials to test hypotheses about jury behavior and develop models of the jury deliberation process (MacCoun, 1989).

Generalizing from the foregoing, one can argue, following Campbell's thesis (1970, 1988), that law is a strategic instrument for effecting social change (Evan, 1965b). If one takes this proposition seriously, then all lawmaking decisions in a society can be conceptualized as a basis for quasi-experiments. This presupposes that one conceives of the legal system of a society in accordance with the principles of scientific method. In other words, public policies are in effect hypotheses to be tested in the laboratory of social reality.

An experimental model of law as an instrument of social change is presented in Figure 15.1. At each cycle of this feedback model, social problems are defined and redefined in the course

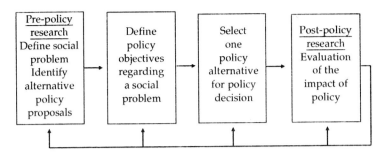

Figure 15.1 An Experimental Model of Law as an Instrument for
Planned Social Change

of prepolicy-making research, and a new set of alternative
policy proposals are identified from which policymakers eventually make a selection. After a policy decision is made, a postpolicy study is undertaken to assess the effectiveness of the
promulgated policy. If this type of model were institutionalized into the fabric of a social system, we would be well on our
way towards achieving what Campbell terms an "experimenting society."

Campbell, who has for many years advocated the concept of
an "experimenting society," acknowledges that it is "a specula-
tive exercise in utopian thought" (Campbell, 1988:291). Taking
as his point of departure the ethos of science and its collective
pursuit of truth, Campbell characterizes the experimenting society in the following terms:

> One that would vigorously try out possible solutions to
> recurrent problems and would make hard-headed, multi-
> dimensional evaluations of outcomes, and when the eval-
> uation of one reform showed it to have been ineffective or
> harmful, would move on to try other alternatives. . . .
>
> The experimenting society will be a *nondogmatic society.*
> While it will state ideal goals and propose wise methods for
> reaching them, it will not dogmatically defend the value
> and truth of these goals and methods against disconfirm-
> ing evidence or criticism.

It will be a *scientific society* in the fullest sense of the word "scientific." The scientific values of honesty, open criticism, experimentation, willingness to change once-advocated theories in the face of experimental and other evidence will be exemplified. . . .

It will be an *accountable, challengeable, due-process society.* There will be public access to the records on which social decisions are made. Recounts, audits, reanalyses, reinterpretations of results will be possible. Just as in science objectivity is achieved by the competitive criticism of independent scientists, so too the experimenting society will provide social organizational features making competitive criticism possible at the level of social experimentation. There will be sufficient separation of governmental powers so that meaningful legal suits against the government are possible. Citizens not a part of the governmental bureaucracy will have the means to communicate with their fellow citizens disagreements with official analyses and to propose alternative experiments. It will be an *open society* (Popper 1945).

It will be a *decentralized society* in all feasible aspects. Either through autonomy or deliberate diversification, different administrative units will try out different ameliorative innovations and will cross-validate those discoveries they borrow from others. The social-system independence will provide something of the replication and verification of successful experiments found in science. . . .

It will be a society committed to *means-idealism* as well as *ends-idealism.* As in modern views of science, the process of experimenting and improving will be expected to continue indefinitely without reaching the asymptote of perfection. In this sense, all future periods will be mediational and transitional, rather than perfect-goal states. Ends cannot be used to justify means, for all we can look forward to are means. The means, the transitional steps, must in themselves be improvements.

It will be a *popularly responsive society,* whose goals and means are determined by collective good and popular preference. Within the limits determined by the common good, it will be a *voluntaristic society,* providing for individual participation and consent at all decision-levels possible. It will be an *equalitarian society,* valuing the well-being and the preferences of each individual equally. (Campbell, 1988:291-296)

It should come as no surprise to the reader that Campbell's vision of an experimenting society has yet to be realized.

There is no such society anywhere today. While all nations are engaged in trying out innovative reforms, none of them are yet organized to adequately evaluate the outcomes of these innovations. . . . Within both capitalist and communist countries there are shared aspects of political processes that work against the emergence of the experimenting society and which may, in the long run, preclude it. (Campbell, 1988:291, 297)

The legal system need not wait for an idealized experimenting society to be brought into existence. It can facilitate the eventual transition to an approximation of this type of society by continuing to acknowledge the need for prepolicy- and postpolicy-making research, as diagrammed in Figure 15.1. In other words, if a legal system is to learn from both its successes and its failures, thereby upgrading its regulatory capabilities and enhancing its legitimacy, it is essential for legal personnel as well as sociologists of law and legal scholars to develop an *experimental* perspective toward the law rather than view the law as a set of commandments engraved in stone. It is not inconceivable that sometime in the twenty-first century, if not sooner, one or more democratic societies will have the courage and wisdom to systematically experiment with law in order to promote the values of justice and democracy.

References

Abel, Richard L. (1982). "Law as Lag: Inertia as a Social Theory of Law." *Michigan Law Review, 80*, 785-809.

Abel, Richard L. and Phillip S. C. Lewis (1988). *Lawyers in Society*. Berkeley: University of California Press.

American Labor Arbitration Awards (1946). New York: Prentice-Hall.

Amnesty International (1978). *Amnesty International Report*. London: Amnesty International.

Amnesty International (1980). *Amnesty International Report*. London: Amnesty International.

Amnesty International (1981). *Amnesty International Report*. London: Amnesty International.

Amnesty International (1982). *Amnesty International Report*. London: Amnesty International.

Amnesty International (1983). *Amnesty International Report*. London: Amnesty International.

Amnesty International (1985). *Amnesty International Report*. London: Amnesty International.

Amnesty International (1986). *Amnesty International Report*. London: Amnesty International.

Amnesty International (1987). *Amnesty International Report*. London: Amnesty International.

Ancel, Marc (1952). "Observations on the International Comparison of Criminal Statistics." *International Review of Criminal Policy*, 41-48.

Antunes, George and A. Lee Hunt (1973). "The Impact of Certainty and Severity of Punishment." *Journal of Criminal Law and Criminology, 64*, 486-493.

Ashby, W. Ross (1968). "Variety, Constraint, and the Law of Requisite Variety." In Walter Buckley (Ed.), *Modern Systems Research for the Behavioral Scientist*, pp. 129-136. Chicago: Aldine.

Aubert, Vilhelm (1969). *Sociology of Law*. New York: Penguin.

Auerbach, Jerold S. (1976). *Unequal Justice*. New York: Oxford University Press.

Banks, Arthur S. and Robert B. Textor (Eds.) (1963). *A Cross-Polity Survey.* Cambridge: MIT Press.

Barkan, Steven M. (1987). "Deconstructing Legal Research: A Law Librarian's Commentary on Critical Legal Studies." *Law Library Journal, 79,* 617-637.

Barnet, R. J. and R. Muller (1974). *Global Reach.* New York: Simon and Schuster.

Bartosic, Florian and Ian D. Lanoff (1972). "Escalating the Struggle against Taft-Hartley Condemners." *University of Chicago Law Review, 39,* 255-294.

Bauer, Raymond A. (Ed.) (1966). *Social Indicators.* Cambridge: MIT Press.

Baxi, U. (1974). "Comment—Durkheim and Legal Evolution: Some Problems of Disproof." *Law and Society Review, 8,* 645-651.

Beck, Randy (1988). "The Faith of the 'Crits': Critical Legal Studies and Human Nature." *Harvard Journal of Law and Public Policy, 11,* 433-459.

Berman, Harold J. (1963). *Justice in the U.S.S.R.: An Interpretation of the Soviet Law.* Cambridge, MA: Harvard University Press.

Bendix, Reinhard (1956). *Work and Authority in Industry.* New York: Prentice-Hall.

Bendix, Reinhard (1960). *Max Weber: An Intellectual Portrait.* New York: Doubleday.

Berelson, B. (1954). "Content Analysis." In Gardner Lindzey (Ed.), *Handbook of Social Psychology,* vol. 1. Cambridge, MA: Addison-Wesley.

Berle, Adolph A. (1952). "Constitutional Limitations on Corporate Activity." *University of Pennsylvania Law Review, 100,* 942-943.

Berle, Adolph A. (1954). *The 20th Century Capitalist Revolution.* New York: Harcourt Brace and World.

Berle, Adolph A. (1958). "Historical Inheritance of American Corporations." In Ralph J. Baker and William L. Cary (Eds.), *Cases and Materials on Corporations,* 3rd ed. Brooklyn: Foundation Press.

Berlin, Isaiah (1969). *Four Essays on Liberty.* London: Oxford University Press.

Bernstein, Irving (1954). "Arbitration." In Arthur Kornhauser, Robert Dubin and Arthur M. Ross (Eds.), *Industrial Conflict.* New York: McGraw-Hill.

Bertalanffy, Ludwig von (1968). *General System Theory: Foundations, Developments and Applications.* New York: Braziller.

Biderman, A. D. (1966). "Social Indicators and Goals." In R. A. Bauer (Ed.), *Social Indicators,* pp. 68-153. Cambridge: MIT Press.

Bilder, Richard B. (1978). "The Status of International Human Rights Law: An Overview." In James C. Tuttle (Ed.), *International Human Rights: Law and Practice,* pp. 1-13. Philadelphia: American Bar Association.

Bisco, Ralph L. (1966). "Social Science Data Archives." *American Political Science Review, 60,* 93-109.

Black, Donald (1976). *The Behavior of Law.* New York: Academic Press.

Blau, Peter M. (1955). *The Dynamics of Bureaucracy: A Study of Interpersonal Relations in Two Government Agencies.* Chicago: University of Chicago Press.

Blau, Peter M. (1973). *The Organization of Academic Work.* New York: John Wiley.

Blau, Peter M. (1977a). "A Macrosociological Theory of Social Structure." *American Journal of Sociology, 83,* 26-54.

Blau, Peter M. (1977b). *Inequality and Heterogeneity.* New York: Free Press.

Blau, Peter M. and Richard A. Schoenherr (1971). *The Structure of Organizations.* New York: Basic Books.

Bohannan, Paul (1968). "Law and Legal Institutions." In *International Encyclopedia of the Social Sciences*, vol. 9, pp. 73-78. New York: Macmillan, Free Press.

Boli-Bennett, J. (1981). "Human Rights or State Expansion? Cross-National Definitions of Constitutional Rights, 1870-1970." In V. P. Nanda, J. R. Scarritt and G. W. Sheperd, Jr. (Eds.), *Global Human Rights: Public Policies, Comparative Measures, and NGO Strategies*. Boulder, Colorado: Westview.

Bonini, Charles P. (1963). *Simulation of Information and Decision Systems in the Firm*. Englewood Cliffs, NJ: Prentice-Hall.

Boulding, Kenneth E. (1953). *The Organizational Revolution*. New York: Harper.

Bredemeier, Harry (1962). "Law as an Integrative Mechanism." In William M. Evan (Ed.), *Law and Sociology*, pp. 73-90. New York: Free Press.

Buckley, Walter (1967). *Sociology and Modern Systems Theory*. Englewood Cliffs, NJ: Prentice-Hall.

Buckley, Walter (Ed.) (1968). *Modern Systems Research for the Behavioral Scientist*. Chicago: Aldine.

Buergenthal, Thomas (1979). "Codification and Implementation of International Human Rights." In Alice H. Henkin (Ed.), *Human Dignity: The Internationalization of Human Rights*, pp. 15-21. New York: Aspen Institute of Humanistic Studies.

Burman, Sandra and Barbara E. Harrell-Bond (Eds.) (1979). *The Imposition of Law*. New York: Academic Press.

Burton, J. W. et al. (1974). *The Study of World Society*. Pittsburgh: University of Pittsburgh International Studies Association.

Buthelezi, M. W. (1987). "Discerning the Divestment Debate." In S. Prakash Sethi (Ed.), *The South African Quagmire: In Search of a Peaceful Path to Democratic Pluralism*. Cambridge, MA: Ballinger.

Campbell, Donald T. (1970). "Legal Reforms or Experiments." *Journal of Legal Education, 23*, 212-239.

Campbell, Donald T. (1988). *Methodology and Epistemology for Social Science*. Chicago: University of Chicago Press.

Carley, Michael (1981). "Political and Bureaucratic Dilemmas in Social Indicators for Policy Making." *Social Indicators Research, 9*, 15-33.

Carlin, Jerome E. (1962). *Lawyers on Their Own*. New Brunswick, NJ: Rutgers University Press.

Carlin, Jerome E. (1966). *Lawyer's Ethics*. New York: Russell Sage Foundation.

Chamberlain, Neil W. (1955). *A General Theory of Economic Process*. New York: Harpers.

Chamberlain, Neil W. (1958). *Labor*. New York: McGraw-Hill.

Cohen, J. R., A. H. Robson and A. Bates (1958). *Parental Authority*. New Brunswick, NJ: Rutgers University Press.

Cohen, Kalman J. and Richard M. Cyert (1965). "Simulation of Organizational Behavior." In James G. March (Ed.), *Handbook of Organizations*. Chicago: Rand McNally.

Coleman, J. S. et al. (1966). *Equality of Educational Opportunity*. Washington, DC: Government Printing Office.

Collective Agreement, Affiliated Dress Manufacturers, Inc., with International Ladies' Garment Workers' Union, 1958-1961.

Collective Bargaining Agreement between International Union, United Automobile, Aircraft, and Agricultural Implements Workers of America (UAW-CIO) and the Ford Motor Company, June 8, 1955.

Collins, Randall (1980). "Weber's Last Theory of Capitalism: A Systemization." *American Sociological Review, 45,* 925-942.

Copeloff, Maxwell (1948). *Management-Union Arbitration.* New York: Harpers.

Cotterrell, Roger (1984). *The Sociology of Law: An Introduction.* London: Butterworths.

Cowan, Thomas N. (1948). "The Relation of Law to Experimental Social Science."*University of Pennsylvania Law Review, 96,* 484-502.

Cowan, Thomas N. (1954a). "The Design of Legal Experiment." *Journal of Legal Education, 6,* 520-538.

Cowan, Thomas N. (1954b). "A Postulate Set for Experimental Jurisprudence." *Philosophy of Science, 18,* 1-5.

D'Amato, A. (1987). *International Law: Process and Prospect.* Dobbs Ferry, NY: Transnational.

David, René (1964). *Les Grands Systèmes de Droit Contemporains.* Paris: Dalloz.

David, René and John E. C. Brierley (1968). *Major Legal Systems in the World Today.* London: The Free Press, Collier-Macmillan.

Davis, Frederic B. (1973). "Administrative Law: Today and Tomorrow." *Journal of Public Law, 22,* 335-355.

Davis, Kenneth Culp (1958). *Administrative Law Treatise,* vols. 1-4. St. Paul, MN: West.

Davis, Kenneth Culp (1961). "Ombudsman in America: Offer to Criticize Administrative Action." *University of Pennsylvania Law Review, 109,* 1057-1076.

Davis, Kenneth Culp (1964). "Behavioral Science and Administrative Law." *Journal of Administrative Law, 17,* 137-154.

Davis, Kenneth Culp (1969). *Discretionary Justice.* Urbana: University of Illinois Press.

Davis, Kenneth Culp (1971). *Administrative Law Treatise,* 1970 Supplement. St. Paul, MN: West.

Davis, Kenneth Culp (1972). *Administrative Law Text,* 3rd. ed. St. Paul, MN: West.

Dennett, D. C. (1978). *Brainstorms: Philosophical Essays on Mind and Psychology.* Cambridge: MIT Press.

Deutsch, K.W. et al. (1966). "The Yale Political Data Program." In Richard L. Merritt and Stein Rokkan (Eds.), *Comparing Nations: The Use of Quantitative Data in Cross-National Research,* pp. 81-94. New Haven: Yale University Press.

Deutsch, K. W. (1968). "The Probability of International Law." In Karl W. Deutsch and Stanley Hoffman (Eds.), *The Relevance of International Law in a Multicultural World.* Cambridge, MA: Schenkman.

Dickens, Linda (1978). "A.S.A.S. and the Union Recognition Procedure." *Industrial Law Journal, 4,* 160-177.

Domhoff, G. William (1967). *Who Rules America?* Englewood Cliffs, NJ: Prentice-Hall.

Downs, Anthony (1967). *Inside Bureaucracy.* Boston: Little, Brown.

Drobak, John N. (1972). "Computer Simulation and Gaming: An Interdisciplinary Survey with a View Toward Legal Applications." *Stanford Law Review, 24,* 712-729.

Drobnig, Ulrich (1972). "The International Encyclopedia of Comparative Law: Efforts Toward a Worldwide Comparison of Law." *Cornell International Law Journal, 5,* 113-129.

Dubin, Robert (1959). "Deviant Behavior and Social Structure: Continuities in Social Structure." *American Sociological Review, 24,* 147-164.

Dupuy, Rene-Jean (1984). "Conclusions of the Workshop." In Rene-Jean Dupuy (Ed.), *The Future of International Law in a Multi-Cultural World,* pp. 469-483. The Hague/Boston/London: Martinus Nijhoff.

Durkheim, Emile (1933). *The Division of Labor in Society.* Glencoe, IL: The Free Press.

Durkheim, Emile (1958). *Professional Ethics and Civic Morals.* Glencoe, IL: The Free Press.

"An Editorial." (1956). *Arbitration Journal,* 11.1, 1, 63.

Ehrlich, E. (1936). *Fundamental Principles of the Sociology of Law,* trans. by Walter L. Moll. Cambridge, MA: Harvard University Press.

Eisenstadt, S. N. and M. Curelaru (1977). "Macro-Sociology: Theory, Analysis, and Comparative Studies." *Current Sociology, 25,* 1-112.

Espiell, H. Gross (1979). "The Evolving Concept of Human Rights: Western, Socialist, and Third World Approaches." In B. G. Ramcharan (Ed.), *Human Rights: Thirty Years After the Universal Declaration,* pp. 41-65. The Hague: Martinus Nijhoff.

Evan, William M. (1957). "Dimensions of Participation in Voluntary Associations." *Social Forces, 35,* 48-53.

Evan, William M. (1959). "Power, Bargaining and Law: A Preliminary Analysis of Labor Arbitration Cases." *Social Problems, 6,* 4-15.

Evan, William M. (1962a). "Transnational Forums for Peace." In Quincy Wright, William M. Evan and Morton Deutsch (Eds.), *Preventing World War III.* New York: Simon and Schuster.

Evan, William M. (1962b). "Public and Private Legal Systems." In William M. Evan (Ed.), *Law and Sociology.* New York: The Free Press.

Evan, William M. (1962c). "Due Process of Law in Military and Industrial Organizations" *Administrative Science Quarterly, 7,* 203-207.

Evan, William M. (1962d). "Introduction: Some Approaches to the Sociology of Law." In William M. Evan (Ed.), *Law and Sociology: Exploratory Essays.* New York: The Free Press.

Evan, William M. (1965a). "Toward a Sociological Almanac of Systems." *International Social Science Journal, 17,* 335-338.

Evan, William M. (1965b). "Law as an Instrument of Social Change." In Alvin Gouldner and S. M. Miller (Eds.), *Applied Sociology: Opportunities and Problems,* pp. 285-293. New York: The Free Press.

Evan, William M. (1966). "The Organization-Set: Toward a Theory of Inter-Organizational Relations." In J. D. Thompson (Ed.), *Approaches to Organizational Design,* pp. 175-190. Pittsburgh: University of Pittsburgh Press.

Evan, William M. (1968). "A Data Archive of Legal Systems: A Cross-National Analysis of Sample Data." *European Journal of Sociology, 9,* 113-125.

Evan, William M. (Ed.) (1971). *Organizational Experiments.* New York: Harper and Row.

Evan, William M. (1972). "An Organization-Set Model of Interorganizational Relations." In M. F. Tuite, M. Radnor and R. K. Chisholm (Eds.), *Interorganizational Decision Making*, pp. 181-200. Chicago: Aldine.

Evan, William M. (1973, August 26). "An Ombudsman for Executives." *New York Times*.

Evan, William M. (1974). "Multinational Corporations and the International Professional Associations." *Human Relations, 27*, 587-625.

Evan, William M. (1975). "The International Sociological Association and the Internationalization of Sociology." *International Social Science Journal, 27*, 385-393.

Evan, William M. (1976a). *Organization Theory*. New York: John Wiley.

Evan, William M. (1976b). *Interorganizational Relations*. London: Penguin.

Evan, William M. (1976c). "Organization Theory and Organizational Effectiveness." *Organization and Administrative Sciences, 7*, 15-28.

Evan, William M. (1977). "Administrative Law and Organization Theory." *Journal of Legal Education, 29*, 106-125.

Evan, William M. (1978, August). "Systems Theory and Sociology of Law." Paper presented at Ninth World Congress of Sociology, Uppsala, Sweden.

Evan, William M. (1980). *The Sociology of Law*. New York: Free Press.

Evan, William M. (Ed.) (1981). *Knowledge and Power in a Global Society*. Beverly Hills, CA: Sage.

Evan, William M. (1984). "Macrosociology, Sociology of Law and Legal Indicators." In Uberto Scarpelli and Vincenzo Tomeo (Eds.), *Società Norme e Valore: Scritti in Onore di Renato Treves*. Milano: Dott. A. Giuffre Editore.

Evan, William M. (1986). "Human Rights, International Law and Legal Indicators." Paper presented at IXth World Congress of Sociology, New Delhi.

Evan, William M. and E. G. Levin (1966). "Status-Set and Role-Set Conflicts of the Stockbroker." *Social Forces, 45*, 73-83.

Evan, William M. and Mildred A. Schwartz (1964). "Law and the Emergence of Formal Organizations." *Sociology and Social Research, 48*, 270-280.

Falk, R. (1975). "A New Paradigm for International Legal Studies Prospects and Proposals." *Yale Law Journal, 84*, 969-1021.

Falk, R. (1983). *The End of World Order*. New York: Holmes and Meior.

Febbrajo, Alberto (1988). "From Hierarchical to Circular Models in the Sociology of Law: Some Introductory Remarks." *European Yearbook in the Sociology of Law*, 3-21.

Fellmeth, Robert C. (1970). *The Interstate Commerce Commission*. New York: Grossman.

Ferencz, B. B. (1988). *Planethood*. Coos Bay, OR: Vision Books.

Forkosch, Morris D. (1958). "American Democracy and Procedural Due Process." *Brooklyn Law Review, 24*, 176-195.

Forrester, Jay W. (1969). *Urban Dynamics*. Cambridge: MIT Press.

Forrester, Jay W. (1971). *World Dynamics*. Cambridge: Wright-Allen.

Freedman, James O. (1972). "Summary Action by Administrative Agencies." *University of Chicago Law Review, 40*, 1-65.

Friedmann, W. (1972). "Human Welfare and International Law—A Reordering of Priorities." In W. Friedmann, L. Henkin and O. Lissitzyn (Eds.), *Transnational Law in a Changing Society*. New York and London: Columbia University Press.

Fuller, L. L. (1964). *The Morality of Law*. New Haven and London: Yale University Press.

Galanter, Marc (1966). "The Modernization of Law." In Myron Weiner (Ed.), *Modernization*, pp. 153-165. New York: Basic Books.

Gamson, William A. (1966). "Rancorous Conflict in Community Politics." *American Sociological Review, 31*, 71-80.

Gastil, Raymond D. (1981). *Freedom in the World: Political Rights and Civil Liberties*. Westport, CT: Greenwood Press.

Gelhorn, Walter (1965). *When Americans Complain*. Cambridge, MA: Harvard University Press.

Gelhorn, Walter (1968). *Ombudsman and Others*. Cambridge, MA: Harvard University Press.

Glaser, William A. (1966). "International Mail Surveys of Informants." *Human Organization, 25*, 78-86.

Glaser, Willliam L. and Ralph L. Boisco (1966). "Plans of the Council of Social Science Data Archives." *Social Science Information, 5*, 71-96.

Glendon, Mary Ann (1975). "Power and Authority in the Family: New Legal Patterns as Reflections of Changing Ideologies." *American Journal of Comparative Law, 23*, 1-33.

Glendon, Mary Ann, Michael Wallace Gordon and Christopher Osakwe (1982). *Comparative Legal Traditions in a Nutshell*. St. Paul, MN: West.

Gold, David (1961). "Lawyers in Politics: An Empirical Exploration of Biographical Data on State Legislation." *Pacific Sociological Review, 4*, 84-86.

Goldberg, Stephen B. (1989). "Grievance Mediation: A Successful Alternative to Labor Arbitration." *Negotiation Journal, 5*, 9-15.

Goldman, Sheldon (1971). "American Judges: Their Selection, Tenure, Variety and Quality." *Current History, 61*, 1-8.

Gollub, Myron (1948). *Discharge for Cause*. State of New York, Department of Labor, Special Bulletin no. 211.

Gordon, Robert W. (1982). "New Developments in Legal Theory." In David Kairys (Ed.), *The Politics of Law*, pp. 281-293. New York: Pantheon.

Gouldner, Alvin W. (1959). "Reciprocity and Autonomy in Functional Theory." In Llewelyn Gross (Ed.), *Symposium on Sociological Theory*, pp. 241-270. Evanston, Il: Row, Peterson.

Grace, Olive and Phillip Wilkinson (1978). *Sociological Inquiry and Legal Phenomena*. New York: St. Martin's Press.

Gray, Herman A. (1948). "Nature and Scope of Arbitration and Arbitration Clauses." In Emmanuel Stein (Ed.), *Proceedings of New York University First Annual Conference on Labor*. New York: Mathew Bender.

Gross, B. M. (1966). "The State of the Nation: Social Systems Accounting." In R. A. Bauer (Ed.), *Social Indicators*, pp. 154-271. Cambridge: MIT Press.

Gross, Leo (1973). "International Terrorism and International Criminal Jurisdiction." *American Journal of International Law, 67*, 508-511.

Gross, N., Ward S. Mason and Alexander W. McEachern (1958). *Explorations in Role Analysis: Studies of the School Superintendency Role*. New York: John Wiley.

Grundstein, Nathan D. (1964). "Administrative Law and the Behavioral and Management Sciences." *Journal of Legal Education, 17*, 121-136.

Gurvitch, Georges (1947). *Sociology of Law*. London: Routledge and Kegan Paul.

Guzzardi, Walter, Jr. (1978, June 19). "How the Union Got the Upper Hand on J. P. Stevens." *Fortune Magazine*, 86-98.

Hage, Jerald (1974, August). "A Longitudinal Test of an Axiomatic Organizational Theory." Paper presented at Eighth World Congress of Sociology, Toronto.

Hale, Robert L. (1952). *Freedom Through Law*. New York: Columbia University Press.

Hall, Jerome (1963). *Comparative Law and Social Theory*. Baton Rouge: Louisiana State University Press.

Halloran, Norbert A. (1974). *Federal Agency Hearings: A Proposed Caseload Accounting System*. Washington, DC: Administrative Conference of the United States.

Hamilton, Walton (1957). *The Politics of Industry*. New York: Knopf.

Hart, H. L. A. (1961). *The Concept of Law*. Oxford: Clarendon.

Hart, Moira (1978). "Union Recognition in America—The Legislative Snare." *Industrial Law Journal, 7*, 201-215.

Hazard, John N. (1977). *Soviet Legal System: Fundamental Principles and Historical Commentary*, 3rd ed. Dobbs Ferry, NY: Oceana Press.

Heinz, John P. and Edward O. Laumann (1978). "The Legal Profession: Client, Interests, Professional Roles and Social Hierarchies." *Michigan Law Review, 76*, 1111-1142.

Henkin, Louis (1976). "Judaism and Human Rights." In *Judaism: A Quarterly Journal of Jewish Life and Thought, 25*, 437.

Henkin, Louis (1981a). "Preface and Introduction." In Louis Henkin (Ed.), *The International Bill of Rights*, ix-31. New York: Columbia University Press.

Henkin, Louis (1981b). "International Human Rights as Rights." In J. Roland Pennock and John W. Chapman (Eds.), *Human Rights*, pp. 257-280. New York: New York University Press.

Henriot, Peter J. (1972). *Political Aspects of Social Indicators: Implications for Research*. New York: Russell Sage Foundation.

Heydebrand, Wolf V. (1973). *Comparative Organizations*. Englewood Cliffs, NJ: Prentice-Hall.

Hickson, D. J., D. S. Pugh and Diana Pheysey (1969, September). "Operations Technology and Organizational Structure: An Empirical Reappraisal." *Administrative Science Quarterly, 14*, 378-398.

Hickson, D. J., C. R. Hinnings, C. J. McMillan and J. P. Schwitter (1974). "The Culture-Free Context of Organization Structure: A Tri-National Comparison." *Sociology, 8*, 50-80.

Hoebel, E. Adamson (1954). *The Law of Primitive Man: A Study in Comparative Legal Dynamics*. Cambridge, MA: Harvard University Press.

Holdaway, Edward and Thomas A. Blowers (1971). "Administrative Ratios and Organization Size: A Longitudinal Examination." *American Sociological Review, 36*, 278-286.

Holsti, O. R. (1969). *Content Analysis for the Social Sciences and Humanities*. Reading, MA: Addison-Wesley.

Horwitz, Morton J. (1977). *The Transformation of American Law 1780-1860*. Cambridge, MA: Harvard University Press.

Humana, Charles (1983). *World Human Rights Guide*. London: Hutchinson.

Humphrey, John P. (1979). "The Universal Declaration of Human Rights: Its History, Impact and Juridical Character." In B. G. Ramcharan (Ed.), *Human Rights: Thirty Years After the Universal Declaration*, pp. 21-37. The Hague: Martinus Nijhoff.

Hunt, Alan (1978). *The Social Movement in Law*. Philadelphia: Temple University Press.

Inkeles, A. (1975). "The Emerging Social Structure of the World." *World Politics, 27*, 467-495.

International Monetary Fund (1989). *World Economic Outlook: A Survey by the Staff of the International Monetary Fund*. Washington, DC: IMF.

Jessup, P. C. (1956). *Transnational Law*. New Haven: Yale University Press.

Jacob, Herbert (1988). *Silent Revolution: The Transformation of Divorce Law in the United States*. Chicago: University of Chicago Press.

Jaffe, Louis L. (1937). "Law Making by Private Groups." *Harvard Law Review, 51*, 213.

Jaffe, Louis L. (1973). "The Illusion of the Ideal Administration." *Harvard Law Review, 86*, 1188-1190.

James, B. and R. C. Simpson (1978). "Grunwick vs. A.C.A.S." *Modern Law Review, 41*, 572-581.

James, Bernard (1977). "Third Party Intervention in Recognition Disputes: The Role of the Commission on Industrial Relations." *Industrial Relations Journal, 8*, 29-40.

Joelson, Mark R. (1963). "Legal Problems in the Dismissal of Civil Servants in the U.S., Britain, and France." *American Journal of Comparative Law, 12*, 147-171.

Johnston, Denis F. and Michael J. Carley (1981). "Social Measurement and Social Indicators." *Annals of the American Academy of Political and Social Science, 453*, 237-253.

Joint Board of Dress and Waistmakers' Union of Greater New York vs. Aywon Dress Co., Inc.-Affiliated Dress Manufacturers, 1939.

Joskow, Paul I. (1973). "Cartels, Competition and Regulation in the Property-Liability Insurance Industry."*Bell Journal of Economics and Management Science, 4*, 426.

Kahn-Freund, O. (1966). "Comparative Law as an Academic Subject." *Law Quarterly Review, 82*, 40.

Kairys, David (Ed.) (1982). *The Politics of Law*. New York: Pantheon.

Kamenka, Eugene (1978). "The Anatomy of an Idea." In Eugene Kamenka and Alice Ehr-Soon Tay (Eds.), *Human Rights*, pp. 1-12. London: Edward Arnold.

Kamenka, Eugene and Alice Erh-Soon Tay (Eds.) (1978). *Human Rights*. London: Edward Arnold.

Kass, B. L. (1966, November). "We Can, Indeed, Fight City Hall: The Office and Concept of Ombudsman." *Administrative Law Review, 19*.

Keohane, J. R. O. and J. S. Nye (Eds.) (1972). *Transnational Relations and World Politics*. Cambridge, MA: Harvard University Press.

Kimberly, John R. (1974, August). "Some Issues in Longitudinal Organizational Research." Paper presented at the Meetings of the American Sociological Association.

Kochan, Thomas A. (1987). "Labor Arbitration and Collective Bargaining in the 1990's: An Economic Analysis." In Walter J. Gershenfeld (Ed.), *Proceedings of* the *Thirty-Ninth Annual Meeting, 1986. Arbitration 1986: Current and Expanding Roles*, pp. 44-60. Washington, DC: Bureau of National Affairs.

Kothari, Rajni (1974). *Footsteps into the Future*. New York: Free Press.

Kristof, Nicholas D. (1988). "What's the Law in China? It's No Secret (Finally)." *New York Times*, November 20.

Kuhn, T. S. (1970). *The Structure of Scientific Revolution*, 2nd ed. Chicago: Chicago University Press.

Kutschinsky, Berl (1966). "Law and Education: Some Aspects of Scandinavian Studies into 'The General Sense of Justice.' " *Acta Sociologica*, 10, 21-41.

Labor Arbitration Reports (1946). Washington, DC: Bureau of National Affairs.

Land, Kenneth C. and Seymour Spilerman (Eds.) (1975). *Social Indicator Models*. New York: Russell Sage Foundation.

Landis, James M. (1960). *Report on Regulatory Agencies to the President Elect*. Washington, DC: Government Printing Office.

Lasswell, H. D. (1963). *The Future of Political Science*. New York: Atherton.

Lasswell, H. D. (1971). *A Preview of Policy Sciences*. New York: Elsevier.

Laszlo, C. A., M. D. Levine and J. H. Milsum (1974). "A General Systems Framework for Social Systems." *Behavioral Science*, 19, 79-92.

Laumann, Edward O. and John P. Heinz (1977). "Specialization and Prestige in the Legal Profession: The Structure of Deference." *American Bar Foundation Research Journal*, 1977, 155-216.

Lazar, Joseph (1953). *Due Process on the Railroads*. Los Angeles: University of California, Institute of Industrial Relations.

Lazarsfeld, Paul F. and Herbert Menzel (1961). "On the Relation Between Individual and Collective Properties." In Amitai Etzioni (Ed.), *Complex Organizations: A Sociological Reader*, pp. 428-429. New York: Holt, Rinehart, and Winston.

Le Grand, Camille E. (1973). "Rape and Rape Laws: Sexism in Society and Law." *California Law Review, 61*, 919-941.

Lidz, Victor (1979). "The Law as Index, Phenomenon and Element—Conceptual Steps Towards a General Sociology of Law." *Sociology Inquiry, 49*, 5-25.

Lillich, Richard B. (1978). "The Role of Domestic Courts in Promoting International Human Rights Norms." In James C. Tuttle (Ed.), *International Human Rights Law and Practice*. Philadelphia: American Bar Association.

Linton, R. (1936). *The Study of Man*. New York: Appleton-Century.

Lipset, Seymour Martin (1959). "Some Social Requisites of Democracy: Economic Development and Political Legitimacy." *Political Science Review, 53*, 69-106.

Lipset, S. M., M. Trow and J. Coleman (1956). *Union Democracy*. New York: Free Press.

Litwak, Eugene (1970). "Toward the Theory and Practice of Coordination Between Formal Organizations." In William R. Rosengren and Mark Lefton (Eds.), *Organizations and Clients*. Columbus, OH: Charles E. Merrill.

Luhman, Niklas (1982). *The Differentiation of Society*. New York: Columbia University Press.

Luhman, Niklas (1985). *A Sociological Theory of Law*, transl. by Elizabeth King and Martin Albrow. London: Routledge and Kegan Paul.

Luhman, Niklas (1986). "The Self-Reproduction of Law and its Limits." In Gunther Teubner (Ed.), *Dilemmas of Law in the Welfare State*. Berlin: Walter de Gruyter.

Luhman, Niklas (1988a). "The Sociological Observation of the Theory and Practice of Law", pp. 23-42. *European Yearbook in the Sociology of Law*.

Luhman, Niklas (1988b). "The Unity of Legal System." In Gunther Teubner (Ed.), *Autopoietic Law: A New Approach to Law and Society*, pp. 21-35. Berlin: Walter de Gruyter.

Luhman, Niklas (1988c). "Closure and Openness: On Reality in the World of Law." In Gunther Teubner (Ed.), *Autopoietic Law: A New Approach to Law and Society*, pp. 335-348. Berlin: Walter de Gruyter.

MacAvoy, Paul W. (1970). *The Crisis of the Regulatory Commissions*. New York: Norton.

MacCoun, Robert J. (1989). "Experimental Research on Jury Decision-Making." *Science, 244*, 1046-1050.

Makela, Klaus (1966). "Public Sense of Justice and Judicial Practice," *Acta Sociologica, 10*, 42-67.

March, J. G. and H. A. Simon (1958). *Organizations*. New York: John Wiley.

Marshall, T. H. (1964). *Class, Citizenship and Social Development*. Garden City, NY: Doubleday.

Maruyama, Magoroh (1963). "The Second Cybernetics: Deviation-Amplifying Mutual Causal Processes." *American Scientist, 51*, 164-179.

Mathews, Donald R. (1954). *The Social Background of Political Decision-Makers*. Garden City, NY: Doubleday.

Maturana, Humberto R. and Francisco J. Varela (1980). *Autopoiesis and Cognition*. Dordrecht, Holland: D. Reidel.

McCamant, J. F. (1981). "A Critique of Present Measures of Human Rights Development." In V. P. Nanda, J. R. Scarritt and G. W. Shepherd, Jr. (Eds.), *Global Human Rights: Public Policies, Comparative Measures, and NGO Strategies*. Boulder, CO: Westview.

McCormick, Charles (1954). *Handbook of the Law of Evidence*. St. Paul, MN: West.

McDougal, M. S. and Lasswell, H. D. (1966). "The Identification and Appraisal of Diverse Systems of Public Order." In R. Falk and S. H. Mendlovitz (Eds.), *The Strategy of World Order, International Law, vol. II*, pp. 44-86. New York: World Law Fund.

McDougal, M. S. and Lasswell, H. D. (1985). "The Identification and Appraisal of Diverse Systems of Public Order." In R. Falk, F. Kratchowil and S. H. Mendlovitz (Eds.), *International Law: A Contemporary Perspective*. Boulder and London: Westview.

McDougal, Myres S. and Florentino P. Feliciano (1961). *Law and Minimum World Public Order*. New Haven, CT: Yale University Press.

McMillan, Charles J. (1973). "The Structure of Work Organization Across Societies." *Academy of Management Journal, 16*, 555-569.

McRuer, James C. (1957). *The Evolution of the Judicial Process*. Toronto: Clarke, Irwin.

Mentschikoff, Soia (1952). "The Significance of Arbitration—A Preliminary Inquiry." *Law and Contemporary Problems, 17*, 698.

Merrill, Fredrick and Linus Schrage (1969). "Efficient Use of Jurors: A Field Study and Simulation Model of a Court System." *Washington University Law Quarterly,* 151-183.

Merritt, Richard L. and Stein Rokkan (Eds.) (1966). *Comparing Nations: The Use of Quantitative Data in Cross-National Research.* New Haven, CT: Yale University Press.

Merryman, John H. (1974). "Comparative Law and Scientific Experiments." In J. N. Hazard and W. J. Wagner (Eds.), *Law in the United States of America in Social and Technical Revolution,* pp. 81-104. Brussels, Belgium: Etablissements Emile Bruylant.

Merryman, John Henry, David S. Clark and Lawrence M. Friedman (1972). *Marriage Stability, Divorce and the Law.* Chicago: University of Chicago Press.

Merryman, John Henry, David S. Clark and Lawrence M. Friedman (1979). *Law and Social Change in Mediterranean Europe and Latin America.* Stanford, CA: Stanford Law School.

Merton, Robert K. (1957). *Social Theory and Social Structure,* rev. ed. Glencoe, IL: Free Press.

Meyer, Marshall W. (1972). *Bureaucratic Structure and Authority.* New York: Harper and Row.

Miller, James Grier (1978). *Living Systems.* New York: McGraw-Hill.

Mills, C. Wright (1956). *The Power Elite.* New York: Oxford University Press.

Milne, A. J. M. (1986). *Human Rights and Human Diversity.* New York: State University of New York Press.

Moody's Industrial (1957). New York: Moody's Investors Service.

Moore, Ernestine M. and James Nix (1953). "Arbitration Provisions in Collective Bargaining Agreements." *Monthly Labor Review, 76,* 261-266.

Moore, Wilbert E. (1951). *Industrial Relations and the Social Order.* New York: Macmillan.

Moore, Wilbert E. (1957). "Management and Union Organizations: An Analytical Comparison." In Conrad M. Arsenberg et al. *Research in Industrial Human Relations.* New York: Harper.

Moore, Wilbert E. (1966). "Global Sociology: The World as a Singular System." *American Journal of Sociology, 71,* 475-482.

Morris, R. T. (1956). "A Typology of Norms." *American Sociological Review, 21,* 610-613.

Murdock, George Peter (1963). *Outline of World Cultures,* 3rd ed. New Haven, CT: Human Relations Area Files.

Murphy, John F. (1974). "Professor Gross's Comments on International Criminal Jurisdiction." *American Journal of International Law, 68,* 306-308.

Nadel, F. (1957). *The Theory of Social Structure.* Glencoe, IL: Free Press.

Nader, Laura and David Serber (1976). "Law and the Distribution of Power." In A. Coser Lewis and Otto N. Larsen (Eds.), *The Uses of Controversy in Sociology.* New York: Free Press.

Nagel, Stuart S. (1962). "Culture Patterns and Judicial Systems." *Vanderbilt Law Review, 16,* 151-152.

Naroll, R. (1983). *The Moral Order.* Beverly Hills, CA: Sage.

National Science Board (1987). *Science and Engineering Indicators—1987.* Washington, DC: Government Printing Office.

Nasatir, David (1967). "Social Science Data Libraries." *American Sociologist, 2,* 207-212.

Nonet, Phillip (1969). *Administrative Justice.* New York: Russell Sage Foundation.

Office of the Federal Register (1973). *Code of Federal Regulations, The President,* Appendix, 1972 Compilation. Washington, DC: Government Printing Office.

Orfield, Lester B. (1953). *The Growth of Scandinavian Law.* Philadelphia: University of Pennsylvania Press.

Organisation for Economic Co-operation and Development (1988). *Main Science and Technology Indicators, 1981-1987.* Paris: OECD.

Pagels, Elaine (1979). "The Roots of Origins of Human Rights." In Alice H. Henkin (Ed.), *Human Dignity: The Internationalization of Human Rights,* pp. 1-8. New York: The Aspen Institute of Humanistic Studies.

Palamountain, Joseph Cornwall (1955). *The Politics of Distribution.* Cambridge, MA: Harvard University Press.

Park, Han S. (1980). "Human Rights and Modernization: A Dialectical Relationship." *Universal Human Rights, 2,* 92-95.

Parsons, Talcott (1961). "An Outline of the Social System." In Talcott Parsons et al. (Eds.), *Theories of Society,* vol. 1, pp. 30-79. New York: Free Press.

Parsons, Talcott (1962). "The Law and Social Control." In William M. Evan (Ed.), *The Law and Sociology,* pp. 56-72. New York: Free Press.

Parsons, Talcott (1966). *Societies: Evolutionary and Comparative Perspectives.* Englewood Cliffs, NJ: Prentice-Hall.

Parsons, Talcott (1978). "Law as an Intellectual Stepchild." In Harry M. Johnson (Ed.), *Social System and Legal Process,* pp. 11-58. San Francisco: Jossey Bass.

Paul, K. (1987). "The Inadequacy of Sullivan Reporting." In S. Prakash Sethi (Ed.), *The South African Quagmire: In Search of a Peaceful Path to Democratic Pluralism.* Cambridge, MA: Ballinger.

Peel, Roy V. (Ed.) (1968). "The Ombudsman or Citizen's Defender: A Modern Institution." *Annals of American Academy of Political and Social Science, 377,* ix-138.

Pennock, J. Roland (1981). "Rights, Natural Rights, and Human Rights—A General View." In J. Roland Pennock and John W. Chapman (Eds.), *Human Rights.,* pp. 1-28. New York: New York University Press.

Podgórecki, Adam, et al. (1973). *Knowledge and Opinion About Law.* London: Martin Robertson.

Podgórecki, Adam (1974). *Law and Society.* London: Routledge and Kegan Paul.

Pollis, A. and Schwab, P. (Eds.), (1974). *Human Rights: Cultural and Ideological Perspectives.* New York: Praeger.

Pool, Ithiel de Sola (1967). "Computer Simulations of Total Societies." In Samuel Z. Klausner (Ed.), *The Study of Total Societies,* pp. 45-65. New York: Anchor Books.

Posner, Richard A. (1970). "A Statistical Study of Antitrust Enforcement." *Journal of Law and Economics, 13,* 419.

Posner, Richard A. (1972). "The Behavior of Administrative Agencies." *Journal of Legal Studies, 1,* 305-347.

Pound, Roscoe (1917). "The Limits of Effective Legal Action." *American Bar Association Journal, 3,* 55-70.

Pound, Roscoe (1923). *Interpretation of Legal History.* New York: McMillan.

Pugh, D. S. et al. (1968). "Dimensions of Organization Structure." *Administrative Science Quarterly, 13,* 65-105.

Pugh, D. S. et al. (1969). "Context of Organizational Structures." *Administrative Science Quarterly, 14,* 91-114.

Rabinowitz, R. W. (1956). "The Historical Development of the Japanese Bar." *Harvard Law Review, 70,* 61-81.

Ramcharan, B. G. (1979). "Implementing the International Covenants on Human Rights." In B. G. Ramcharan (Ed.), *Human Rights: Thirty Years After the Universal Declaration,* pp. 159-195. The Hague: Martinus Nijhoff.

Raskin, A. H. (1959, May 11). "A Contrast in Unions." *New York Times.*

Retzlaff, Ralph H. (1965). "The Use of Aggregate Data on Comparative Political Analysis." *Journal of Politics, 28,* 797-817.

Rheinstein, Max (Ed.) (1954). *Max Weber on Law in Economy and Society.* Cambridge, MA: Harvard University Press.

Rheinstein, Max (1972). *Marriage Stability, Divorce and the Law.* Chicago: University of Chicago Press.

Riesman, David (1962). "Law and Sociology: Recruitment, Training, and Colleagueship." In William M. Evan (Ed.), *Law and Sociology,* pp. 12-55. New York: Free Press.

Rose, Arnold M. (1954). *Theory and Method in the Social Sciences.* Minneapolis: University of Minnesota Press.

Rose, Arnold M. (1961). "On Individualism and Social Responsibility." *European Journal of Sociology, 2,* 161-169.

Rosenberg, Maurice (1964). *Pre-Trial Conference and Effective Justice: A Controlled Test in Personal Injury Litigation.* New York: Columbia University Press.

Ross, H. Laurence (1977). "Deterrence Regained: The Cheshire Constabulary's Breathalyser Blitz." *Journal of Legal Studies, 6,* 241-249.

Rowat, D. C. (1968). *The Ombudsman: Citizen's Defender,* 2nd ed. London: George, Allen, and Unwin.

Rowe, W. D. (1968). "A Model of Bureaucratic Growth Using GPSS." In Arnold Okene (Ed.), *Second Conference on Applications of Simulation.* New York: SHARE, ACM, IEEE, SCI.

Rueschmeyer, Dietrich (1973). *Lawyers and Their Society.* Cambridge, MA: Harvard University Press.

Ruml, Beardsley (1950). "Corporate Management as a Locus of Power." In Edward N. Cahn (Ed.), *Social Meaning of Legal Concepts,* no. 3. New York: New York University School of Law.

Russet, Bruce et al. (Eds.) (1964). *World Handbook of Political and Social Indicators.* New Haven, CT: Yale University Press.

Sarat, Austin (1975). "Knowledge, Attitudes and Behavior." *American Politics Quarterly, 3,* 3-24.

Savatier, Rene (1952). "Law and Progress of Techniques." *International Social Science Bulletin, 4,* 309-319.

Scarman, Lord Justice (1977). *Report of a Court of Inquiry into a Dispute Between Grunwick Processing Laboratories Limited and Members of the Association of Professional, Executive, Clerical and Computer Staff,* Cmnd 8922. London: H.M.S. Stationery Office.

Schlesinger, Rudolf B. (1961). "The Common Core of Legal Systems: An Emergent Subject of Comparative Study." In Kurt H. Nadelman, Arthur T. von Mehren and John N. Hazard (Eds.), *XXth Century Comparative and Conflict Law: Legal Essays in Honor of Hessel E. Yntema,* pp. 65-79. Leiden: A. W. Sythoff.

Schlossberg, Stephen I. (1988). "Challenge and Change." In Gladys W. Gruenberg (Ed.), *National Academy of Arbitrators: Proceedings of the Fortieth Annual Meeting, 1987. Arbitration 1987: The Academy at 40,* pp. 13-24. Washington, DC: The Bureau of National Affairs.

Schneider, Eugene V. (1957). *Industrial Sociology.* New York: McGraw-Hill.

Schwartz, Bernard and H. W. R. Wade (1972). *Legal Control of Government: Administrative Law in Britain and the United States.* Oxford: Clarendon.

Schwartz, R. D. (1961). "Field Experimentation in Sociological Research." *Journal of Legal Education, 13,* 401-410.

Schwartz, R. D. (1974). "Legal Evolution and the Durkheim Hypothesis: A Reply to Professor Baxi." *Law and Society Review, 8,* 653-668.

Schwartz, R. D. and J. C. Miller (1964). "Legal Evolution and Societal Complexity." *American Journal of Sociology, 70,* 159-169.

Scoble, H. M. and L. S. Wiseberg (1981). "Problems and Comparative Research on Human Rights." In Ved P. Nanda, James R. Scarritt and George W. Shepherd, Jr. (Eds.), *Global Human Rights: Public Policies, Comparative Measures and NGO Strategies,* pp. 147-171. Boulder, CO: Westview.

Selznick, Phillip (1949). *TVA and the Grass Roots: A Study in the Sociology of Formal Organizations.* Berkeley: University of California Press.

Selznick, Phillip (1959). "Sociology of Law." In Robert K. Merton, Leonard Broom and Leonard S. Cottrell (Eds.), *Sociology Today.* New York: Basic Books.

Sheldon, Eleanor B. and Wilbert E. Moore (Eds.), (1968). *Indicators of Social Change.* New York: Russell Sage Foundation.

Sheldon, Eleanor B. and Kenneth C. Land (1972). "Social Reporting for the 1970's: A Review and Programmatic Statement." *Policy Sciences, 3,* 137-151.

Shelleff, L. S. (1975). "From Restitutive Law to Repressive Law: Durkheim's Division of Labor in Society Revisited." *European Journal of Sociology, 16,* 16-45.

Shister, Joseph (Ed.) (1956). *Readings in Labor Economics and Industrial Relations.* Philadelphia: Lippincott.

Shue, H. (1980). *Basic Rights: Subsistence, Affluence and U.S. Foreign Policy.* Princeton, NJ: Princeton University Press.

Shulman, Harry (n.d.). *Opinions of the Umpires: Ford Motor Co. and UAW-CIO, 1943-1946.*

Shulman, Harry (1955). "Reason, Contract and Law in Labor Relations." *Harvard Law Review, 68,* 999-1024.

Shulman, Harry (1956). "The Arbitration Process." In Joseph Shister (Ed.), *Readings in Labor Economics and Industrial Relations.* New York: Lippincott.

Sigler, J. A. (1968). "A Cybernetic Model of the Judicial System." *Temple Law Quarterly, 41,* 398-427.

Singh, Nagendra (1982). *Human Rights and the Future of Mankind.* Atlantic Highlands, NJ: Humanities Press.

Singh, Ram (1979). "Towards Applicable Theory in Industrial Relations Using a Systems Approach." *Journal of Applied Systems Analysis, 6,* 15-24.

Skilton, Robert H. (1952). *Industrial Discipline and the Arbitration Process.* Philadelphia: Labor Relations Council of the Wharton School of Finance and Commerce, University of Pennsylvania.

Skjelsbaek, K. (1972). "The Growth of International Nongovernmental Organizations in the Twentieth Century." In J. R. O. Keohane and J. S. Nye (Eds.), *Transnational Relations and World Politics,* pp. 70-92. Cambridge, MA: Harvard University Press.

Smigel, Erwin O. (1969). *The Wall Street Lawyer.* Bloomington, IN: Indiana University Press.

Sprudzs, Adolf (1980). "The International Encyclopedia of Comparative Law: A Bibliographical Status Report." *American Journal of Comparative Law, 27,* 93-104.

Standen, Jeffery (1986). "Critical Legal Studies as an Anti-Positivist Phenomenon." *Virginia Law Review, 72,* 983-998.

Starke, J. G. (1978). "Human Rights and International Law." In Eugene Kamenka and Alice Ehr-Soon Tay (Eds.), *Human Rights,* pp. 113-131. London: Edward Arnold.

Stigler, George G. and Claire Friedland (1962). "What Can Regulators Regulate? The Case of Electricity." *Journal of Law and Economics, 5,* 1-16.

Strauss, Donald B. (1949). *Hickey-Freeman Company and Amalgamated Clothing Workers of America: A Case Study.* Washington, DC: National Planning Association.

Strouse, James C. and Richard P. Claude (1976). "Empirical Comparative Rights Research: Some Preliminary Tests of Development Hypotheses." In Richard P. Claude (Ed.), *Comparative Human Rights,* pp. 51-67. Baltimore, MD: Johns Hopkins University Press.

Sumner, William Graham (1906). *Folkways.* Boston, MA: Ginnard.

Sutherland, Edwin H. (1949). *White Collar Crime.* New York: Holt, Rinehart, and Winston.

Tapp, June Louin and Felice J. Levine (1974). "Legal Socialization: Strategies for an Ethical Legality." *Stanford Law Review, 27,* 1-72.

Taylor, Charles Lewis and Michael C. Hudson (Eds.), (1972). *Political and Social Indicators,* 2nd ed. New Haven, CT: Yale University Press.

Teubner, Gunther (1983a). "Substantive and Reflexive Elements in Modern Law." *Law and Society Review, 17,* 239-285.

Teubner, Gunther (1983b). "Autopoiesis in Law and Society: A Rejoinder to Blankenburg." *Law and Society Review, 18,* 291-301.

Teubner, Gunther (1988a). *Autopoietic Law: A New Approach to Law and Society.* Berlin: Walder de Gruyter.

Teubner, Gunther (1988b). "Hypercycle in Law and Organization: The Relationship Between Self-Observation, Self-Construction and Autopoiesis." In *European Yearbook in the Sociology of Law,* pp. 43-79.

The President's Advisory Council on Executive Organization (1971). *A New Regulatory Framework: Report on Selected Independent Regulatory Agencies.* Washington, DC: Government Printing Office.

Thibaut, J. Laurens Walker and E. Allen Lind (1972). "Adversary Presentation and Bias in Legal Decision Making." *Harvard Law Review, 86,* 387.

Timasheff, N. S. (1939). *An Introduction to the Sociology of Law.* Cambridge, MA: Harvard University Committee on Research in the Social Sciences.

Trubek, David M. (1972). "Max Weber on Law and the Rise of Capitalism." *Wisconsin Law Review, 730.* (Quoted in Alan Watson, [1981] *The Making of the Civil Law,* p. 230. Cambridge, MA: Harvard University Press)

Trubek, David M. (1984). "Where the Action Is: Critical Legal Studies of Empiricism." *Stanford Law Review, 36,* 575.

Trubek, David M. and John Esser (1989). " 'Critical Empiricism' in American Legal Studies: Paradox, Program, or Pandora's Box." *Law and Social Inquiry, 14,* 3-52.

Turner, Johnathan H. (1980). "Legal System Evolution: An Analytical Model." In William M. Evan (Ed.), *The Sociology of Law,* pp. 377-394. New York: Free Press.

Turner, James S. (1970). *The Chemical Feast.* New York: Grossman.

Tumin, Melvin (1956). "Some Dysfunctions of Institutional Imbalances." *Behavioral Science, 1,* 218-223.

United Automobile Workers (1957-58). *First Annual Report of the Public Review Board to the membership of the UAW.*

United Nations (1980). *United Nations Action in the Field of Human Rights.* New York: United Nations.

United Nations (1983). *Multilateral Treaties Deposited with the Secretary-General.* New York: United Nations.

United Nations (1988). *Statistical Yearbook,* 1985-1986. New York: United Nations.

U.N. Economic and Social Council, Report by the Secretariat, "Criminal Statistics: Standard Classification of Offenses." E/CN 5/357, March 2, 1959 (Mimeo).

Umpire, Ford Motor Co., and UAW-CIO (1948). *Discharge for Theft,* Case nos. 5867, 5869, 5872, 5990. Highland Park, Local 400, Opinion A-256.

U.S. Bureau of the Census (1954). *Census of Manufacturers, vol. II, Industry Statistics.* Washington, DC: Government Printing Office.

U.S. Department of Commerce, Bureau of Census (1980). *Social Indicators III.* Washington, DC: Government Printing Office.

U.S. Department of Labor, Bureau of Labor Statistics (1942-1952). *Arbitration of Labor-Management Grievances: Bethlehem Steel Company and United Steelworkers of America,* Bulletin no. 1159.

U.S. Department of State (1979). *Country Reports on Human Rights Practices for 1978.* Washington, DC: Government Printing Office.

U.S. Department of State (1984). *Country Reports on Human Rights Practices for 1983.* Washington, DC: Government Printing Office.

Ury, William L., Brett, Jeanne M. and Goldberg, Stephen (1988). *Getting Disputes Resolved.* San Francisco, CA: Jossey-Bass.

Vanyo, James P. (1971). "Dynamics of the Legal Process and Environmental Law." *California Trial Lawyers Journal, X ,* 44-50.

Vanyo, James P. (1974). "The Legal System: Can It Be Analyzed to Suit the Scientist?" In William A. Thomas (Ed.), *Scientists in the Legal System: Tolerated Meddlers or Essential Contributors?* pp. 55-66. Ann Arbor, MI: Ann Arbor Science Publishers.

Varela, Francisco (1979). *The Principle of Autonomy.* New York: North Holland.

von Bertalanffy, Ludwig (1968). *General System Theory.* New York: G. Braziller.

Wai, D. M. (1979). "Human Rights in Sub-Saharan Africa." In Adamantia Pollis and Peter Schwab (Eds.), *Human Rights: Cultural and Ideological Perspectives,* pp. 115-144. New York: Praeger

Watson, Alan (1974). *Legal Transplants: An Approach to Comparative Law.* Charlottesville: University of Virginia Press.

Watson, Alan (1978). "Comparative Law and Legal Change." *Cambridge Law Journal, 37,* 313-336.

Watson, Alan (1981). *The Making of Civil Law.* Cambridge, MA: Harvard University Press.

Watson, Alan (1983). "Legal Change, Sources of Law and Legal Culture." *University of Pennsylvania Law Review, 131,* 1121-1157.

Watson, Alan (1985). *The Evolution of Law.* Baltimore: Johns Hopkins University Press.

Watson, Alan (1987). "Legal Evolution and Legislation." *Brigham Young University Law Review,* 353-379.

Weber, Max (1947). *Theory of Social and Economic Organization,* trans. by A. M. Henderson and Talcott Parsons. New York: Oxford University Press.

Weber, Max (1950). *General Economic History.* Glencoe, IL: Free Press.

Weber, Max (1954). *Law in Economy and Society,* trans. by Edward Shils and Max Rheinstein. Cambridge, MA: Harvard University Press.

Weedon, Jr., D. R. (1987). "The Evolution of the Sullivan Principle." In S. Prakash Sethi (Ed.), *The South African Quagmire: In Search of a Peaceful Path to Democratic Pluralism.* Cambridge, MA: Ballinger.

Weitzman, Lenore J. (1985). *The Divorce Revolution: The Unexpected Social and Economic Consequences for Women and Children in America.* New York: Free Press.

Whitney, Fred (1957). *The Collective Bargaining Argument.* Bloomington, IN: Indiana University School of Business, Bureau of Business Research.

Wigmore, John H. (1928). *A Panorama of the World's Legal Systems.* St. Paul, MN: West.

Wigmore, John H. (1940). *A Treatise on the Anglo-American System of Evidence in Trials at Common Law.* Boston: Little, Brown.

Wilking, L. H. (1987). "Should the U.S. Corporations Abandon South Africa?" In S. Prakash Sethi (Ed.), *The South African Quagmire: In Search of a Peaceful Path to Democratic Pluralism.* Cambridge, MA: Ballinger.

Whitney, Fred (1957). *The Collective Bargaining Agreement.* Bloomington: Indiana University School of Business, Bureau of Business Research.

Witte, Edwin E. (1952). *Historical Survey of Labor Arbitration.* Philadelphia: University of Pennsylvania Press.

Woetzel, Robert K. (1974). "Professor John F. Murphy's Letter on Professor Gross's Comments on International Terrorism and International Criminal Jurisdiction." *American Journal of International Law, 68,* 717-718.

World Bank (1989). *World Tables, 1988-1989 Edition.* Baltimore: Johns Hopkins University Press.

World Peace Through Law Center (1965). *Law and Judicial Systems of Nations.* Washington, DC: World Peace Through Law Center.

Wright, Quincy (1966). "Toward a Universal Law for Mankind." In Richard A. Falk and Saul H. Mendlovitz (Eds.), *Toward a Theory of War Preventions*, vol. 1. New York: World Law Fund.

Wyzanski, Charles E., Jr. (1979). "The Philosophical Background of the Doctrines of Human Rights." In Alice H. Henkin (Ed.), *Human Dignity: The Internationalization of Human Rights*, pp. 9-13. New York: Aspen Institute of Humanistic Studies.

Zeisel, Hans (1973). "Reflections on Experimental Techniques in the Law." *Journal of Legal Studies*, 2, 107-124.

Zeisel, Hans, Harry Kalven and Bernard Bucholz (1959). *Delay in the Court.* Boston: Little, Brown.

Zeleny, Milan (1980). *Autopoiesis, Dissipative Structures and Spontaneous Social Orders.* Boulder, CO: Westview Press (for the American Association for the Advancement of Sciences).

Zimring, Franklin and Gordon Hawkins (1971). "The Legal Threat as an Instrument of Social Change." *Journal of Social Issues*, 27, 33-48.

Author Index

Subject Index

action, theory of, 29

administrative law, 86-108; and judicial law, 89; component of social-structure model, 86; constitutional bases of, 90; delegation of powers in, 90-94; FCC as organization-set model of, 102-103; focal organization in, 101; life-cycle hypothesis of, 95; limits of powers of, 110; problems in, 96; organization-set model of, 86-108; quasi-field experiments in, 107; regulatory agencies in, 93-95; research strategies in, 106-108; role of ombudsman in, 92; stages of development of, 90-91; specialization in, 100; trends in, 89-96; variables in, 104-105; vis-à-vis sociology of law, 87

Administrative Procedure Act of 1946, 91

Age Discrimination Act of 1967, 234

Amalgamated clothing and Textile Workers Union *vs.* J. P. Stevens & Co., 110-115, 120; *see also* collective bargaining

American Arbitration Association, 142

American Bar Association, 79, 96

American Medical Association, in malpractice suits, 130

Americanists, 49

Amnesty International, 189, 200, 205, 206, 207, 240

Amnesty International and laws, 200-207; as part of international law, 184-213; juridical rules in, 187; implementation of, 184-187; in Third World countries, 196-198, 207; legal indicators in, 187-195; on human rights, 180-216; transnational, 200-213; *see also* human rights issues

antipositivist philosophy, 36-37

Anti-Slavery Movement, 227

arbitration, legalistic approach to, 149-153; *see also* collective bargaining

autopoietic law, theory of, 32, 38-46; definition of, 40; systems of, 41, 45

Bill of Rights, 57, 124

Bureau of Labor Statistics, 142, 147

bureaucracies, in law profession, 170; Weber's theory of, 87, 88, 97

capitalist societies, legal order in, 36; superstructure of, 24

Categorical Imperative, of Immanuel Kant, 201

Civil Rights Act of 1964, 157, 158, 226, 234; class hegemony, 24; implementation of, 158

About the Author

William M. Evan is Professor of Sociology and Management at the University of Pennsylvania. He received his B.A. at the University of Pennsylvania and his Ph.D. at Cornell University. Prior to joining the faculty of the University of Pennsylvania he taught at Princeton University, Columbia University, and M.I.T. In 1971-1972, he was the Ford Visiting Professor of Sociology at the Graduate School of Business of the University of Chicago, and in 1978-1979 he was a Visiting Fellow at Wolfson College, Oxford. The author of numerous articles for various professional journals, he is also the author or editor of *Preventing World War III* (with Quincy Wright and Morton Deutsch) (1962), *Law and Sociology* (1962), *Organizational Experiments* (1971), *Organization Theory* (1976), *Interorganizational Relations* (1976, 1978), *The Sociology of Law* (1980), *Knowledge and Power in a Global Society* (1981), and *The Arms Race and Nuclear War* (1987). His principal current research and teaching interests are sociology of law, organization theory, and problems of war and peace.

M

TOMMY DONBAVAND'S FUNNY  SHORTS

MY GRANNY BIT MY BUM

WRITTEN BY TOMMY DONBAVAND
ILLUSTRATED BY LEE ROBINSON

EDGE
FRANKLIN WATTS
LONDON·SYDNEY

Franklin Watts
First published in Great Britain in 2016 by The Watts Publishing Group

Credits
Executive Editor: Adrian Cole
Design Manager: Peter Scoulding
Cover Designer: Cathryn Gilbert
Illustrator: Lee Robinson

HB ISBN 978 1 4451 4617 1
PB ISBN 978 1 4451 4633 1
Library ebook ISBN 978 1 4451 4618 8

Printed in China

BRENT LIBRARIES	
HAR	
91120000322961	
Askews & Holts	19-Apr-2017
JF SHORT CHAPTER	£6.99

Franklin Watts
An imprint of
Hachette Children's Group
Part of The Watts Publishing Group
Carmelite House
50 Victoria Embankment
London EC4Y 0DZ

An Hachette UK Company
www.hachette.co.uk

www.franklinwatts.co.uk

Contents

Chapter One:
Bite!

It started out as an average Sunday. I slept in, watched some TV, did my homework. Then we all went round to my granny and granddad's house for the evening.

But things got weird after we'd finished our dinner. My dad and granddad were dozing off in front of a snooker match on TV. My mum and granny were in the kitchen, making another pot of tea and having a natter about whatever it is women

talk about when they're alone. Knitting

probably, and their husbands. And soup.

I dunno.

As for me — I was sprawled across the floor in front of the electric fire, reading a story on a local news website. Two men had robbed a corner shop near my school! Apparently, they'd burst in, tied up the owner and stolen all the money from the till. And they'd got away with it, too.

The article described the men, saying one was tall and thin, and the other was short and chubby. And it said they were both very dangerous and should not be approached by members of the public.

Wow! Nothing like that ever happens around here. I've lived in this town ever since I was born, and the most exciting thing I can remember was when Uncle Henry found a boa constrictor snake in his back garden. Animal rescue turned up to catch it, plus three ambulances in case anyone ended up bitten. Or constricted. The 'snake' turned out to be a bit of garden hose with a dead mouse stuck in one end.

So, there I was, reading about a real-life local action story, when my granny's cat — Mr Grimsdale — waddled over. He usually lies in front of the fire, and I think he was a bit jealous of me taking his spot 'cos he kept nudging me in the ribs with his head.

I tried to push him away a couple of times, but he's so fat the best I could do was roll him onto his back. He seemed happy enough with that and stayed there.

That's when my granny came in with a glass of lemonade and a plate of Jammie Dodger biscuits for me.

"Here you go, William, love!"

"Gran!" I said. "Please call me Billy. All my friends do."

"Nothing wrong with a good name like William," she said.

"Except it makes me sound seventy years old," I pointed out.

My gran just winked and stepped over
to put my drink down. But she didn't
spot Mr Grimsdale lolling about, and she
accidentally stood on his tail. It must have
hurt, because the cat screeched so loud it
made my brain buzz.

My granny jumped back, dumping half
a dozen Jammie Dodgers and a glass of
lemonade into my sleeping dad's lap.
He shot up in the air, showering Granddad
with what was left of his lukewarm cup
of tea.

Granddad shouted "Peanuts!" (I've no
idea why), and threw a cushion at the TV.
It missed, but hit my granny on the back
of her head. That knocked her false teeth
out of her mouth and sent them flying —
and they bit me hard right on my bum.

I didn't know it at the time, but things
were soon going to get a lot worse...

15

The following morning, I was walking to school with my best friend, Owen. You'd like Owen — he's funny, but a bit weird. He loves monsters, like mummies and zombies, but he thinks vampires are real and disguised as late-night road sweepers.

Told you. Weird.

Anyway, I was telling Owen about the bite on my bum just as we passed the Post Office. Mr Khan, the owner, was opening up early so the long queue of people waiting outside could get warm.

"Good morning, Owen and William!" he called out as we passed, switching on his bright shop sign. I opened my mouth to reply but, suddenly, I started to feel a bit ... strange.

I told Owen so.

"I feel a bit strange," I said.

Owen frowned. "Have you got, like, a buzzing noise in your head?" he asked.

"Yeah," I said, nodding. "Now you come to mention it, I have!"

"I bet your arms and legs feel stiff," Owen said.

"That's right!" I agreed.

"And your eyes?"

"What about them?"

"Are they really, really itchy — like you just want to claw them out of their sockets with your bare fingers, then throw them on the floor and stamp them into the ground, spreading sticky, gooey eye juice everywhere?"

I blinked. "No, not really."

"Don't know what your problem is then," said Owen. "Sorry."

Fat lot of help he was!

Then my body went all wonky.

My spine twisted and bent forwards, my ears grew larger, and a faint moustache sprouted on my top lip. My hair turned grey — with a pink tint — and my fingernails were long and painted a pale, shimmering gold.

Even my clothes changed! One minute I was wearing my usual boring school uniform. The next, I was dressed in a sensible coat, a chiffon headscarf and a pair of boots that appeared to be made from yeti skin.

Oh, and I was carrying the heaviest handbag in the universe.

The transformation complete, I threw back my head and shouted: "Young people of today have no respect for their elders!"

And then I did a really loud, incredibly stinky fart.

"What's happened to me?" I croaked.

"I don't know how to tell you this, Billy," said Owen with a gulp. "But I think you're a were-granny!"

Chapter Two:
Billy!

"A were-what?" I demanded — and jumped at the sound of my own voice. It was a lot more high-pitched than I remembered it.

"A were-granny!" said Owen. "You know — like a werewolf, but with old lady bits instead of fangs and fur."

"Do were-grannies even exist?"

Owen shrugged. "I've never heard of one," he said. "But then, I've never seen my best mate transform into an old age pensioner right in front of me before."

I shuffled as quickly as I could to the hair salon next door to the Post Office, and turned to examine my reflection in the window. It was weird seeing someone else — an elderly woman — staring back at me instead of the usual-looking boy. When I blinked, she blinked. When I turned to the side, she did the same.

I briefly wondered what she would do if I tried a karate move.

"Did anyone else see what happened?" I asked. "Mr Khan, or anyone in the Post Office queue?"

"I don't think so," said Owen. "They were all too keen to get inside out of the cold."

"It is a bit nippy out today," I said, pulling my coat around me. "I wonder if Mr Khan's got all four bars of his shop heater on…"

Owen giggled. "You're starting to sound like a granny as well now!"

I sighed. "Why has this happened?" I said. "And how?"

"It must have been that bite you got from your granny's false teeth," Owen said. "You've been infected with old lady DNA. Probably."

"But, I was bitten last night," I pointed out. "Why didn't I transform then? Why wait until now?"

"Werewolves don't change when they're first bitten, either," said Owen. "They only get hairy when the full moon is out..." He peered up at the sky.

"I doubt there's going to be a full moon out at..." I paused to check the clock in the Post Office window, "...quarter-to-nine in the morning."

"Quarter-to-nine!" said Owen. "We'd better get a move on if we don't want to be late for school."

"I can't go to school looking like this!" I cried. "I'm at least 50 years too old!"

Owen nodded. "I'm pretty sure you'd lose your place on the football team, too."

"So, what do we do?"

"Something must have triggered your transformation," said Owen, thinking hard. "Like the moon does with a werewolf..."

My eyes grew wide, the glittery eye-shadow sparkling. "And if we can work out what that trigger was, we might be able to find a way to reverse it!" I exclaimed.

"OK," said Owen, pacing up and down. "You went all granny about ten minutes ago, just as we passed the queue outside the Post Office." He stopped and looked at me. "Do you think one of them cast a spell on you?"

"They're old people, Owen," I said. "Not witches and wizards..."

"Alright, then... Mr Khan said good

morning, didn't he?"

"Then he switched on the Post Office sign..."

We both froze.

"The light from the Post Office sign!" I gasped. "It shone on me just like the moon does on werewolves!"

"Come on, then," urged Owen, grabbing my arm. "Let's get you away from that light."

We couldn't move very quickly — well, I couldn't move very quickly — but our idea seemed to work. The further we got from the Post Office and its bright red and yellow sign, the more I began to feel like myself again.

My back straightened up, the wrinkles smoothed out of my skin, and my hair reverted to its usual mop of brown. I felt the layers of make-up melting away (which was very weird), my fingernails were once again bitten too far down, and my upper lip was quickly hair-free!

By the time we reached the school gates even my uniform was back in place.

"We did it!" I grinned.

Owen checked his watch. "Yeah, but we're ten minutes late for double history. We're going to get a detention from Mr Parker."

"Trust me," I said. "It's better than going granny!"

But we didn't have to worry about detention in the end. When we finally got to class, there was a new figure taking the register: a young man in a badly fitting suit.

"Come along, boys, hurry up!" he said as we crashed in through the door.

"Where's Mr Parker?" I asked.

"He's off sick," said the new guy. "I'm Mr Wells, your supply teacher for the day. Now, take your seats while I finish the register."

Owen and I shared a high-five as we made our way to our seats at the back of the room. We'd solved my pesky pensioner problem, avoided detention for being late — and now we were going to have fun winding up the poor, unsuspecting supply teacher.

"Now," said Mr Wells, opening the register again. "Where were we ... ah yes ... Rachel Shields?"

"Here, sir."

"Yousuf Usman?"

"Sir!"

"William Tucker?"

"You can call me Billy if you like, sir!" I said with a grin. But my smile fell as I reached into my rucksack for my pencil case. My bag was filled with boiled sweets, packets of tissues and a carefully folded raincoat, covered with a flowery design.

Cautiously, I pulled my hand back above the desk. The skin was all wrinkly, and my nails were long and painted gold.

"Owen!" I hissed, but he was already staring at me in horror.

"Whatever your trigger is, it's not the Post Office sign!" he gulped. "You're transforming again!"

33

Chapter Three: Bluff!

Thankfully, Owen and I sat right at the back of the class in history — so everyone was facing away from us when I transformed. Mr Wells also had his back to us, writing today's topic — the Second World War — on the board.

So, no one saw me shrink back into my old lady form. They missed my school uniform vanishing and the thick woollen coat appearing in its place. And no one spotted my hair turn pale pink and wrap itself up in the purple headscarf.

In fact, I could have sat there for the whole lesson without anyone noticing, if I hadn't shouted: "Back in my day, this was all fields as far as the eye could see!"

I suddenly became aware that everyone was staring at me. One or two jaws even dropped.

"Excuse me..." said Mr Wells. "Can I help?"

Before I could reply, Owen jumped to his feet. "This is my granny!" he blurted out. "Billy had to go to the dentist at short notice and I brought my granny in to help me in school!"

Mr Wells blinked. "Help you?"

"Yes," said Owen. "You're allowed to take a dictionary into English class, and you can use calculators in maths... So I brought my granny in to help me in case there were any difficult bits in today's history lesson."

His voice wobbled a bit near the end of his explanation, but I had to give him top marks for quick thinking.

Everyone turned back to Mr Wells, waiting

for his reaction. It wasn't at all what I expected.

"What a marvellous idea!" he said, hurrying over. "Thank you for coming in, Mrs…"

"…Wrinkles," I said, glancing at the back of my hand. I know! But it was the first thing that came into my head.

"Mrs Wrinkles?" repeated the teacher.

"Yes," I said, smiling. There was no going back now. "But you can call me Doris!"

"OK then, Doris," said Mr Wells as he led me to the front of the class. "You say you can remember this area before the school was built, when it was just fields?"

"I can indeed!" I said, beginning to enjoy myself.

"And, when was that, if you don't mind my asking?"

I looked up at the topic Mr Wells had written on the board. "Oh, during the war."

Our teacher almost clapped his hands together with joy. "So you had first-hand experience of life in wartime?"

"Er ... yes," I said.

At the back of the room, Owen slid down in his chair.

"Then perhaps you can tell our pupils exactly what daily life was like during those dark years..."

"Yes, of course."

I smiled sweetly to my classmates, but inside I was screaming to myself: What

are you doing, you fool! You don't know
anything about the war apart from what
you've seen in old documentaries! Stop
talking and get out of here now!

I cleared my throat. "The main difference
between life today and back in the Second
World War was that ... er ... everyone in
wartime lived in black-and-white. The world
didn't turn to colour until the 1960s."

There was a flurry of scribbling as everyone wrote this down in their books.

"What?" said Mr Wells. I took his frown as a sign that I should continue.

"It wasn't easy, being in black-and-white," I explained. "Everyone was always getting cheese mixed up with soap, and it was impossible to play snooker 'cos all the balls looked the same, and rainbows were rubbish."

"No," said Mr Wells, gesturing for the class to put their pens down. "I don't think..."

But I was on a roll. "Everyone used to hope that they didn't get a Valentine's Day card on 14th February because they all had

40

poems inside that started with 'Roses are grey, violets are grey...'"

"Thank you, Mrs Wrinkles!" said Mr Wells, ushering me towards the door.

I continued talking all the way. "It was really easy to get tomatoes confused with ping-pong balls, and all squirrels were grey, even the red ones."

Mr Wells pushed me out of the classroom and slammed the door. Seconds later, Owen was also thrown out, straining with my heavy handbag.

"So, what do we do now?" he asked, gladly handing the bag over.

I fixed him with a firm stare. "We go back to the source of the problem!"

We caught the bus to my granny's house. I found a senior citizen's bus pass at the bottom of my bag, along with enough loose change to pay for Owen. Luckily, we were alone on the top deck when I changed back again, and quickly lost fifty years.

We had just reached her door, when Gran opened it and smiled. "Billy," she said. "I've been expecting you. Hello, Owen. Come in, both of you."

I was halfway down the hall before I realised what she had said. "You called me Billy!" I gasped.

"Of course I did," said Gran. "You don't want me to use your full name and start another transformation to old age, do you?"

"So, that's what your trigger is!" cried Owen. "It's when people call you Willia—" Gran clamped a hand over his mouth before he could finish saying my name.

"I said, we don't want Billy to change again! At least, not right now..."

We went into the kitchen, where my granny put the kettle on. "So, you know what's been happening to me?" I asked.

Gran nodded. "Exactly what I've been going through for the past 62 years," she said.

Chapter Four: Battle!

I stared at her. "You're a were-granny, too?"

"Yes," she said, with a sigh. "I was bitten when I was just ten years old."

Owen scowled. "But, you're already... I mean, you aren't... What I mean is..."

"You mean I'm already old," said Gran, pouring the tea. "It is true that — if anyone ever calls me Elizabeth instead of Liz — I don't change much these days. But it was very different when I was younger. More difficult to conceal our precious gift."

"Gift!" I exclaimed, spitting out a mouthful of tea. "How can this be a gift?"

"You have been given special powers, Billy!" Gran said. "And, with great power—"

"I know this one!" grinned Owen. "It's from Spider-Man! With great power comes great responsibility!"

"No, that's not it," said my gran. "I was going to say — with great power, comes great big pants."

I blinked. "Pants?"

"Yes," said Gran. "That's your first lesson. Always wear big, comfortable pants when you're in your older form. You'll thank me one day."

"Lessons?" I queried. "You mean you're going to train me to be a granny?"

"I've already started!" said Gran, jumping up and grabbing her coat. "And we haven't a moment to lose. Follow me…"

So, Owen and I trailed after Gran as she dragged us to a coffee morning, knitting shop, bakery, charity store and bingo game.

She taught me which kind of boiled sweets to keep in my bag, how to correctly tuck a handkerchief up the sleeve of my cardigan, and when the best time was to shout at a group of youngsters hanging around on the street corner.

By the time we reached the bench outside the Post Office, I was exhausted! Owen and I collapsed.

"You two boys wait here while I nip in and pick up my pension," said Gran. "I didn't get the chance this morning."

I stretched out as she disappeared inside,

only for someone to trip over my feet as he made to follow my granny.

"Watch it!" snarled a tall, thin guy.

"Sorry!" I said, pulling my feet in quickly.

The thin guy's mate — a short, chubby man — glared at me as he scurried into the Post Office after his friend.

I stretched out on the bench again, trying

to think of a way to change my name from William to Billy in the school register. If I could do that—

Wait a minute! Two men — one tall and thin, and the other short and chubby?

I grabbed the front of Owen's jumper. "I think the Post Office is about to be robbed!" I hissed.

"What?"

"Go and call the police!" I ordered. "I have to go and help my granny!"

I crashed in through the doors of the Post Office just as the tall robber was tying up Mr Khan.

The other bad guy had hold of my granny's arm. "Lock the door behind you!" the villain snarled.

I did as I was told, locking the two robbers, Gran, Mr Khan and myself in the shop.

"Now, where's the safe?" said the thin guy, disappearing into the back room.

When he'd gone, Mr Khan turned to me and tried to talk through the gag over his face. "Mmmpph-mmph-mppphher-mphhheffmmpphhh."

Gran winked at me. "I think Mr Khan is

saying 'Good afternoon, Master William',"
she said.

"Quiet!" snapped the chubby robber.
"You three are our hostages. We'll do the...
talking..." His voice trailed away as my
transformation hit me with full force.

I bent over, ruffled my thin moustache, and then snapped my head up to glare at the bad guy through old lady eyes.

"Wh-what?" sputtered the chubby robber. "How did you...?"

"Let's just say we don't like it when things get granti-social!" I cackled.

"I presumed you'd just come in here for a STAMP!" snarled Gran, stomping on her captor's foot with a sensible shoe.

The fat guy yelled out in pain and began to hop around. I quickly pulled out a handful of boiled sweets from my handbag, and rolled them across the floor. I'm not sure exactly what kind of sweets grannies like to buy, but these things were indestructible. Instead of being crushed

beneath the chubby robber's foot, he rolled

on them and came crashing to the floor.

I took the opportunity to whack him a few times with my handbag, then I whipped off my headscarf and used it to tie his hands behind his back.

"Untie me, you old-aged weirdo!" the robber barked.

"You want to mind your language, sunshine!" I said. Then I whipped the snotty handkerchief from up my sleeve and stuffed it into his mouth.

Just then, the tall guy appeared from the back room. He had bundles of money piled high in his arms. He spotted his chubby friend on the floor and groaned. "Why have I always got to sort these things out myself?" he demanded, dumping the cash on the counter.

He stepped out from behind the till
area — to find himself faced by my granny
holding a pair of glinting knitting needles.

"What are you going to do with those
things?" he chuckled. "Make me a sweater?"

"More like a straitjacket!" declared Gran,
then she leapt into action. It was amazing!
She was like some sort of knitting ninja

— dancing around her opponent in a blur, poking the needles through his jumper, grabbing lengths of wool and knitting them back in a new position.

Within minutes, the tall robber's arms were knitted behind his back, and his mouth was completely covered.

I slumped back against the wall as I changed back into a boy, just in time to see the police break down the Post Office door and rush inside. Owen was with them.

"You did it!" he cried as officers raced to untie Mr Khan. "You stopped them!"

I grinned. "Nothing your average were-granny couldn't handle!"

But Owen didn't reply. He was staring back out into the street at an old man wearing a green jacket.

"What's wrong?" I asked.

"You see that guy out there?" whispered Owen. "The one with the beard?"

I nodded. "What about him?"

Owen swallowed hard. "I think he might be a grampire!"

TOMMY DONBAVAND'S FUNNY SHORTS

They'll have you in stitches!

978 1 4451 4676 8

978 1 4451 4673 7

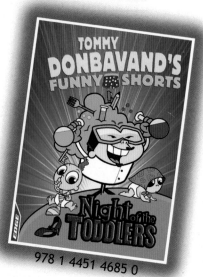

978 1 4451 4685 0